Lynda Weinman's | Hands-On Training

Macromedia®

Dreamweaver® 8
Beyond the Basics

Includes Exercise Files and Demo Movies

lynda.com

By Joseph Lowery

Macromedia® Dreamweaver® 8 Beyond the Basics Hands-On Training

By Joseph Lowery

lynda.com/books | Peachpit Press
1249 Eighth Street • Berkeley, CA • 94710
800.283.9444 • 510.524.2178 • 510.524.2221(fax)
http://www.lynda.com/books
http://www.peachpit.com

lynda.com/books is published
in association with Peachpit Press,
a division of Pearson Education
Copyright ©2007 by lynda.com

ISBN: 0-321-22856-1

0 9 8 7 6 5 4 3 2 1

Printed and bound in the
United States of America

H•O•T Credits

Director of Product Development and Video Production: Tanya Staples

Operations Manager: Lauren Harmon

Project Editor: Karyn Johnson

Production Coordinator: Tracey Croom

Compositors: David Van Ness, Myrna Vladic

Developmental Editor: Jennifer Eberhardt

Copyeditor: Kim Wimpsett

Proofreader: Haig MacGregor

Interior Design: Hot Studio, San Francisco

Cover Design: Don Barnett

Cover Illustration: Bruce Heavin (bruce@stink.com)

Indexer: Julie Bess, JBIndexing Inc.

Video Editors and Testers: Alex Marino, Scott Cullen, Eric Geoffroy

H•O•T Colophon

The text in *Macromedia Dreamweaver 8 Beyond the Basics H·O·T* was set in Avenir from Adobe Systems Incorporated. The cover illustation was painted in Adobe Photoshop and Adobe Illustrator.

This book was created using QuarkXPress and Microsoft Office on an Apple Macintosh using Mac OS X. It was printed on 60 lb. Influence Matte at Courier.

Table of Contents

Introduction

A Note from Lynda Weinman

Most people buy computer books to learn, yet it's amazing how few books are written by teachers. Joseph and I take pride this book was written by experienced teachers, who are familiar with training students in this subject matter. In this book, you'll find carefully developed lessons and exercises to help you learn Dreamweaver 8—one of the most capable Web development tools available today.

This book is targeted at intermediate- to advanced-level Web designers and Web developers who are looking for a way to learn about the more complex and powerful features of Dreamweaver 8 quickly and easily. The premise of the hands-on approach is to take you to the next level quickly with Dreamweaver 8 while you actively work through the lessons in this book. It's one thing to read about a program and another experience entirely to try the product and achieve measurable results. Our motto is, "Read the book, follow the exercises, and you'll learn the program." I have received countless testimonials, and it is our goal to make sure this motto remains true for all our Hands-On Training books.

This book doesn't set out to cover every single aspect of Dreamweaver 8, and it doesn't try to teach you how to hand-code a Web site from scratch. What we saw missing from the bookshelves was a process-oriented tutorial teaching readers advanced principles, techniques, and tips in a hands-on format.

I welcome your comments at **dw8btbthot@lynda.com**. If you run into any trouble while you're working through this book, check out the technical support link at **www.lynda.com/books/HOT/dw8btb**.

Joseph and I hope this book will enhance your skills in Dreamweaver 8 and Web design in general. If it does, we have accomplished the job we set out to do!

—Lynda Weinman

About lynda.com

lynda.com was founded in 1996 by Lynda Weinman and Bruce Heavin in conjunction with the first publication of Lynda's revolutionary book *Designing Web Graphics*. Since then, lynda.com has become a leader in software training for graphics and Web professionals and is recognized worldwide as a trusted educational resource.

lynda.com offers a wide range of Hands-On Training books, which guide users through a progressive learning process using real-world projects.

lynda.com also offers a wide range of video-based tutorials, which are available on CD and DVD and through the lynda.com Online Training Library. lynda.com also owns the Flashforward Conference and Film Festival.

For more information about lynda.com, check out **www.lynda.com**. For more information about the Flashforward Conference and Film Festival, visit **www.flashforwardconference.com**.

Product Registration

Register your copy of *Macromedia Dreamweaver 8 Beyond the Basics HOT* today, and receive the following benefits:

- FREE 24-hour pass to the lynda.com Online Training Library with more than 13,000

professionally produced video tutorials covering more than 199 topics by leading industry experts and teachers

- News, events, and special offers from lynda.com

- The lynda.com monthly newsletter

To register, visit **www.lynda.com/register/HOT/dreamweaver8btb**.

Additional Training Resources from lynda.com

To help you master and further develop your skills with Dreamweaver 8, register to use the free, 24-hour pass to the lynda.com Online Training Library, and check out the following video-based training resources:

Dreamweaver 8 Essential Training
with Garrick Chow

Dreamweaver 8 Beyond the Basics
with Daniel Short

Dreamweaver 8 Dynamic Development
with Daniel Short

Studio 8 Web Workflow
with Abigail Rudner

About Joseph Lowery

Joseph Lowery has been working with Dreamweaver since before it was born. After hearing the buzz about a hot new Web authoring tool, Joe joined the Dreamweaver beta program and began exploring. His best-selling *Dreamweaver Bible* books have been published in 11 languages and have sold more than 400,000 copies. Joseph has also written about Macromedia Fireworks and Macromedia Contribute and last year released *CSS Hacks and Filters*.

Fascinated by Dreamweaver's advanced capabilities, Joe began developing extensions. Several of his extensions have won awards and claim the ultimate honor of being included in the released versions of Dreamweaver and Fireworks.

Joe currently works as the director of marketing for WebAssist, the leading provider of Adobe extensions. He continues his long-standing love affair with New York City, with his other long-standing love affair, his wife, Debra, and their daughter, Margot. Oh, and the pretty one in his picture on the back of the book is the family golden retriever, Star.

Acknowledgments from Joseph Lowery

I'm very, very appreciative of the ongoing support and encouragement from everyone at lynda.com. From Garo Green to Bruce Heavin to Michael Ninness, thank you for working so hard to get this project—and I hope many more—underway. Tanya Staples has been a superb (and patient, oh-so patient) project director for whom I am extremely grateful. I'd like to thank Jennifer Eberhardt and Lauren Harmon for their editorial guidance. I'd especially like to single out the book's beta testers, Alex Marino and Scott Cullen, for their careful attention and welcome suggestions; you made the book better than I could alone. In fact, everyone involved in the book process has been fantastic—a hearty and deep felt thank you from the heart of the East Village.

How to Use This Book

The following sections outline important information to help you make the most of this book.

The formatting in this book

This book has several components, including step-by-step exercises, commentary, notes, tips, sidebars, and video tutorials. Step-by-step exercises are numbered. File names, folder names, commands, keyboard shortcuts, and Web addresses are in bold so they pop out easily, such as **filename.htm**, the **images** folder, **File > New**, **Ctrl+click**, and **www.lynda.com**. Captions and commentary are in dark gray text: This is commentary.

Interface screen captures

I took most of the screen shots in the book on a Windows computer using Windows XP, as I do most of my design, development, and writing on Windows. I also own and use Macs, and I note important differences between the two platforms when they occur.

What's on the Dreamweaver 8 HOT CD-ROM?

You'll find a number of useful resources on the **Dreamweaver 8 HOT CD-ROM**, including the following: exercise files, video tutorials, and information about product registration. Before you begin the hands-on exercises, read the following sections so you know how to set up the exercise files and video tutorials.

Exercise files

The files required to complete the exercises are on the **Dreamweaver 8 HOT CD-ROM** in a folder called **exercise_files**. These files are divided into chapter folders, and you should copy each chapter folder onto your desktop before you begin the exercise for that chapter. For example, if you're about to start Chapter 5, copy the **chap_05** folder from the **exercise_files** folder on the **Dreamweaver 8 HOT CD-ROM** onto your desktop. For uncluttered storage, store them in another folder you create called **DW 8 Beyond**.

On Windows, when files originate from a CD, they automatically become write protected, which means you cannot alter them. Fortunately, you can easily change this attribute. For complete instructions, read the "Making exercise files editable on Windows computers" section on page xii.

Once you've copied the files to your desktop, you'll find it's easiest to work with them if you create a site in Dreamweaver 8. Your site should use the folder on your desktop containing the exercise files as the local site root and should be named **DW 8 Beyond**; if you plan on working through the exercises in the book, I recommend that you copy all the files in the exercise_files folder to your site root.

HTM versus HTML

All the exercise files on the **Dreamweaver 8 HOT CD-ROM** end with the **.htm** extension. As you design Web sites, you may see HTML (**H**yper**T**ext **M**arkup **L**anguage) files using the **.html** extension. You can name your files either way, and any browser will recognize the file.

Video tutorials

Throughout the book, you'll find references to video tutorials. In some cases, these video tutorials reinforce concepts explained in the book. In other cases, they show bonus material you'll find interesting and useful. To view the video tutorials, you must have Apple QuickTime Player installed on your computer. If you do not have QuickTime Player, you can download it for free from Apple's Web site at **www.apple.com/quicktime**.

To view the video tutorials, copy the videos from the **Dreamweaver 8 HOT CD-ROM** to your hard drive. Double-click the video you want to watch, and it will automatically open in QuickTime Player. Make sure the volume on your computer is turned up so you can hear the audio content.

If you like the video tutorials, refer to the "Product Registration" section earlier in this introduction, and register to receive a free pass to the lynda.com Online Training Library, which is filled with more than 13,000 video clips from more than 199 different tutorials.

Making exercise files editable on Windows computers

By default, when you copy files from a CD to a Windows computer, they are set to read-only (write protected). This will cause a problem with the exercise files because you will need to edit and save many of them. You can remove the read-only property by following these steps:

1 Open the **exercise_files** folder on the **Dreamweaver 8 HOT CD-ROM**, and copy one of the subfolders, such as **chap_02**, to your desktop.

---

2 Open the **chap_02** folder you copied to your desktop, and choose **Edit > Select All**.

---

3 **Right-click** (Windows) or **Ctrl+click** (Mac) one of the selected files, and choose **Properties** from the contextual menu.

---

4 In the **Properties** dialog box, select the **General** tab. Turn off the **Read-Only** check box to make the selected files in the **chap_02** folder editable.

Making file extensions visible on Windows computers

By default, you cannot see file extensions, such as **.htm**, **.fla**, **.swf**, **.jpg**, **.gif**, or **.psd** on Windows computers. Fortunately, you can change this setting easily. Here's how:

1 On your desktop, double-click the **My Computer** icon.

Note: If you (or someone else) has changed the name, it will not say My Computer.

---

2 Choose **Tools > Folder Options** to open the **Folder Options** dialog box. Select the **View** tab.

---

3 Turn off the **Hide extensions for known file types** check box to make all the file extensions visible.

Dreamweaver 8 System Requirements

Windows

- 800 MHz Intel Pentium III processor (or equivalent) and newer

- Windows 2000, Windows XP

- 256 MB RAM (1 GB recommended to run more than one Studio 8 product simultaneously)

- 1024 x 768, 16-bit display (32-bit recommended)

- 650 MB available disk space

Mac

- 600 MHz PowerPC G3 and newer

- Mac OS X 10.3, 10.4

- 256 MB RAM (1 GB recommended to run more than one Studio 8 product simultaneously)

- 1024 x 768, thousands of colors display (millions of colors recommended)

- 300 MB available disk space

Getting Demo Versions of the Software

If you'd like to try demo versions of the software used in this book, you can download them at the following locations:

Firefox: www.getfirefox.com

Dreamweaver 8: www.adobe.com/products/dreamweaver/

Fireworks 8: www.adobe.com/products/fireworks/

Contribute 3: www.adobe.com/products/contribute/

Flash 8: www.adobe.com/products/flash/flashpro/

Coldfusion MX 7: www.adobe.com/products/coldfusion/

NOTE:

Special Thanks

Special thanks to the Dominique Sillet (**www.littleigloo.com**) for the design of the Starfish Vacations brand and Web site used throughout the exercises in this book.

Special thanks to istockphoto.com (**www.istockphoto.com**), specifically the photographers listed below, for providing the stock photos used in the exercises in this book:

Yanik Chauvin, Jamey Ekins, Jean-Bernard Emond, David Freund, Benjamin Goode, Virgil Graham, Donald Gruener, Terry Healy, Charles Humphries, Christopher Messer, Stephanie Phillips, Chris Schmidt, Gerda Smets, Jay Spooner, Jennifer Trenchard and Holger Wulschlaeger

1

Getting Started

Dreamweaver 8 is a beauty of a program. With it and just basic HTML (**H**yper**T**ext **M**arkup **L**anguage) understanding, you can create a working Web site with all the essentials—text, graphics, and links. What really makes Dreamweaver 8 shine is its depth. The more time you spend with the program, the further you can take your sites. One of the most common responses I hear when I demonstrate Dreamweaver 8 at conferences is, "I didn't know you could do that!" Well, you can—and this book shows you how.

Designing CSS Layouts

Use Dreamweaver 8 to craft CSS (**C**ascading **S**tyle **S**heets) layouts and reap the benefits of faster loading times, easier-to-read code, and more flexible designs. Dreamweaver 8 takes CSS to the next level with its enhanced design-time rendering and overhauled CSS implementation. In addition, Dreamweaver 8 offers a number of visual aids specifically designed to help your workflow: **CSS Layout Outlines**, **CSS Layout Background**, and **CSS Layout Box Model**. Open the **Style Rendering** toolbar to design page layouts for screen, print, and other mediums.

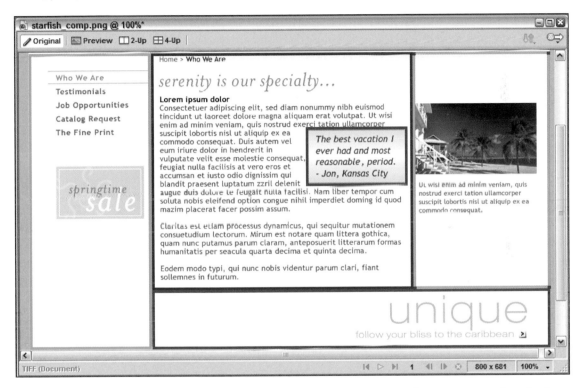

Chapter 2, *"Designing Layouts with CSS,"* and Chapter 3, *"Creating CSS Column Layouts,"* describe how to create pages from the ground-up using CSS in Dreamweaver 8.

Creating Pure-CSS Navigation

Streamline your navigation with CSS and ordered lists—for either vertical or horizontal navigation bars. In addition, CSS navigation is easy to change; adding or removing items is as simple as changing a bulleted list item. The advanced CSS-rendering capabilities in Dreamweaver 8 give you the same in-browser experience you have with modern CSS-compliant browsers such as Safari and Firefox.

Chapter 4, *"Building CSS Navigation Systems,"* explains how to build CSS navigation in Dreamweaver 8, and Chapter 5, *"Taking CSS Further,"* describes how to integrate templates with CSS, create magazine-style layouts, and apply CSS hacks.

Automating Production with Templates

Work smarter, not harder, with advanced Dreamweaver 8 template features. Leverage the power of the template expression architecture to do less work in the production phase of site creation. Whether you want to automatically create named anchors and their corresponding links on a FAQ (Frequently Asked Questions) page, set up "previous" and "next" links in a series of pages, or provide alternative CSS style sheets and properties at design time, templates are the way to go.

Chapter 6, *"Working with Advanced Templates,"* explains how to make the most of template expressions with repeating regions, navigation, and CSS.

Coding Faster Than Ever

Get more out of **Code** view than you ever have before. With the new **Coding** toolbar, you can more quickly select and manipulate your code. The new code collapse feature is terrific for hiding sections of your code so you can hone in on just what you want to see. One surefire way to push your productivity through the roof—whether you're in **Code** or **Design** view—is to take advantage of the **Insert** bar's **Favorites** category.

Chapter 7, *"Utilizing Rapid Coding Techniques,"* covers how to use all these features, and more, to gain productivity.

Incorporating RSS Feeds

Bring a wealth of fresh information to your site, every day, with RSS (**R**eally **S**imple **S**yndication) feeds. The new XML (e**X**tensible **M**arkup **L**anguage) features allow you to incorporate standard or dynamically generated information streams. Best of all, you can style the feeds within Dreamweaver 8 and get a clear view of how your page will look when published.

Chapter 8, *"Setting Up an XML Feed,"* describes how to create an XML data file and how to integrate an XML feed on both the client and on the server.

Building Ajax-Driven Pages

Set up smoother, more exciting interactions for your site visitors with Ajax-powered pages. Ajax (**A**synchronous **J**ava**S**cript and **X**ML) allows users to choose the data they want to see and refresh only the appropriate portions of your page, not the whole page. With one or two commonly available code libraries, you can incorporate Ajax technology into your sites today.

Chapter 9, *"Implementing Ajax in Dreamweaver,"* gives step-by-step instructions on how to use this new technology to enhance your users' experience when visiting your Web site.

Using Flash Designer Fonts

Overcome Web font limitations with accessible, CSS-compliant Adobe Flash headlines. Using a technique known as sIFR (**s**calable **I**nman **F**lash **R**eplacement), you can substitute boring, everyday Web browser fonts with designer-selected typefaces. Done correctly, your new, improved typography will work with your CSS style sheets while remaining friendly to search engines.

Chapter 10, *"Incorporating sIFR Text,"* covers how to implement sIFR in Dreamweaver 8.

Working Collectively

Expand productivity throughout your organization by developing team-oriented Dreamweaver 8 sites. When properly used, the check-in/check-out system makes it possible to spread the workload for major sites more effectively. Other features, such as Design Notes, streamline the team's to-do lists.

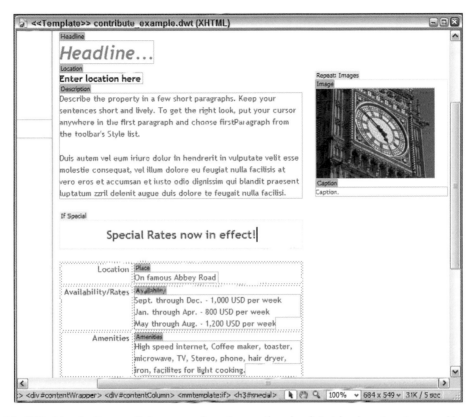

Chapter 11, *"Working in Groups,"* shows you how to use the check-in/check-out system and how to incorporate Design Notes into your workflow.

Designing for Contribute

When Contribute was introduced, a whole new market for Dreamweaver designers emerged. Now, Dreamweaver designers can create sites for small-businesses, educational facilities, non-profits and other markets—without having to worry about maintaining the content. Designing sites for Contribute users to maintain, however, is far different from designing them for yourself to manage.

Chapter 12, *"Designing for Contribute,"* describes how to set up Contribute administration from within Dreamweaver, how to build Contribute-friendly templates, and how to structure your CSS correctly with Contribute in mind.

Optimizing Your Site for Search Engines

Search engine optimization is an essential Web developer skill—and one Dreamweaver 8 can help you master. Whether you're adding **<meta>** tags, developing a site map, or submitting your site to Google, Dreamweaver 8 can make your sites more accessible to search engines.

Chapter 13, *"Optimizing for Search Engines,"* shows you how to optimize your pages for search engines, develop a site map, and craft a Google sitemap.

Outputting Accessible Forms

Make it easy for your site visitors—all your site visitors—to provide the information you need in a usable format. Forms are Web constants, but they often don't get the attention they deserve. With Dreamweaver 8, you can apply fieldsets and add legends to improve your forms' readability and ease of use.

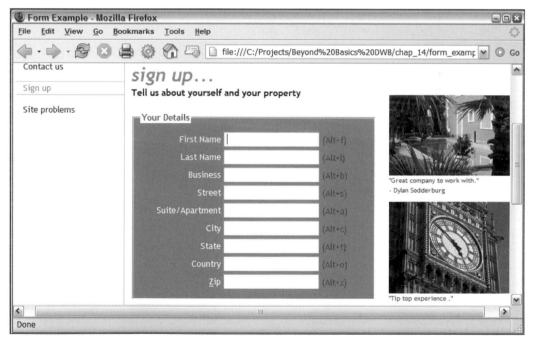

Chapter 14, *"Building Usable Forms,"* describes how to add fieldsets and legends to your forms, how to style form elements, and how to make your forms accessible.

Integrating Podcasts and Video

Turn your Web pages into media-rich environments. Dreamweaver 8 includes all the tools you need to add podcasts to your site and extend your site's reach to MP3 players and beyond. Import Flash video for an in-page video experience available to almost everyone instantaneously.

Chapter 15, *"Integrating Multimedia Content,"* covers how to create podcasts and add Flash video to your site.

Now that you've gotten a sense of what you can do with Dreamweaver 8, let's get to it! The next chapter starts with an exploration of crafting CSS layouts—from starting graphic compositions to completing Dreamweaver 8 Web pages.

2

Designing Layouts with CSS

Layout design for Web pages has evolved significantly in the past few years. Table-based layouts are becoming a technique of the past as more Web designers are turning to CSS (**C**ascading **S**tyle **S**heets). Pages structured with CSS are more flexible, easier to maintain, and faster to download.

When working with a CSS-based design versus a table-based design, you'll need to slice your comps differently—regardless of whether you're editing images with Adobe Fireworks or Adobe Photoshop. Although you'll probably find yourself using fewer slices with CSS, the challenge is understanding which portions of your graphics can be manipulated by CSS to create layouts. In this chapter, you'll practice slicing stand-alone foreground images as well as background graphics that repeat in one direction.

Most CSS-based layouts rely on several positioning techniques. To accomplish sophisticated designs, you'll need a firm grasp of two CSS properties: **position** and **float**. I'll discuss these properties—and their values—in detail to give you the foundation needed to integrate sliced graphics with CSS. You'll also learn how to work with the enhanced **CSS Styles** panel in Dreamweaver 8.

Finally, you'll use your newfound CSS skills to craft a distinctively styled Web page, with a magazine-style layout, an oversized graphic, and flowing text.

Slicing Graphic Comps for CSS Layouts

Converting a graphic comp into a Web page layout is an art in itself. Many of today's designers grew up mastering the art of slicing graphics to create table-based layouts, but CSS-based layouts require a different skill set. When designers look at comps intended for table-based layouts, they tend to regard the design as a complete picture, with areas denoted for text and other page content. Often designers reproduce a page as a single outer table with many cells or nested tables.

With a CSS-based layout, however, a comp is more correctly regarded as the sum of its parts. Typically, the CSS page is structured around semantic elements such as the company logo, navigation, main content, and sidebar. Converting the comp requires extracting the elements corresponding with the page's CSS structure.

Moreover, CSS has built-in graphic capabilities perfectly capable of substituting for many standard image components. For example, you don't need to include a slice of any rectangular area comprised of a flat color. Likewise, you can easily reproduce simple borders in CSS, which results in much more flexible layouts. Complex, graphic-oriented borders often require a much smaller slice than necessary with table-based designs. These CSS capabilities translate easily to a real Web page benefit: smaller file size.

You can include graphics in CSS layouts in one of two ways: either as foreground graphics or as background graphics. **Foreground graphics** are images inserted as `<img>` tags, and they require an `alt` attribute for accessibility purposes. **Background graphics** are images applied through CSS `background-image` properties. Much of the design flexibility of CSS comes from the power inherent in the `background-image` property: You can display a background image once or have it repeat either horizontally or vertically—or both. This means you must carefully slice repeated background images so they display properly.

Although the process may vary according to the design, you can generally follow four steps when preparing a comp's graphics for a CSS layout:

1. **Visualize the CSS layout:** Plan your CSS layout to determine which slices and what type— foreground or background—are necessary to convert the comp into a Web page.

2. **Slice the foreground elements:** Earmark those portions of the layout to be inserted as `<img>` tags, including any elements essential to the page's contextual meaning.

3. **Slice the background elements:** Slice layout areas that form the underlying graphic structure of the comp, giving special attention to repeating images.

4. **Export the slices:** Extract properly named comp images to the site's folder for easy identification.

The key to thinking in CSS when looking at a graphic comp is being able to see the page in boxes. In CSS layouts, `<div>` tags are the primary building blocks—and are just as rectangular. The most important aspect about these layout boxes is that, for the most part, they do not overlap. True, many CSS-based pages incorporate floating or absolutely positioned elements inside a larger `<div>` tag, but these do not form the core structure of the page. CSS layouts primarily comprise distinct rectangular regions.

An equally important facet of CSS layout regions is that they do not intersect content. Again, this generalization is a rule made to be broken, but when you're first composing your pages, it's a good one to follow.

In the first exercise, you will look at a completed comp in Fireworks and learn how to turn it into a CSS layout by performing the initial step, visualization.

1 | Visualizing the Layout

In this exercise, you'll examine a comp in Fireworks and visualize how to convert it to a CSS-based layout. The visualization process has two phases. First, you'll envision the major sections of the page; outer `<div>` tags will represent each of these areas. Next, you'll mentally drill down into the design to figure out how you can separate the page elements into what will become the inner `<div>` tags.

To help you visualize the layout, the comp includes two layer groups: one for the major divisions and another for the more detailed areas. Initially, these layers are turned off, but during this exercise you'll turn them on, one at a time, to see why I chose each area to be its own group.

Note: You'll need Fireworks to complete the first four exercises. If you own Adobe Studio 8, you should already have Fireworks 8 installed, because it is part of the Studio 8 suite of applications. If you have a stand-alone version of Dreamweaver 8, you can download a trial version of Fireworks 8 from Adobe's Web site at **www.adobe.com**.

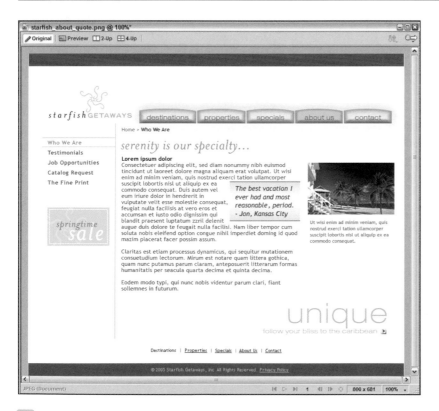

1 In Fireworks, open **starfish_comp.png** from the **chap_02** folder you copied to your desktop. If you're asked whether you'd like to maintain the appearance or replace the fonts, click **Maintain Appearance**. Make sure the Fireworks **Layers** panel is visible. If not, choose **Window > Layers**, or press F2.

When you initially look at the comp, your eye is likely to be attracted to the content area, with the captioned image and graphic-enhanced pull quote—that's looking at the page as a site visitor.

Now, look at the page again but as a CSS designer. First, identify those areas stretching the full width of the comp. The most obvious one is the dark gray border at the top; at the bottom of the page, you'll find its counterpart, which contains the footer links. Both of these areas are adjacent to other full-width sections and, as such, can be represented as full **<div>** tags.

2 In the **Layers** panel, click the **plus** sign (Windows) or the **triangle** (Mac) to expand the **Major CSS Divs** layer. Click the **eye** icon next to the **Header** object to turn on visibility.

Note: If you're more familiar with Photoshop than Fireworks, what you know as layer groups are **layers** in Fireworks; in addition, layers in Photoshop are **objects** in Fireworks.

Tip: When you turn on visibility, you'll see a thick red line surrounding the upper portion of the comp. I've incorporated this outline to help you identify the **<div>** area.

Both the upper dark gray border and the section immediately beneath it (which includes the logo and the primary navigation) can reside within a single, outer **<div>** tag. Why? Well, both sections stretch the full width of the comp and are adjacent to each other. Later, you'll use nested **<div>** tags with this outer **<div>** tag to separate the border from the logo and navigation sections. Each of these **<div>** sections will translate to a specific CSS style.

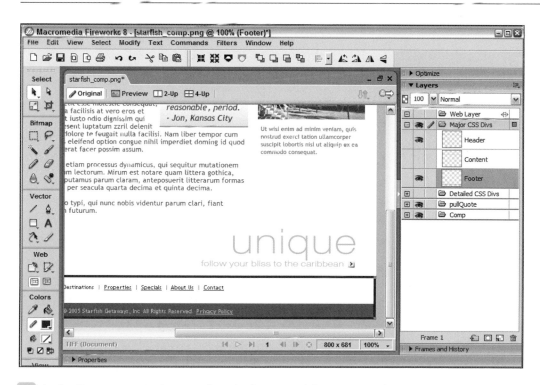

3 In the **Document** window, scroll to the bottom of the comp. In the **Layers** panel, click the **eye** icon next to the **Footer** object to turn on visibility.

When you turn on visibility, you'll see a thick blue line surrounding the lower portion of the starfish_comp.png comp. This area designates the lower **<div>** tag and encompasses both the bottom dark gray border and the footer links.

Again, both the dark gray border and the footer section span the comp's width and are adjacent to each other. Therefore, you can group them into an outer **<div>** tag.

You might be wondering why the area with the large **unique** text is not also included in this same outer **<div>** tag. If you look at the left side of the page, you'll notice a thin, light gray line separating the left-column navigation from the main content. Because this line extends all the way to the footer section, it stops the **unique** text from going the full width and becoming part of the main footer **<div>** tag.

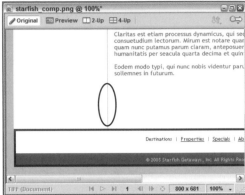

4 In the **Layers** panel, click the **eye** icon next to the **Content** object to turn on visibility.

This time, a thick green rectangle surrounds the secondary navigation in the left column, the primary content area, the photograph and caption in the right column, and the lower featured section with the **unique** text.

All these areas fill the full width of the comp, and you can now see the three main parts of the page—header, content, and footer—from a CSS perspective. When you start working in Dreamweaver 8, one of your first tasks will be to create CSS rules to correspond to these three comp sections. With the outer **<div>** tags visualized, you're ready to begin noting the nested areas.

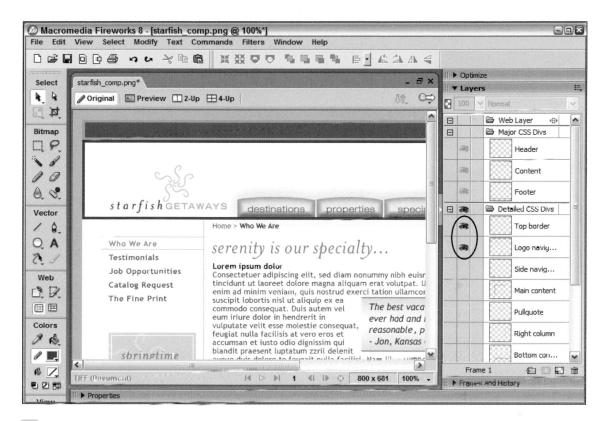

5 In the **Layers** panel, click the **eye** icon next to the **Major CSS Divs** layer to turn off visibility. Click **plus** sign (Windows) or **triangle** (Mac) to expand the **Detailed CSS Divs** layer. Click the **eye** icons next to the **Top border** and **Logo navigation** layers to turn on visibility.

As noted previously, the dark gray border should obviously be a separate `<div>` tag. Whereas you might consider slicing this section for a table-based layout, with CSS, you can easily replace a graphic with a `background-color` attribute.

The logo and primary navigation do not appear so overtly as a single `<div>` tag—until you visualize them with a rectangle, like the red one shown in the illustration here. The key factor to note is that the bottom of the logo graphic is inline with the bottom of the navigation. This alignment keeps both elements together in a single, nested `<div>` tag.

Clicking the eye icon is a quick way to turn on visibility for a single object. But if you have multiple objects, you need a faster method. Dragging down the column of eye icons is a quick way to turn on visibility for adjacent objects, as you'll see in the next step. This technique definitely beats clicking each eye icon individually.

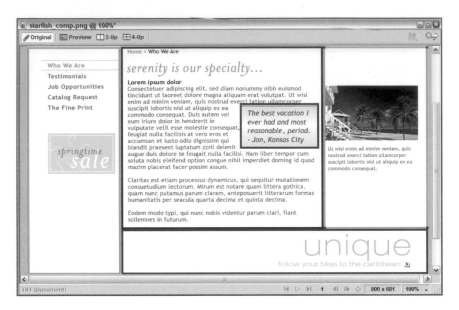

6 In the **Layers** panel, position your cursor in the **eye** icon column next to the **Side navigation** layer, drag down the column to turn on visibility for the **Side navigation**, **Main content**, **Pullquote**, **Right column**, and **Bottom content** objects, and then release the mouse.

Each of the outlined areas will translate to a separate inner `<div>` tag in Dreamweaver 8 CSS—and all of them will reside in the outer `<div>` tag. Notice each of these areas, with one exception, does not overlap any other area, as shown in the illustration here.

The exception is the pull quote block, which I highlighted as a separate `<div>` tag for one primary reason. The pull quote has a gradient background, so you must isolate it during the slicing process. If you intend to place the `background-image` property behind text, it needs an outer element, such as a `<div>` tag. The other two image elements—the sale graphic in the left column and the picture in the right—require no containing element to be positioned properly.

---

7 In the **Layers** panel, click the **eye** icons next to the **Footer links** and **Bottom border** objects to turn on visibility.

Now, you can see all nine inner `<div>` tags required for the comp. The next step is to examine each of these `<div>` tags to determine what, if any, graphic slices you need in order to reproduce the design in CSS. Here's how I suggest approaching each of the inner `<div>` tags:

Top border: Use a flat color handled by the CSS `background-color` property; no slicing is needed.

Logo navigation: The logo requires a separate slice, which you can place either in the foreground or in the background of a `<div>` tag. One tip is to put omnipresent elements, such as the logo, in the background to avoid needless repetition by screen readers. The second element in this section, the primary navigation, can also go either way. For now, you'll skip the navigation buttons, but you'll learn how to work with them in Chapter 4, *"Building CSS Navigation Systems."*

Side navigation: Use text to handle only the secondary navigation links, and slice the sale graphic as a foreground image.

Main content: This should include all the text, unless you use a graphic for the headline. No slicing is needed.

Pullquote: Slice the gradient portion of the pull quote for background use.

Right column: Use a combination of a foreground slice (the picture) and text.

Bottom content: The graphic text in this section definitely needs to be understood to be accessible, so a foreground slice is the way to go.

Footer links: Use text only; no slicing is needed.

Bottom border: This section mirrors the top border and, as such, requires no slicing.

---

8 Choose **File > Save**, or press **Ctrl+S** (Windows) or **Cmd+S** (Mac). Leave **starfish_comp.png** open for the next exercise.

Congratulations! You have finished the first step in slicing a graphic comp for CSS layout: visualizing the components. You now know which portions of the layout you will insert as **<img>** tags.

In the next exercise, you will complete the second step of the process: slicing the foreground elements.

---

2 | Slicing Foreground Elements

Slicing foreground images is a straightforward process. In Fireworks, foreground images often are single objects on their own layers; you can also easily group several images into one object. The **Insert Slice** command is ideal for converting individual objects to slices. Another, more hands-on approach is to use the **Slice** tool to draw a rectangle around the desired image. In this exercise, you will learn both of these techniques.

Foreground images have certain characteristics that differentiate them from background images. For example, a foreground image must be nonrepeating; only CSS background properties have the ability to tile or repeat along an axis. Foreground images also typically include an `alt` attribute—such as `"follow your bliss to the caribbean"` for a photo of an island paradise—to facilitate accessibility requirements. Also, you must place any image used as a link in the foreground.

---

1 If you followed the previous exercise, **starfish_comp.png** should still be open in Fireworks. If it's not, complete Exercise 1, and then return to this exercise.

In all, you'll create five foreground images by slicing in this exercise: the photograph, the sale notice in the left column, and the three elements in the bottom content area (the two graphic text blocks and the clickable arrow).

---

2 In the **Layers** panel, click the **eye** icons next to the **Major CSS Divs** and **Detailed CSS Divs** layers to turn off the visibility of these layers. Click the **eye** icon next to **Comp** to turn on the visibility of the layer.

Before getting started with slicing, you need to hide the previously viewed visualizations.

Most of the graphics to be sliced reside in a single layer group, Comp, because I created the initial composition in Photoshop. When you open a PSD file in Fireworks, the application converts all the layers to objects and places them in a single layer group. The pull quote graphics are in another layer group in Fireworks.

---

3 In the comp, **right-click** (Windows) or **Ctrl+click** (Mac) the beach photo. From the contextual menu, choose **Insert Rectangular Slice**. If necessary, display the **Property Inspector** by choosing **Window > Properties**. In the **Property Inspector**, name the slice **beach_photo**, and press **Enter** (Windows) or **Return** (Mac). If necessary, from the **Property Inspector Slice export settings** list, select **JPEG – Better Quality** to export the slice as a JPEG.

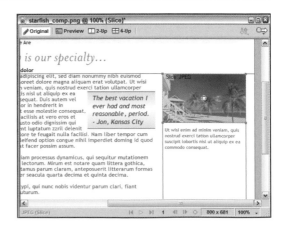

Because names for slices cannot contain spaces in Fireworks, you must substitute underscores or hyphens. When you export a slice, Fireworks uses its name for the file name.

Tip: Single images are the easiest type of objects to slice. You can also choose Edit > Insert > Rectangular Slice to create a slice.

---

4 In the **Optimize** panel, select **GIF** from the **Export File Format** list, and select **Exact** from the **Indexed Palette** list. In the **Comp** layer, click **springtime**. Hold down the **Shift** key, and click **sale outer frame** to multiple-select five files. Choose **Edit > Insert > Rectangular Slice**. When prompted by Fireworks to create one slice or multiple slices, click **Single**. In the **Property Inspector**, type **springtime_sale**, and press **Enter** (Windows) or **Return** (Mac) to name the slice.

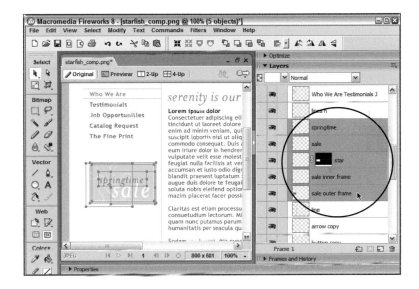

You set the optimization controls for the entire page before slicing any further objects because the remaining foreground slices all use the same export options.

You can also select graphic elements comprising multiple objects in the Document window; however, it's often difficult to avoid selecting adjacent or overlapping objects, such as the background. Although you could also group these objects and then apply the rectangular slice, it's not really necessary.

---

5 In the comp, click the **unique** text object to select it, hold down the **Shift** key, and then click the tagline **follow your bliss to the caribbean** to multiple-select the objects. Choose **Edit > Insert > Rectangular Slice**. When prompted by Fireworks to create one slice or multiple slices, click **Multiple**.

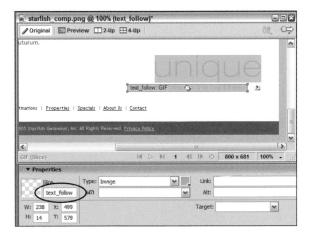

6 Click anywhere on the page to deselect both text objects, and then click the **unique** slice. In the Property Inspector, name the slice **text_unique**. Click the **follow your bliss to the caribbean** slice to select it, and in the **Property Inspector**, name the slice **text_follow**.

The Multiple slice option is a great time-saver, but you must make sure only one slice is selected when you're naming them.

Tip: Name graphic text with the prefix **text_** so it's easy to find when you get ready to import it in Dreamweaver 8.

---

7 In the **Tools** panel, select the **Zoom** tool, and create a rectangle around the boxed arrow below the **text_unique** slice. With the expanded view of the object visible, select the **Slice** tool in the **Tools** panel. Create a rectangular slice around the magnified object. In the **Property Inspector**, name the slice **box_arrow**.

Although you could select the two objects making up the box_arrow graphic and let Fireworks create the slice for you with the Insert Rectangular Slice command, it's good to know you have the option to draw slices manually.

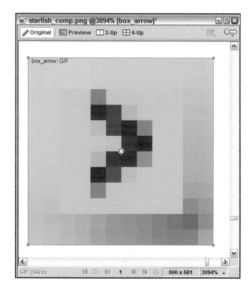

---

8 Choose **File > Save**, or press **Ctrl+S** (Windows) or **Cmd+S** (Mac). Leave **starfish_comp.png** open for the next exercise.

In this exercise, you learned how to determine the portions of your layout that should be foreground images, and you learned how to slice them. In the next exercise, you'll see how to recognize and prepare background graphics.

EXERCISE

3 | # Preparing Background Images and Gradients

CSS allows you to determine whether an image repeats when placed in the background. In some situations, the procedure for slicing background images is the same as for foreground images. When the image does not repeat, the slicing method matches the foreground technique. When you want graphics to repeat, on the other hand, you must slice them manually and precisely. Moreover, if you're placing the graphic behind text, you'll need to perform additional steps. You'll get a chance to practice background slicing for both repeating and nonrepeating elements in this exercise.

1 If you followed the previous exercise, **starfish_comp.png** should still be open in Fireworks. If it's not, complete Exercise 2, and then return to this exercise.

2 In the **Comp** layer, click the **logo** object. Choose **Edit > Insert > Rectangular Slice**. Click the newly created slice, and in the **Property Inspector**, name the slice **main_logo**.

Because the logo is a nonrepeating background image, it doesn't require any special slicing technique.

3 In the **Layers** panel, click the **plus sign** (Windows) or **triangle** (Mac) next to **pullQuote** to expand the layer, and click the **eye** icons next to the **Pull quote text**, **Top line**, and **Bottom line** layers to turn off visibility. Click the **padlock** icon next to **Comp** to lock the layer.

Selecting the proper background image for the gradient requires a fair bit of manipulation, and it's important to isolate the Gradient object. By turning off visibility and locking layers, you have successfully isolated Gradient.

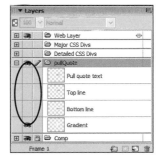

4 In the comp, click the **Gradient** object, and choose **Edit > Clone**. In the **Layers** panel, double-click the newly created **Gradient** object. In the **Property Inspector**, name the object **Large Gradient**. Choose **Modify > Transform > Numeric Transform**. In the **Numeric Transform** dialog box, choose **Scale** from the pop-up menu, and set the values for width (**W**) and height (**H**) to **200%**. Make sure the **Scale attributes** check box is turned on, and click **OK**.

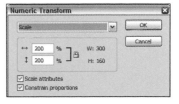

Because you're placing this gradient behind text, it's good practice to double the size of the image before slicing. Why? Should page visitors increase the size of their text, the pull quote area will expand; if the gradient remains at the original size, the background image will not be able to expand, thus breaking the design. To achieve this goal, I like to clone a gradient and slice the copy so the original design remains intact.

You may have noticed that the object's name contains a space. Spaces are legal when naming objects; however, as mentioned previously, you can't use them when naming slices.

---

5 In the **Document** window, click the **Gradient** object to display the **gradient handles**. Drag the **top handle** down so it aligns with the top of the graphic; then drag the **bottom handle** to the bottom of the gradient.

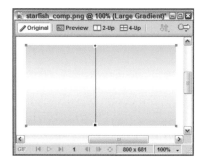

This step is not one you may always need to apply, but it is necessary with this particular gradient. When you apply this slice in Dreamweaver 8, as well as in browsers, using CSS, you basically reduce the lightness of the gradient by half. To get a shade closer to the comp, you need to adjust the gradient handles. Although this will have the effect of darkening the gradient slightly when the text expands, it's worth the trade-off.

---

6 In the **Tools** palette, select the **Slice** tool, and create a slice over the center of the large gradient, as shown in the illustration here. Make the slice **10 pixels wide** and the same height as the gradient by adjusting the width (**W**) and height (**H**) values in the **Property Inspector**. Position the slice so it starts at the top of the gradient and ends at the bottom. In the **Property Inspector**, name the slice **pullquote_bg**. From the **Slice export settings** list, select **JPEG – Better Quality**.

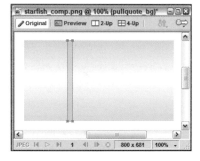

When slicing gradients, you should slice in the middle of the gradient rather than on either side; this ensures you don't capture any unwanted surrounding space.

Even if you're pretty good at creating slices by dragging, inevitably you'll end up fine-tuning the slice position and size with the Property Inspector. Use the width and height fields in Property Inspector to get the correct dimensions and make sure the slice's and the gradient's Y coordinates match.

---

7 Choose **File > Save**, or press **Ctrl+S** (Windows) or **Cmd+S** (Mac). Leave **starfish_comp.png** open for the next exercise.

In this exercise, you learned how to choose background images from your comp and prepare them for slicing. In the next exercise, you'll export the sliced graphics.

---

4 | Exporting Slices

In the previous exercise, you did all the hard work. Now, you have all the slices—both foreground and background—defined. Exporting slices in Fireworks is a one-step operation, but it's important to make sure your settings are correct; if they aren't, you could end up with a great number of unwanted images in your output folder. In this exercise, you'll set up your slices for exporting to Dreamweaver 8.

---

1 If you followed the previous exercise, **starfish_comp.png** should still be open in Fireworks. If it's not, complete Exercise 3, and then return to this exercise.

---

2 In the **Layers** panel, click the **Web Layer** layer to select all the slices in the comp. In the toolbar, click the **Export** icon. Alternatively, you can choose **File > Export**.

Because the logo is a nonrepeating background image, it doesn't require any special slicing technique.

---

3 In the **Export** dialog box, navigate to the **chap_02/assets** folder. Leave whatever is currently listed in the **File name** box. From the **Export** pop-up menu, choose **Images Only**. From the

Slices pop-up menu, choose **Export Slices**. Turn on the **Selected slices only** check box to export only the chosen slices, and make sure the **Include areas without slices** check box is turned off. Click **Export**.

Fireworks outputs all the selected sliced files, each with its own specified optimization and name. Because you turned on the Selected slices only check box, Fireworks ignores the file name noted in the dialog box (by default, the name of the first slice in the graphic). You cannot delete it, however, because Fireworks requires a value—any value—in the File name box.

---

4 Choose **File > Open**. In the **Open** dialog box, navigate to the **chap_02/assets** folder, and verify all the files you selected have been exported. Click **Cancel**.

In all, you should see seven new files: five foreground images and two background images. With the slicing done, you're ready to begin putting the slices to work in Dreamweaver 8.

5 Choose **File > Save**, or press **Ctrl+S** (Windows) or **Cmd+S** (Mac). Close **starfish_comp.png**, and press **Ctrl+Q** (Windows) or **Cmd+Q** (Mac) to quit Fireworks.

VIDEO: | **photoshop.mov**

In the previous few exercises, you learned how to prepare graphical content for your Web page in Fireworks. You can also use Photoshop to achieve the same results. To learn more about using Photoshop to prepare your graphical content, check out **photoshop.mov** in the **videos** folder on the **Dreamweaver 8 HOT CD-ROM**.

Working with Positioning and Floats

Taken together, the **position** and **float** properties are the core engine driving CSS layouts. Without them, CSS-based designs simply would not exist.

In all, the **position** property accepts four values. The first, **static**, is essentially the default value and reflects exactly where the page elements are in the flow of the document. If you look at a Dreamweaver 8 page consisting of a series of **<div>** tags without any CSS styling, and then look at the same page after you've styled all the **<div>** tags with a **position: static** declaration, you won't see any difference. Because this property essentially has no variation in positioning, the **position: static** declaration is rarely used; if that's what you want, you can simply omit the positioning property from the CSS declaration block for any given rule.

The other three positioning values—**relative**, **absolute**, and **fixed**—are far more meaningful. The key to understanding these values is a concept known as the **containing block**. Every tag in an HTML (**H**yper**T**ext **M**arkup **L**anguage) page is within at least one other element (nested). If no tags are nested, the **<html>** tag is the containing block. When one **<div>** tag is nested within another, the outer **<div>** tag becomes the containing block. As you'll see, the way each position value relates to the containing block underscores the differences between them.

The position: relative declaration

The **position: relative** declaration is perhaps the most misunderstood of all the CSS positioning

attributes. The point of confusion comes from the term **relative**. What is a **<div>** tag styled with **position: relative** relative to? The somewhat surprising answer is, the **<div>** tag. In other words, the containing block is the element itself. When you combine the **left** and **top** properties with a **position: relative** declaration, the styled element moves relative to its current position in the flow of the document.

For example, let's say a design has a photo, an **<h1>** heading, and a paragraph of text, all in one column.

You can create a CSS style for the **<h1>** tag and assign it a **position: relative** declaration, like so:

```
h1 {
    position: relative;
    left: 20px;
    top: 30px;
}
```

In this case, the **<h1>** tag moves 20 pixels to the left and 30 pixels down from its current position in the flow of the document. In fact, it moves so much out of the flow of the document that it overlaps the paragraph below it.

In truth, **position: relative** is used in combination with **left** and **top** far less frequently than by itself. When used alone, **position: relative** resets the starting coordinates for any nested element styled with **position: absolute**, discussed next.

The position: absolute declaration

The **position: absolute** declaration gives CSS designers the power to place any content at any specified location, outside the document flow. Using **position: absolute** depends on the containing block to determine what the **left** and **top** values are relative to. For this positioning attribute, the containing block is the nearest ancestor element styled with a **position: relative**, **position: fixed** declaration or another **position: absolute** declaration; or, if such an ancestor element does not exist, the root **<html>** tag is the containing block.

For example, you can add the following CSS rule to a page:

```
#columnContent {
    position: absolute;
    left: 100px;
    top: 25px;

}
```

The affected column is rendered 100 pixels from the left of the page and 25 pixels from the top—totally obscuring the logo.

To wrap the column in a **<div>** tag, use the **position: relative** declaration. Because the new **<div>** tag—which, as the nearest ancestor tag, now becomes the containing block—appears in the code flow after the logo, the column is rendered 100 pixels from the left and 25 pixels from

---

NOTE:

The Curative Powers of Position: Relative

The **position: relative** declaration has also proved valuable for clearing up Microsoft Internet Explorer 6 CSS display problems. One general Internet Explorer debugging tactic is to apply a **position: relative** declaration to content selectors within a **<div>** tag not rendering properly. For example, let's say you have a **<div>** tag with an ID of **#sidebar**, and the headings and paragraph content do not immediately display in Internet Explorer. In this situation, you can create a style like this:

```
#sidebar h1 { position: relative; }
```

This style has no effect on any other modern browser; the affected **<h1>** tag cannot contain any other element, and it remains in the current flow of the document. It will, however, cause Internet Explorer 6 to render the missing content correctly.

the top of the wrapping **<div>** tag, not from the top of the page.

Dreamweaver 8 treats elements styled with **position: absolute** differently from those with the other positioning values. Any **<div>** tag with a **position: absolute** style appears with a border and handle in the upper-left corner. This appearance stems from a long Dreamweaver 8 history of working with **<div>** tags absolutely positioned with inline CSS as layers. If you select the handle, the **Layer Property Inspector** appears. You can also drag the handle to a new location, and the new values are written into the applicable CSS rule.

The position: fixed declaration

As the name implies, the **position: fixed** declaration has the ability to keep an element in a specified location, even if the rest of the page is scrolling. This is possible because the containing block is not a page element at all, but rather the viewport. The **viewport** is the frame you're looking through for a given medium: When the medium is a browser, the viewport is the browser window.

For example, say you always want your company logo to remain onscreen, no matter what. One way to do that is to use the **position: fixed** declaration, like this:

```
#logo {
  position: fixed;
  left: 10px;
  top: 10px;
}
```

When the page appears in an expanded browser window, no real difference is visible. All elements appear in their proper positions.

If the browser window is shortened, a scroll bar appears. When the site visitor scrolls down the page, the column section (the photo, heading, and paragraph) moves up, but the logo stays in the same position. This effect is visible only in a CSS-compliant browser such as Firefox or Safari; you won't see the fixed effect in Dreamweaver 8.

To make the example a bit clearer, I added a **z-index: 10** declaration to the **#logo** CSS rule in the illustration shown here. This has the effect of putting the **#logo <div>** tag in front of the one containing the column.

Internet Explorer and Position: Fixed

Support for **position: fixed** is lacking in both Internet Explorer 5 and 6. However, you can simulate the effect by using conditional comments. **Conditional comments** are a mechanism for passing CSS styles and other code to Internet Explorer. Best of all, the code validates properly because conditional comments use a standard HTML comment as the shell. To achieve a **position: fixed** cross-browser effect for the example in this section, you need to slightly rework the previous code. Instead of using **position: fixed** in the #**logo** CSS rule, replace it with **position: absolute** and add the following CSS rule after the #**logo** rule is declared:

```
html>body div#logo { position: fixed; }
```

Because of the differences between Internet Explorer 5 and 6, you need two separate conditional comments. For Internet Explorer 5, you use the following code:

```
<!–[if IE 5]>
<style type="text/css">
body {
  overflow: hidden;
}
div#logo {
  height: 100%;
  overflow: auto;
}
</style>
<![endif]–>
For Internet Explorer 6, you use the following:
<!–[if IE 6]>
<style type="text/css">
html {
  overflow: hidden;
}
div#logo {
  height: 100%;
  overflow-y: auto;
}
</style>
<![endif]–>
```

Both conditional comments work the same way: They hide content that cannot be shown in the browser window (the overflow) within the main document element. Internet Explorer 5 considers the **<body>** tag to be the main document element, and version 6 considers it to be the **<html>** tag.

The float property

One other property is equally important for CSS layout: **float**. As you'll see in the examples later in the chapter in Exercise 5, the **float** property is key for integrating text and images, as well as for constructing more complex layouts such as multiple columns. In its basic usage, the **float** property acts like the HTML `align="left"` or `align="right"` attribute. When you include the **float: left** declaration in a CSS style rule, the styled tag—often an image—appears flush left in the container, and any text flows around the styled tag's right side.

The reverse is true for a **float: right** declaration.

In HTML, inline tags represent images. The **float** property takes an additional value when applied to block-level tags like **<div>** tags. Many CSS layout designs rely on the **float** property applied to **<div>** tags to display columns side by side. You can accomplish this goal using a number of techniques; perhaps the simplest is to assign **float: left** (or **float: right**) declarations to each **<div>** tag

you want to render as a column. Additionally, you should give each column a width, either of a fixed size in pixels or of a percentage.

For example, to lay out two columns next to each other, your CSS might look like this:

```
#content {
    width: 400px;
    float: left;
}
#columnContent {
    width: 205px;
    float: left;
}
```

The two **<div>** tags follow one another in the HTML code.

Wherever possible, it's best to assign a width to any CSS style that uses the **float** property. Floats are one of the most problematic of CSS properties for browsers to render, and you can rectify numerous errors by declaring a width for the **float** property. In the next exercise, you'll practice incorporating images into your layout.

5 | Applying Comp Images to a Layout

Since you've mastered slicing images and know a little bit about positioning and floats, it's time to dive into Dreamweaver 8 and begin integrating the images into a layout. For the purposes of this exercise, I have already constructed a basic CSS layout. By using this existing layout, you'll learn the different CSS techniques required for incorporating both foreground and background images.

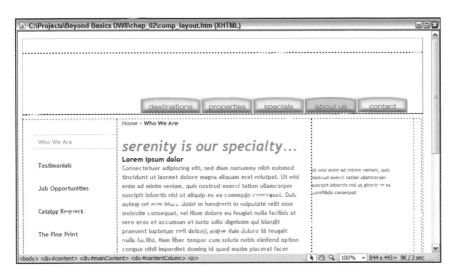

1 In Dreamweaver 8, open **comp_layout.htm** from the **chap_02** folder you copied to your desktop. In the **Document** toolbar **Visual Aids** menu, make sure the **CSS Layout Outlines** and **CSS Layout Box Model** options are on.

Both the CSS Layout Outlines and CSS Layout Box Model options are new—and extremely useful— additions to the Visual Aids menu of Dreamweaver 8. The CSS Layout Outlines option places a dotted border around any **<div>** tags. Select any **<div>** tag when the CSS Layout Box Model option is on, and Dreamweaver indicates any padding, margin, or borders both visually and with numeric values.

2 In the top **<div>** tag on the page, position your cursor in **#topborder**. In the **CSS Styles** panel, switch to **Current** mode, and make sure the **Show Only Set Properties** view (at the bottom of the panel) is selected. In the **Properties** pane, click **Add Property**. In the **Property** column, type **background-color**, and press **Enter** (Windows) or **Return** (Mac). Click the color swatch, and choose the third darkest gray, **#666666**, as shown in the illustration here.

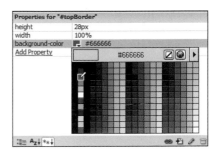

One of the key concepts to remember when creating CSS layouts is that you can re-create almost any flat color in CSS without sliced graphics.

Tip: If you were having trouble pinpointing the background color, you could sample the color directly from the comp by positioning your graphics program and Dreamweaver 8 side by side and moving your eyedropper from Dreamweaver to the image in your graphics program.

---

3 Position your cursor in the **<div>** tag at the bottom of the page, and repeat the previous step to add a new **background-color** property with a value of **#666666** to **#bottomBorder**.

---

4 Position your cursor in the **#topNavigation** **<div>** tag, located directly below the **#topBorder** **<div>** tag you assigned a **background-color** property to in the previous step. In the **CSS Styles** panel, click **Edit Style**. In the **CSS Rule definition for X** dialog box, click the **Background** category. Click **Browse**, navigate to the **chap_02/assets** folder, click **main_logo.gif** to select it, and click **OK**. From the **Repeat** pop-up menu, choose **no-repeat**. From the **Horizontal position** pop-up menu, choose **30**. From the **Vertical position** pop-up menu, choose **50**. Click **OK**.

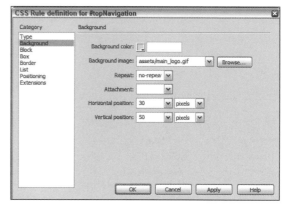

Here, the logo resides in the background of a **<div>** tag. By default, a background image repeats both horizontally and vertically, or **tiles**, to fill the available space. By choosing no-repeat for the Repeat pop-up menu, the image appears only once. You can set the coordinates for the background image through the **background-position** property, represented in the CSS Rule definition for X dialog box by the combined Horizontal position and Vertical position pop-up menus. The **background-position** property uses the given values (which can also be percentages) as offsets from the upper-left corner of the **<div>** tag.

NOTE:

Background Versus Foreground Logos

Why place the logo image in the background rather than the foreground? Pros and cons exist for both possibilities. Some designers want the logo in the foreground because they use the logo as a somewhat subtle, de facto link to the homepage. Although such a convention is widely applied, it's not universally recognized. Other designers think it's better to simply use a Home button in the main navigation. A clear reason to push an image to the background is to avoid the constant repeating of the alt text when someone using a screen reader browses the site.

5 Position your cursor in the right content column, in front of the placeholder text. Press **Enter** (Windows) or **Return** (Mac), and then press the **up arrow** key once to move your cursor to the newly created line above the paragraph. In the **Insert** bar, click the **Common** category, and click the **Image** button. In the **Select Image Source** dialog box, click **beach_photo.jpg**, and then click **OK**.

As you might expect, placing certain foreground images into a CSS layout is straightforward. The right content column includes a substantial **padding-top** value, 95 pixels, to force the top of the image to align with the text in the main content area.

---

6 Position your cursor in the **#contentFeature <div>** tag located beneath the main and right column content areas. In the **Insert** bar, click the **Image** button, and then click **text_unique.gif**. Click **OK** to insert the graphic. In the **Property Inspector Alt** field, type **Unique**. Press the **right arrow** key to move off the image, and press **Shift+Enter** (Windows) or **Shift+Return** (Mac) to insert a line break.

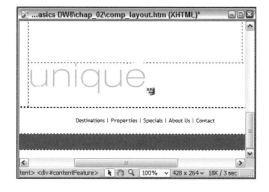

The bottom content section comprises three foreground images: two text graphics and a boxed arrow. Here, you are using foreground graphics expressly because you want screen readers to be able to find the **<alt>** tag of the text images and "click" the boxed arrow image. The design calls for the two text images to be placed one on top of the other, so a simple line break, or **
** tag, works. If you required more spacing control, you could insert the images into separate paragraphs and space them through CSS margin styles.

---

7 In the **Insert** bar, click the **Image** button again. In the **Select Image Source** dialog box, click **text_ follow.gif**. In the **Property Inspector Alt** field, type **follow your bliss to the caribbean**. Press the **right arrow** key to move off the selected image, add a space, and click **Image**. In the **Select Image Source** dialog box, click **box_arrow.gif**, and click **OK**. From the **Property Inspector Class** list, choose **arrowBox**. To move all elements to the right, choose **<div#contentFeature>** from the **Tag Selector**. Then, in the **CSS Styles** panel **Properties** pane, click **Add Property**, and type **text-align**. Press **Enter** (Windows) or **Return** (Mac), and choose **right** from the list.

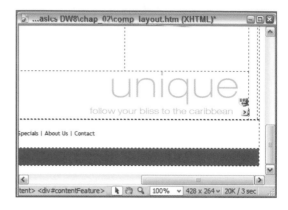

In this step, you added the remaining two foreground images, one inline with the other. You applied a previously created style, **arrowBox**, to the arrow graphic to give it some needed padding. You also added the `text-align: right` declaration to the containing `<div>` tag to move the content flush right.

The final graphic element to add to the layout is the pull quote—or more specifically, the background for the pull quote. You'll actually extract the pull quote from the content by using a styled `<span>` tag.

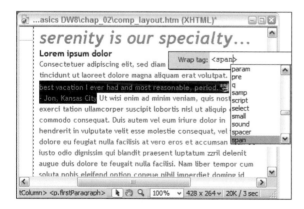

8 In the placeholder text of the main content area, select the second sentence. Press **Ctrl+T** (Windows) or **Cmd+T** (Mac) to open the **Quick Tag Editor** in **Wrap** mode. Type **span** in the tag brackets, as shown in the illustration here, and press **Enter** (Windows) or **Return** (Mac).

9 In the **Tag Selector**, **right-click** (Windows) or **Ctrl+click** (Mac) the **<span>** tag, and choose **Set Class > pullQuote**. In the **CSS Styles** panel, click **Edit Rule**. In the **CSS Rule definition for X** dialog box, click the **Background** category. Click **Browse**, and navigate to the **chap_02/assets** folder. Click **pullquote_bg.jpg** to select it, and click **OK**. From the **Repeat** list, choose **repeat-x**. From the **Horizontal position** pop-up menu, choose **50%**. From the **Vertical position** pop-up menu, choose **50%**. Click **OK**. In the **Document** toolbar, choose **Visual Aids > Hide all Visual Aids**.

Here you put to practice the technique discussed when slicing the double-sized background gradient. By declaring the `repeat: repeat-x` declaration, you tile the image, which is 10 pixels wide, across the containing element, the pull quote box. Setting the positioning property to a 50% width and a 50% height has the effect of scaling the image to half its size, which displays the gradient as designed.

10 Choose **File > Save**, or press **Ctrl+S** (Windows) or **Cmd+S** (Mac). Close **comp_layout.htm**.

In this chapter, you learned how to visualize CSS layouts in your graphics editor as well as differentiate between foreground and background graphics. This is definitely an area where practice makes perfect. Because designs vary greatly, the more designs you examine, the better you'll be able to see how you can structure a comp in CSS. You also learned how to slice both standard and repeating graphics and then how to apply those graphics to your layouts in Dreamweaver 8.

In the next chapter, you'll develop a full two-column layout from scratch and learn how to convert it to a three-column layout and back again.

3

Creating CSS Column Layouts

For all the benefits of using CSS to create your page layouts—more flexibility, less code, faster download—this technique does have one big drawback: the learning curve. Although inserting layout elements, primarily `<div>` tags, is easy in Dreamweaver 8, understanding where those elements go is something else altogether. In this chapter, you'll learn how to create the two most common layouts, those with two and three columns. Both layout variations include a header section and a footer section, and you can easily modify them to fit your particular needs.

Crafting a Two-Column CSS Layout

Most two-column layouts have a similar basic structure. A header area spans the top of the page, and a footer area goes across the bottom. A content section appears in between—the meat (or the tofu) in the sandwich, if you will. This content region contains the page's columns and is almost always the largest of the layout's three main zones (header, content, and footer) when the page is finished and filled with text, images, and other media. Frequently, an outer section surrounds all three areas to control the overall page's positioning and size.

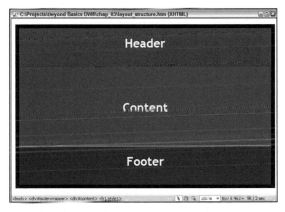

Two-column layouts often start with just one column for the three main regions.

Numerous variations are possible within the content region. For two-column layouts, the most typical scenario is one narrow column on the left, which is most often used for navigation, and a wider main content column. The narrow column can actually appear on the left or right of the content column but is usually a fixed width. The content column takes up the balance of the space.

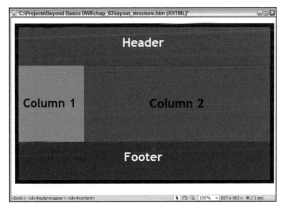

In a two-column design, one column is typically wider than the other.

The outer wrapper acts as a constraint to make sure the two columns, taken together, are the same width as the header and footer. If you want the layout to extend the full width of the browser window, you can set the outer wrapper's width to 100 percent. Alternatively, set the outer wrapper to a fixed width, such as 800 pixels, to keep the layout the same width regardless of the browser window dimensions. In the following exercise, you'll create the basic structure for a CSS layout in Dreamweaver 8.

1 | Setting Up the Page Structure

Enough with the theory—let's build a page! In this exercise, you'll create a new page and begin defining and applying the associated CSS. The page will follow the concepts outlined in the previous section. You'll start with a minor bit of housekeeping that will help you write better, more concise code.

---

1 Copy the **chap_03** folder from the **Dreamweaver 8 HOT CD-ROM** onto your desktop.

---

2 Choose **Edit > Preferences** (Windows) or **Dreamweaver > Preferences** (Mac). In the **Preferences** dialog box, click the **CSS Styles** category. Under **Use shorthand for**, turn on the **Font, Background, Margin and padding, Border and border width,** and **List-Style** check boxes. Click **OK**.

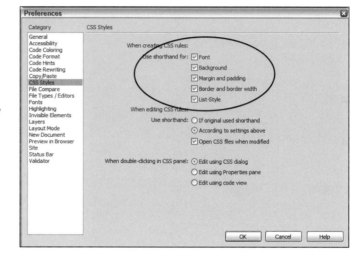

CSS shorthand combines both selectors and properties and can significantly reduce the size of your CSS file. For example, let's say you want to set both the top and bottom margins to **0px** and the side margins to **auto**. Without CSS shorthand, the code looks like this:

```
#container {
  margin-top: 0px;
  margin-right: auto;
  margin-bottom: 0px;
  margin-left: auto;
}
```

However, by turning on the Margin and padding check box, you dramatically reduce the amount of code:

```
#container {
  margin: 0px auto;
}
```

It's also important to familiarize yourself with CSS shorthand syntax because many of the more advanced designs found on the Web use it exclusively.

---

3 In the **Files** panel, open **two_col_layout.htm** from the **chap_03** folder you copied to your desktop. In the **Document** toolbar, make sure the **CSS Layout Box Model** and **CSS Layout Outlines** options are on.

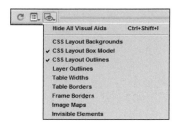

To give you a head start, I've already given two_col_layout.htm a title; otherwise, the page is blank. The first phase of creating a new CSS structure is to define the core layout styles.

---

4 In the **CSS Styles** panel, click **New CSS Rule**. In the **New CSS Rule** dialog box, click the **Advanced** radio button under **Selector Type** to set the selector. Type **#outerwrapper** in the **Selector** field to name it. Under **Define in**, click the **This document only** radio button, which is currently unselected, and click **OK**.

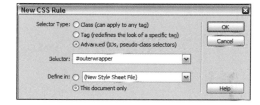

All the basic CSS layout rules will be ID selectors like **#outerwrapper** because each **<div>** tag they are assigned to is unique on the page.

You might be wondering why you're defining the rule in the current document. After all, isn't using external style sheets considered a best practice for a CSS-based site? Everyone, including myself, agrees that's true. However, the first time you develop a basic page layout in CSS, it's far easier to keep all the styles in the same page; with this method, you need to maintain only a single document, and debugging and testing the layout are much faster. You will, of course, need to move the embedded CSS styles to an external style sheet prior to building additional pages.

---

5 In the **CSS Rule definition for #outerwrapper** dialog box, click the **Box** category. Set **Width** to **800 pixels**. Turn off the **Same for all** check box for **Margin**, and set **Top** to **0 pixels**, **Right** to **auto**, **Bottom** to **0 pixels**, and **Left** to **auto**. Click **OK** when you're done.

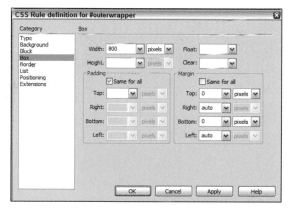

For this design, the layout width is fixed at 800 pixels. By assigning this value to the style controlling the outer wrapper's **<div>** tag, you can set all the other layout styles to 100 percent width, and the design will never get wider than the desired pixel width. As noted previously, setting the left and right margins of the outer element to **auto** has the effect of centering the design; with **0** for the top and bottom margins, the upper and lower borders will hug the browser window.

6 In the **CSS Styles** panel, click **New CSS Rule**. In the **New CSS Rule** dialog box, type **#header, #content, #footer** in the **Selector** field. Click **OK**. In the **CSS Rule definition for #header, #content, #footer** dialog box, click the **Box** category, and set **Width** to **100%**. Click **OK**.

It's a good idea to group selectors whenever they have a common property and value; once you have defined them in this way, you can make major changes to all three selectors in one step. Here, all the major layout rules share a width of 100 percent, which will be restricted by *#outerwrapper*'s fixed-width value of 800 pixels.

NOTE:

Getting Quick Percentages

Although all Dreamweaver 8 interfaces present a **percentage** option in the adjacent pop-up menu, Dreamweaver 8 also offers a faster way to apply a percentage setting. In the field where the number value appears, type both the number and a percent sign; for example, type **100%**. Press the **Tab** key to confirm your entry, and Dreamweaver 8 automatically removes the percent sign and selects **percent** from the pop-up menu. That's definitely faster!

---

7 Click anywhere in the **Document** window. In the **Insert** bar, click the **Common** category, and click **Insert Div Tag**. In the **Insert Div Tag** dialog box, leave the **Insert** pop-up menu set to **At insertion point**, and from the **ID** pop-up menu, choose **outerwrapper**.

Because the **<body>** section of the page is empty, you can place the first layout **<div>** tag where the cursor is currently (the top of the page). When you insert it, you'll see an outlined **<div>** tag because the CSS Layout Outlines option is on. Also, you'll see this placeholder text: Content for id "outerwrapper" Goes Here.

---

8 In the **Insert** bar, click the **Common** category, and click **Insert Div Tag**. In the **Insert Div Tag** dialog box, choose **After start of tag <div id="outerwrapper">** from the **Insert** pop-up menu. From the **ID** pop-up menu, choose **header**, and click **OK**. In the **Document** window, select **placeholder content** for the **outerwrapper <div>** tag, and press **Delete**.

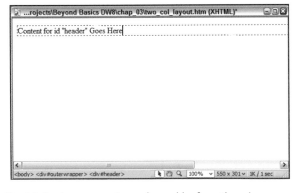

To place the header **<div>** tag within the **outerwrapper <div>** tag, you must insert it after the tag starts and before it ends. Dreamweaver 8 places the code for the header **<div>** tag directly after the **<div id="outerwrapper">** code and before the placeholder content, which makes the header content appear above the **outerwrapper** content. Because no true **outerwrapper** content exists outside the major layout **<div>** tags, you can safely remove the placeholder text.

---

9 In the **Insert** bar, click the **Common** category, and click **Insert Div Tag**. In the **Insert Div Tag** dialog box, choose **After tag <div id="header">** from the **Insert** pop-up menu. From the **ID** pop-up menu, choose **content**, and click **OK**.

The first of the final two **<div>** tags follows directly after the header **<div>** tag. By placing it directly after the header **<div>** tag, it remains within the **outerwrapper <div>** tag.

10 In the **Insert** bar, click the **Common** category, and click **Insert Div Tag** one last time. In the **Insert Div Tag** dialog box, choose **After tag <div id="content">** from the **Insert** pop-up menu. From the **ID** pop-up menu, choose **footer**, and click **OK**.

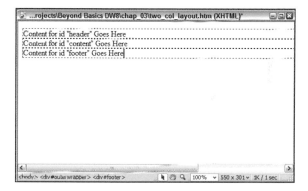

You need to define one last CSS style. To bring the page to the edges of the browser, you'll need to set the **<body>** tag to a **0** margin. While you're defining the **<body>** tag, it's also a good idea to declare the font for the page.

11 In the **CSS Styles** panel, click **New CSS Rule**. In the **New CSS Rule** dialog box, under **Selector Type**, click the **Tag** radio button, and type **body** in the **Tag** field. In the **CSS Rule Definition Type** category, click **Trebuchet MS** in your Dreamweaver 8 **Font** list to select it. (If you have not previously set up **Trebuchet MS** in the **Font** list, choose **Edit Font List**, and add the font family **Trebuchet MS, Verdana, sans-serif**. If you're unclear on how to do this, see the sidebar "Adding Font Families.") Click the **Box** category, and set **Margin** to **0**. Click **OK**.

The basic CSS structure of the page is now complete, and you're ready to begin filling in the major **<div>** tags.

12 Choose **File > Save**, or press **Ctrl+S** (Windows) or **Cmd+S** (Mac). Leave **two_col_layout.htm** open for the next exercise.

In this exercise, you created the basic layout for a two-column page using CSS styles and **<div>** tags. Next, you'll focus on the header section of the page and lay the foundation for the primary navigation.

NOTE:

Adding Font Families

Dreamweaver 8 comes with a core selection of font families that work for a great deal of Web design. However, you can always customize your font selections. Once you do, your enhanced options are available on every site.

At the bottom of every **Font** list, whether in the **Property Inspector**, in the **CSS Rule definition for X** dialog box, or even in **Code** view, you'll find the **Edit Font List** option. Click **Edit Font List** to open the **Edit Font List** dialog box. The current font families appear in the upper area, labeled **Font list**, and a list of your system fonts appears in the lower-right area, labeled **Available Fonts**. Select any entry from the **Available Fonts** list, and click the **Add** (<<) button to place the selected font in the **Chosen Font** pane. Add fonts to the same pane to create a font family, such as **Trebuchet MS, Verdana, sans-serif**. It's always best to include one of the generic fonts (cursive, decorative, fantasy, monospace, sans-serif, or serif) as the final member of your font family, just in case the user doesn't have any of the fonts you selected.

2 | Building the Header and Navigation

Many headers include a logo and the primary navigation and maintain a constant width and height. Oftentimes, a dark gray border crosses the top of the header while framing the page. In this exercise, you will continue building the two-column layout you began in the previous exercise. Specifically, you will build a two-column version of the page comp in Chapter 1, *"Getting Started."* A two-column design is one of the most common layouts on the Web.

1 If you followed the previous exercise, **two_col_layout.htm** should still be open in Dreamweaver. If it's not, complete Exercise 1, and then return to this exercise.

2 In the **CSS Styles** panel, click **New CSS Rule**. In the **New CSS Rule** dialog box, click the **Advanced** radio button under **Selector Type**, and type **#header** in the **Selector** field. Click **OK**. In the **CSS Rule definition for #header** dialog box, click the **Border** category, and turn off all three **Same for all** check boxes. For the **Top** border, set **Style** to **Solid**, **Width to 28 pixels**, and **Color** to **#666666**.

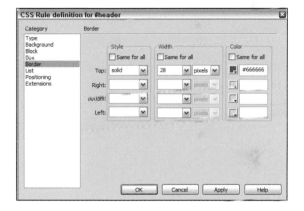

Even though you defined **#header** as part of a group selector in the previous exercise, it still requires some individual styles. You can easily add the thick dark gray border to the top of the **#header**. Because you turned on shorthand for border attributes, you write this declaration as follows: `border-top: 28px solid #666666`.

Note: If you worked your way through the exercises in Chapter 2, *"Designing Layouts with CSS,"* you'll probably notice you handled the top border differently. In that chapter, you established a separate `<div>` tag, styled with a `background-color` property. Both techniques are valid, depending on the graphic used for the border and the browser compatibility desired. With a flat color, such as the solid gray in this example, the border style applied here works well in modern browsers.

3 While still in the **CSS Rule definition for #header** dialog box, click the **Positioning** category, and choose **relative** from the **Type** pop-up menu. Set **Height** to **122 pixels**. Click **OK**.

You need the `relative` positioning attribute because the `<div>` tag this style is applied to will contain an absolutely positioned style. You'll recall from Chapter 2, *"Designing Layouts with CSS,"* that unless you want to position the `<div>` tag relative to the upper left of the document, absolutely positioned `<div>` tags must be within a relative positioned `<div>` tag. Finally, you specify the height of the `#header` style to match the comp.

4 In the **#header** `<div>` tag, delete the placeholder content. In the **CSS Styles** panel, make sure **#header** is selected, and in the **Properties** pane, click **Add Property**. Type **background** in the **Property** column, and press **Enter** (Windows) or **Return** (Mac). In the **Value** column, type **url(assets/main_logo.gif) no-repeat 50px 46px**. Press **Enter** (Windows) or **Return** (Mac).

As shown in Chapter 2, *"Designing Layouts with CSS,"* the logo appears as a background image. Like with the `border` CSS property, you can com-

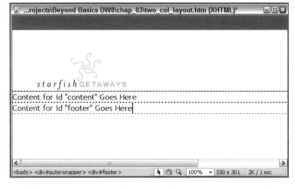

bine the various background properties in a single series of values. The two final pixel values represent the horizontal and vertical (or, if you prefer, *x* and *y*) coordinates for the left and top of the image, respectively.

5 In the **CSS Styles** panel, click **New CSS Rule**. In the **New CSS Rule** dialog box, click the **Advanced** radio button under **Selector Type**, and type **#navbar** in the **Selector** field. Click **OK**. In the **CSS Rule definition for #navbar** dialog box, click the **Positioning** category, and choose **absolute** from the **Position** pop-up menu. In the **Placement** section, type **30px** in the **right** field and **4px** in the **bottom** field. Click **OK**.

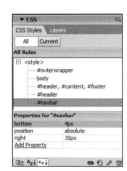

The main navigation will appear in an absolutely positioned `<div>` tag. Although you could determine offset values from the left and top corner of the containing `<div>` tag, **#header**, it's much easier to use the `right` and `bottom` properties, because `#navbar` is designed to appear nearly flush right and at the bottom of the area.

6 In the **Insert** bar, click the **Common** category, and click **Insert Div Tag**. In the **Insert Div Tag** dialog box, choose **After start of tag <div id="header">** from the **Insert** pop-up menu. From the **ID** pop-up menu, select **navbar**, and click **OK**.

With the properly styled **<div>** tag in place, it's time to add the navigation elements. For this exercise, you'll apply a series of images previously exported from Adobe Fireworks.

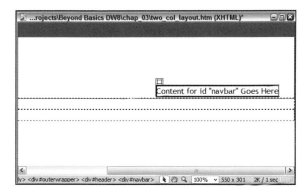

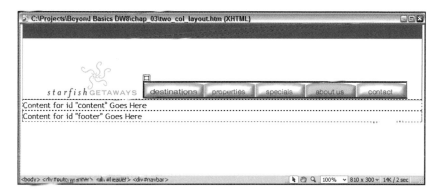

7 Select the placeholder text in the **#navbar <div>** tag, and delete it. In the **Insert** bar, click **Image**. Navigate to the **assets/topNav** folder, and select **destinations.gif**. After the image is added to the page, press the **right arrow** key. Using the same series of steps, add the following images: **properties.gif**, **specials.gif**, **about_us_f2.gif**, and **contact.gif**.

This inserts each image side by side; no additional positioning is necessary. To demonstrate how to indicate the current page, I've applied the image exported from frame 2 of the About Us symbol.

8 Choose **File > Save**, or press **Ctrl+S** (Windows) or **Cmd+S** (Mac). Leave **two_col_layout.htm** open for the next exercise.

In this exercise, you styled the header section to add a company logo and primary navigation. In the next exercise, you'll create and apply the styles for the two columns in the layout.

NOTE:

Learning More About Creating Navigation

If you want to make the navigation bar interactive, you need to add links to each image along with **Swap Image** behaviors. Chapter 4, *"Building CSS Navigation Systems,"* discusses navigation in full.

3 | Containing the Content

The content area is the most sophisticated page area. With a two-column structure at its heart, this area incorporates the side navigation as well as a split content section. In all, you require four separate CSS styles and `<div>` tags to achieve the goals of the design: `#content` (the outer wrapper for the area), `#navColumn` (the side navigation), `#contentColumn` (main text and image region), and `#contentFeature` (the highlighted section below the `#contentColumn` `<div>` tag). In this exercise, you'll create the styles for each column, apply them to separate `<div>` tags, and insert placeholder content.

---

1 If you followed the previous exercise, **two_col_layout.htm** should still be open. If it's not, complete Exercise 2, and then return to this exercise.

---

2 In the **CSS Styles** panel, click **New CSS Rule**. In the **New CSS Rule** dialog box, click the **Advanced** radio button under **Selector Type**, and type **#content** in the **Selector** field. Click **OK**. In the **CSS Rule definition for #content** dialog box, select the **Type** category, and set **Size** to **.8 ems**. Click the **Box** category, turn off the **Same for all** check box for **Padding**, and then set **Top** to **10 pixels**. Click the **Positioning** category, and set **Overflow** to **Auto**. Click **OK**.

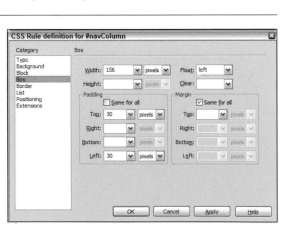

As with the `#header` style, you are establishing rules specific to the `#content` style. You're making the text a bit smaller than usual (about 10 points instead of 12), and you're giving the content a bit of room to breathe at the top.

The `overflow: auto` declaration is an important one because it keeps content in floated `<div>` tags from breaking through their container elements. For several years, designers handled the same issue by inserting a blank `<div>` tag with a `clear: both` style. Although this largely worked, it added an unnecessary markup element for presentation only—exactly what CSS is meant to avoid.

---

3 In the **CSS Styles** panel, click **New CSS Rule**. In the **New CSS Rule** dialog box, click the **Advanced** radio button under **Selector Type**, and type **#navColumn** in the **Selector** field. Click **OK**. In the **CSS Rule definition for #navColumn** dialog box, click the **Text** category, set **Size** to **1 ems** and **Line height** to **150%**. Click the **Box** category, and set **Width** to **156 pixels** and **Float** to **left**. Turn off the **Same for all** check box for **Padding**, and type **30** for both **Top** and **Left**. Click **OK**.

The links in the side navigation are simply text, so you can easily set up the design of them here. You're applying a static width because the overall layout is not intended to expand. Floating this column is a key aspect to creating a two-column design.

---

4 In the **Insert** bar, click the **Common** category, and click **Insert Div Tag**. In the **Insert Div Tag** dialog box, choose **After start of tag <div id="#content">** from the **Insert** pop-up menu, and choose **navColumn** from the **ID** pop-up menu. Click **OK**.

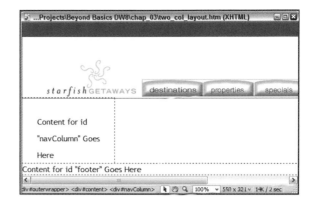

5 Remove the placeholder text **Content for id "navColumn" Goes Here**. Type the following text, with each phrase on its own line: **Who We Are**, **Testimonials**, **Job Opportunities**, **Catalog Request**, and **The Fine Print**. In the **CSS Styles** panel, click **New CSS Rule**. In the **New CSS Rule** dialog box, click the **Class** radio button under **Selector Type**, and type **.currentLink** in the **Name** field. Click **OK**.

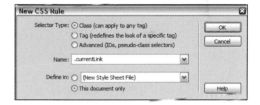

6 When the **CSS Style Definition** dialog box opens, click the **Type** category, and set **Color** to **#006699**. Click the **Box** category, and turn off the **Same for all** check boxes for **Padding** and **Margin**. Set **Padding Left** to **10 pixels** and **Margin Left** to **-10 pixels**. Click the **Border** category, turn off the **Same for all** check boxes for **Padding** and **Margin**, and set both the **Top** and **Bottom** settings to **solid**, **1 pixel**, and **#CCCCCC**. Click **OK**. Choose the top paragraph in the side navigation, and from the **Property Inspector Style** list, choose **currentLink**.

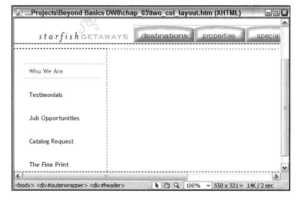

This applies the **.currentLink** style to whatever page is currently displayed. The most interesting aspects of this style are the top and bottom borders. You achieve the effect of starting 10 pixels in and continuing to the edge of the **<div>** tag through the dual **padding-left** and **margin-left** settings. The negative 10-pixel **margin-left** value compensates for the **padding-left** value and keeps the text aligned with the borders.

The navigation text style matches the design, including indicating the current page. However, as you'll see in Chapter 4, *"Building CSS Navigation Systems,"* additional CSS work is necessary to keep the same look and feel when you apply links.

7 In the **CSS Styles** panel, click **New CSS Rule**. In the **New CSS Rule** dialog box, click the **Advanced** radio button under **Selector Type**, and type **#contentColumn** for **Selector**. Click **OK**. In the **CSS Rule definition for #contentColumn** dialog box, click the **Type** category, and set **Color** to **#666666**. Click the **Box** category, set **Width** to **583 pixels**, and set **Float** to **Left**. Turn off the **Same for all** check box for **Padding**, set **Right** to **20 pixels**, and set **Left** to **10 pixels**. Click the **Border** category, turn off all three **Same for all** check boxes, and set **Bottom** to **solid, 1 pixel**, and **#CCCCCC**. Click **OK**.

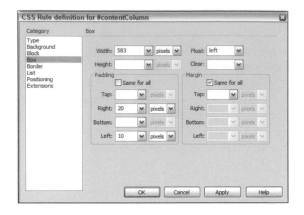

The #contentColumn style is the second of the two major columns on the page; again, it is floated left. Both of the float: left columns stand side by side—but only because they are the right widths. For this design, all columns are static, so you're using set pixel widths.

Remember that the outer width of the container style is 800 pixels. The navigation column takes up 186 pixels (156 pixels in width plus 30 in left padding); the content column makes up the difference (583 pixels in width plus 20 in left padding plus 10 in right padding plus 1 equals 614). If you added one more pixel to the width, padding, margin, or border, the content column would drop below the navigation column. This sets the light, 1-pixel border on the left of the column to expand as needed.

Figuring out the proper measurements is a key requirement when designing CSS layouts.

---

8 In the **Insert Div Tag** dialog box, from the **Insert** pop-up menu, choose **After tag <div id="navColumn">**, and from the **ID** pop-up menu, choose **mainContent**. Click **OK**.

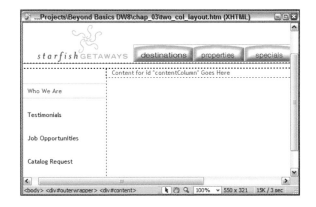

---

9 In the **Files** panel, open **page_text.htm** from the **chap_03** folder you copied to your desktop. Press **Ctrl+A** (Windows) or **Cmd+A** (Mac) to select all the text, press **Ctrl+C** (Windows) or **Cmd+C** (Mac) to copy the file, and then close the file. Select the placeholder text **Content for id "contentColumn" Goes Here**, and press **Ctrl+V** (Windows) or **Cmd+V** (Mac) to replace the place-holder phrase with the copied content.

Rather than have you spend your time entering dummy text, I thought I'd give you a little break. Enjoy!

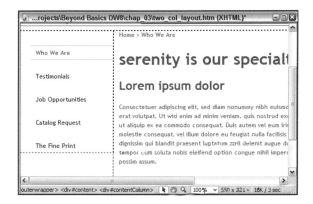

NOTE:

Styling the Content (Extra Credit)

Although the chapter's focus is on layouts, some folks—myself included—just aren't satisfied until the page is completely styled. If you fall into that camp or just want to have a bit of practice creating and applying styles, this sidebar is for you! Add five more styles to the page:

#breadcrumb: Set the style to `font-size: 11px`, `font-weight: bold`, and `color: #000000` and apply to the paragraph at the top of the content column: **Home > Who We Are**.

.currentSection: Set the style to `color: #666666` and apply to the text **Home >**.

#content h1: Set the style to `font-size: 2.25em`, `font-style: italic`, and `color: #609DC9` and `margin-bottom: 0px`; this style is applied automatically.

#content h2: Set the style to `font size: 1.1em`, `color: #000000`, and `margin-bottom: 0px`. and `margin-top: 0px`; this style is applied automatically.

.firstParagraph: Set the style to `margin-top: 0px` and apply it to the first full paragraph of placeholder text.

1. In the **CSS Styles** panel, click **New CSS Rule**. In the **New CSS Rule** dialog box, click the **Advanced** radio button under **Selector Type**, and type **#contentFeature** for **Selector**. Click **OK**. In the **CSS Rule definition for #contentFeature** dialog box, click the **Block** category, and set **Text align** to **right**. Click the **Box** category, and set

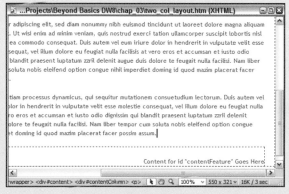

Width to **100%**. Turn off the **Same for all** check box for **Padding**, and set **Top** to **20 pixels**. Click **OK**. Select the last paragraph in the content area, and press the **right arrow** key to move past the closing **<p>** tag. In the **Insert** bar, click the

continues on next page

NOTE:

Styling the Content (Extra Credit) *continued*

Common category, and click **Insert Div Tag**. In the **Insert Div Tag** dialog box, leave the **Insert** pop-up menu set to the default **At insertion point**, and choose **contentFeature** from the **ID** pop-up menu. Click **OK**.

The **#contentFeature** style sets up an area that sits below the main content. To keep it lined up, you define the style at 100 percent width, with some padding on the top to separate the two sections. The technique for placing the **#contentFeature** **<div>** tag ensures that it appears within the **#contentColumn <div>** tag but after the content.

2. Choose **File > Save**, or press **Ctrl+S** (Windows) or **Cmd+S** (Mac). Leave **two_col_layout.htm** open for the next exercise.

10 Choose **File > Save**, or press **Ctrl+S** (Windows) or **Cmd+S** (Mac). Leave **two_col_layout.htm** open for the next exercise.

In this exercise, you specified styles within each column of the content area and applied them to format the side navigation and the main content area. In the next exercise, you'll set the styles for the footer area of the page.

NOTE:

Retracing Previous Steps

If you're working through this book in sequence, you'll recall filling in the **#contentFeature** **<div>** tag in Chapter 2, *"Designing Layouts with CSS."* If you'd like to include example content in this area, insert the necessary images. Here's a reminder: This **<div>** tag has three images—**text_unique.gif**, **text_follow.gif**, and **box_arrow.gif**.

4 | Building the Footer

In some ways, the **#footer** style is a mirror image of the **#header** style. Both have a single border (one on the top, the other on the bottom) containing the same dimensions and color. Both are applied to **<div>** tags on either side of the content area but inside the overall containing wrapper. The **#footer** style, however, better illustrates the idiom "Less is more." Unlike the **#header** style, the **#footer** style has no height requirement, just a bit of padding. In this exercise, you'll style the footer section and insert necessary content.

1 If you followed the previous exercise, **two_col_layout.htm** should still be open. If it's not, complete Exercise 3, and then return to this exercise.

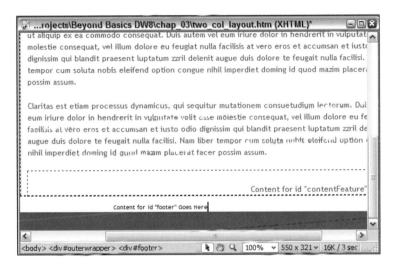

2 In the **CSS Styles** panel, click **New CSS Rule**. In the **New CSS Rule** dialog box, click the **Advanced** radio button under **Selector Type**, and type **#footer** for **Selector**. Click **OK**. In the **CSS Rule definition for #footer** dialog box, click the **Text** category, and set **Size** to **.625 ems**. Click the **Block** category, and set **Text align** to **center**. Click the **Box** category, turn off the **Same for all** check box for **Padding**, and set **Top** to **1 ems**. Click the **Border** category, turn off all three **Same for all** check boxes, and set **Bottom** to **solid**, **28 pixels**, and **#666666**. Click **OK**.

You're applying the ems measurement to ensure the text in this section resizes properly if the browser font size changes. The text size, .625 ems, is approximately equivalent to a 10-point font when viewed at the browser's default settings. Although a bit of space appears above the placeholder text, notice none appears between the text and the border. You'll adjust that in the next step.

molestie consequat, vel illum dolore eu feugiat nulla facilisis at vero eros et accumsan et iust

dignissim qui blandit praesent luptatum zzril delenit augue duis dolore te feugait nulla facilisi.

tempor cum soluta nobis eleifend option congue nihil imperdiet doming id quod mazim placer

possim assum.

Claritas est etiam processus dynamicus, qui sequitur mutationem consuetudium lectorum. Dui

eum iriure dolor in hendrerit in vulputate velit esse molestie consequat, vel illum dolore eu fe

facilisis at vero eros et accumsan et iusto odio dignissim qui blandit praesent luptatum zzril de

augue duis dolore te feugait nulla facilisi. Nam liber tempor cum soluta nobis eleifend option

nihil imperdiet doming id quod mazim placerat facer possim assum.

Content for id "contentFeature"

Destinations | Properties | Specials | About Us | Contact

`<body> <div #outerwrapper> <div #footer> <p>` | 100% | 550 x 321 | 16K / 3 sec

3 Delete the placeholder text **Content for id "footer" Goes Here**. In its place, type the following: **Destinations | Properties | Specials | About Us | Contact**. With your cursor at the end of the line you just typed, choose **Paragraph** from the **Format** list in the **Property Inspector**.

Although it may be tempting to add a `padding-bottom` declaration to the `#footer` style, it's always best to use standard, syntactically correct HTML (HyperText Markup Language) first. Often the application of a `<p>` tag to a single line of text does the trick—without additional CSS coding.

---

4 Choose **File > Save**, or press **Ctrl+S** (Windows) or **Cmd+S** (Mac). Leave **two_col_layout.htm** open for the next exercise.

In this exercise, you learned how to style a footer region to hold typical content. In the next exercise, you'll learn how to take your two-column design and convert it to a three-column layout.

---

5 | Converting to a Three-Column CSS Layout

As you saw in the previous exercises when developing the two-column layout, the **float** property is key. Although you set each column to **float: left**, you could have just as easily set to them to **float: right**—as long as you apply the property consistently. The same is true of a third column.

In this exercise, you'll convert the two-column design to a three-column version. The techniques involved are pretty straightforward. First, you'll define a new style and insert the associated **<div>** tag. Next, you'll reduce the existing content column in width to accommodate the new column. Then, you'll create a new wrapper **<div>** tag to enclose the two columns. Finally, you'll move the bottom section to properly span both content columns.

To make the exercise more universally applicable, you'll also learn a technique to make it easy to switch layouts from one page to another, just by changing a class in the **<body>** tag.

---

1 If you followed the previous exercise, **two_col_layout.htm** should still be open in Dreamweaver. If it's not, complete Exercise 4, and then return to this exercise.

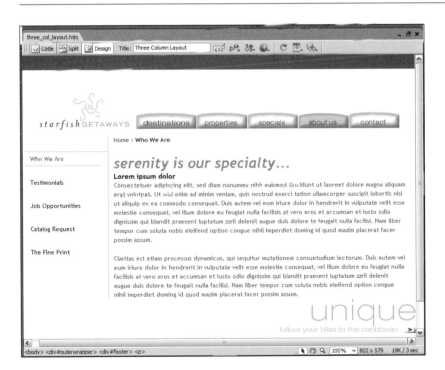

2 In the **Files** panel, open **three_col_layout.htm** from the **chap_03** folder you copied to your desktop.

This page applies all the same layout techniques discussed in the previous exercises in this chapter. However, I've added some content and formatting to give the page a more finished look.

---

3 In the **Document** window, place your cursor anywhere in the main content area. From the **Tag Selector**, choose **<div#contentColumn>**. In the **CSS Styles** panel, switch to **Current** mode. In the **Properties** pane, change the **width** value from **583px** to **378px**. Select the border value, and delete it.

By selecting any styled tag and then viewing the CSS Styles panel in Current mode, you can really hone in on all the properties applicable to a selection. Later in this exercise, you'll create a containing style with a border to replace the one you removed in this step.

With the #contentColumn style narrowed and unneeded border removed, you're ready to create and apply the style for the third column.

4 In the **CSS Styles** panel, click **New CSS Rule**. In the **New CSS Rule** dialog box, click the **Advanced** radio button under **Selector Type**, and type **#rightColumn** for **Selector**. Click **OK**. In the **CSS Rule definition for #rightColumn** dialog box, set **Size** to **.8 ems** and **Color** to **#666666**. Click the **Box** category, and set **Width** to **205 pixels** and **Float** to **left**. Turn off the **Same for all** check box for **Padding**, and set **Top** to **95 pixels**. Click **OK**.

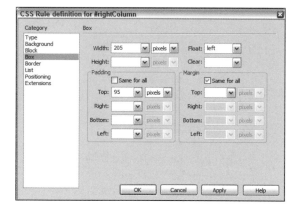

The chosen width fits within the formula without taking too much attention from the main content area. To make sure the right column is a secondary focus, you're making the text a bit smaller and adding padding to keep any content aligned with the first paragraphs of the #contentColumn area.

5 In the **Insert** bar, click the **Common** category, and click **Insert Div Tag**. In the **Insert Div Tag** dialog box, from the **Insert** pop-up menu, choose **After tag <div id="contentColumn">**. From the **ID** pop-up menu, choose **rightColumn**, and click **OK**.

All three columns (navigation, main content, and side content) are visible on the page now. This layout has a problem, however. The #contentFeature section is under the #contentColumn section, and it really needs to span both the #contentColumn and #rightColumn sections. To fix this issue, you'll need to add and apply a containing style around the two columns.

6 In the **CSS Styles** panel, click **New CSS Rule**. In the **New CSS Rule** dialog box, click the **Advanced** radio button under **Selector Type**, and type **#contentWrapper** for **Selector**. Click **OK**. In the **CSS Rule definition for #contentWrapper** dialog box, click the **Box** category, and set **Width** to **613 pixels** and **Float** to **left**. Click the **Border** category, turn off all the **Same for all** check boxes for **Padding**, and set **Left** to **solid**, **1 pixel**, and **#CCCCCC**. Click **OK**.

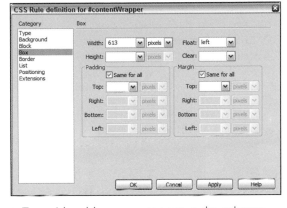

Why is another wrapper required? With columns, it's always best to float two columns next to each other; floating more than two is often problematic with browsers. To avoid problems, you can group the columns.

In the next step, you'll enclose both the `#contentColumn` and `#rightColumn` `<div>` tags with your newly created style, thus grouping them. To accomplish this, you'll first need to select the two columns in the code.

---

7 Place your cursor anywhere in the **#contentColumn** area, and choose **<div#contentColumn>** from the **Tag Selector**. Switch to **Code** view, and click one of the **collapse** buttons to the left of the selected code. Select both the newly collapsed code and the complete **<div>** tag below it. In the **Insert** bar, click the **Common** category, and click **Insert Div Tag**. In the **Insert Div Tag** dialog box, from the **Insert** pop-up menu, choose **Wrap around selection**, and from the **ID** pop-up menu, choose **contentWrapper**. Click **OK**.

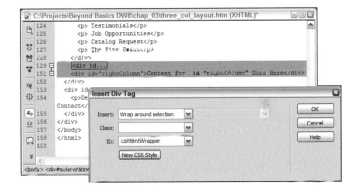

Code collapse is a Dreamweaver 8 innovation that makes selecting multiple adjacent **<div>** tags much easier. The code automatically expands after you insert the new **<div>** tag.

The last step to complete the three-column layout is to move the `#contentFeature` `<div>` tag.

8 In the **Document** window, select the **text_unique.gif** graphic, and then choose **<div#contentFeature>** from the **Tag Selector**. Press **Ctrl+X** (Windows) or **Cmd+X** (Mac) to cut the selected **<div>** tag. Place your cursor in the placeholder text for the **#rightColumn <div>**, and select **<div#rightColumn>** from the **Tag Selector**. Press the **right arrow** key to move past the selection, and press **Ctrl+V** (Windows) or **Cmd+V** (Mac) to paste the copied **<div>** tag.

Here's another application of the technique I like to think of as "visualizing the code": When you choose any element in the Tag Selector, Dreamweaver 8 selects the entire tag and all its contents. Pressing the left or right arrow key allows you to move your cursor in the code before or after the selected tag.

You can easily revert the three-column layout you just constructed to a two-column structure. In fact, it's even easier than modifying the two-column layout in the first place.

It's not uncommon for sites to have both two- and three-column layouts intermixed. You can use the same CSS style sheet for either layout with a few simple enhancements. This technique, known as **body classes**, relies on adding a class to the **<body>** tag. You reference the class through a CSS style rule that adjusts the width of the `#contentColumn` section to fit the two-column variation.

---

9 From the **CSS Styles** panel, click **New CSS Rule**. In the **New CSS Rule** dialog box, click the **Advanced** radio button under **Selector Type**, and type **body.twoColumn #contentColumn** for **Selector**. Click **OK**. In the **CSS Rule definition for #contentColumn** dialog box, click the **Box** category, and set **Width** to **583**. Click **OK**.

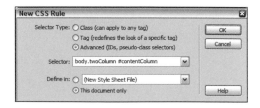

The Advanced selector type is extremely flexible. In this step, you're creating a rule that affects the `#contentColumn` style when the `<body>` tag has a class of `.twoColumn`. You'll notice you're setting the width to the same value you used when creating the two-column layout.

Now, you're all set up to make the switch back to a two-column design.

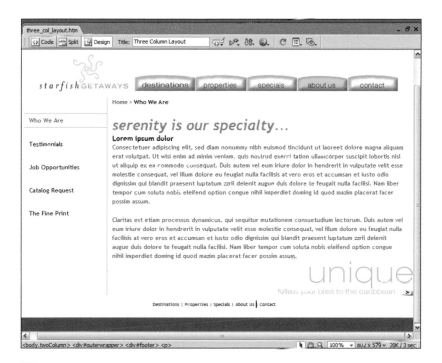

10 Place your cursor in the right-column placeholder text. From the **Tag Selector**, choose `<div#rightColumn>`, and press **Delete**. Once again from the **Tag Selector**, **right-click** (Windows) or **Ctrl+click** (Mac) the `<body>` tag, and choose **Class > twoColumn**.

The body class technique is extremely useful for switching between a series of layouts. As the example stands, the three-column layout is the default, and the two-column design takes effect only when the body class is set to `.twoColumn`. You could, of course, explicitly set up a `body.threeColumn #contentColumn` rule with a narrower width and then apply the `.threeColumn` class to the `<body>` tag.

11 Choose **File > Save**, or press **Ctrl+S** (Windows) or **Cmd+S** (Mac). Close **two_col_layout.htm**.

In this chapter, you learned how to construct a CSS layout for a two-column design. You also learned how to convert the two-column layout to a three-column version and set up the page to easily switch back and forth. In the next chapter, you'll design and implement a variety of navigation systems, all in CSS.

Building CSS Navigation Systems

CSS has expanded the realm of possibilities when it comes to Web site navigation. Designers now have a choice between navigation bars consisting completely of graphics or those built with a mix of text, graphics, and CSS.

CSS navigation has several key advantages. First, CSS navigation is extremely easy to manage: You can quickly add and remove entire navigation elements and just as easily adjust labels. Second, the flexibility inherent in CSS is highly useful when it comes to navigation—you can change a navigation bar from horizontal to vertical by switching a few CSS declarations. And with just a little more CSS magic, your horizontal navigation bar can become a tabbed interface.

In this chapter, you'll learn how to structure your pages to set them up properly for CSS navigation techniques. I'll describe various navigation styles—horizontal, vertical, and tabbed—in detail so you can apply the techniques to your own pages. In addition, you can accomplish more elaborate navigation designs by adding JavaScript to the mix. This chapter details the JavaScript code and CSS necessary to add a sliding panel to your site for on-demand navigation.

Understanding CSS and Navigation

CSS-based navigation typically relies on the bulleted, or **unordered**, list to form the HTML content. The unordered list is a perfect candidate to be transformed into graphical navigation because you can render such lists without leading bullets and in either orientation—vertical or horizontal. Additionally, you can easily display background graphics behind the list.

Each item in a list used for navigation is an HTML link, which allows for multistate formatting. In addition to the default state, linked list items also offer hover, visited, and active (clicked) modes. Most commonly, the `a:link` and `a:visited` CSS selectors are grouped, as are `a:hover` and `a:active`. This strategy leads to a two-state button depicting the default (mouse off) and hover (mouse over) conditions.

Perhaps the best reason to use lists as the basis for CSS navigation is their potential hierarchical structure. Any list item can include multiple subitems, just as a main navigation element can have a submenu with numerous elements. You can use many techniques for displaying such complex list navigation through a combination of CSS and JavaScript. Patrick Griffiths and Dan Webb developed one of the first versions (**www.htmldog.com/articles/suckerfish/dropdowns**).

The final reason for using unordered lists to create CSS navigation is what happens when CSS is disabled. The linked list degrades cleanly, and even complex navigation with multiple subitems remains perfectly navigable.

1 | Crafting Horizontal Navigation Bars

In this exercise, you'll build a horizontal navigation bar from scratch. After you've inserted the unordered list using HTML, you'll focus on styling the list with CSS. In addition to creating standard styles for the navigation list items, you'll also create a style to apply to the navigation item representing the current page. Once you're done, you'll be able to modify the button labels easily and, if desired, add a new navigation element or remove an existing one—all as easily as changing a bulleted list item.

---

1 Copy the **chap_04** folder from the **Dreamweaver 8 HOT CD-ROM** onto your desktop.

2 In the **Files** panel, open **horizontal_nav.htm** from the **chap_04** folder you copied to your desktop. Place your cursor in the text **Content for "navbar" div goes here**.

So you have a good starting point for this exercise file, I have removed the main navigation; only a **\<div\>** tag with the ID **navbar** remains. The **\<div\>** tag is absolutely positioned with the header **\<div\>**. In addition, I previously created and imported all the graphics for this exercise into the Dreamweaver 8 site so you can focus on the navigation.

---

3 In the **navbar <div>** tag, delete the placeholder text. In the **Property Inspector**, click **Unordered List**, and type the following five items, each as a separate list item: **destinations, properties, specials, about us**, and **contact**. Select the **destinations** item, and in the **Property Inspector**, type # (a number sign) in the **Link** field to create a link; repeat this process for the other four list items you created.

Believe it or not, that's all the HTML you'll need to create the horizontal navigation bar—all the remaining steps are CSS oriented. The first CSS task is to set the general font characteristics for the navigation items.

---

4 From the **Tag Selector**, choose **<div#navbar>**. In the **CSS Styles** panel, switch to **Current** mode. In the **Properties** pane, click the **Add Property** link, type **font-family**, and then press **Enter** (Windows) or **Return** (Mac). Choose **Geneva, Arial, Helvetica, sans-serif** from the list. Click the **Add Property** link again, type **font-size**, and then press **Enter** (Windows) or **Return** (Mac). Type **0.9em**, and then press **Enter** (Windows) or **Return** (Mac).

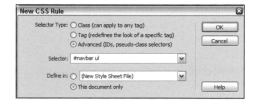

Because the **#navbar** CSS rule already existed, you have to add only a couple of declarations to specify the look and feel of the font for the navigation items. The CSS Current mode is great for quickly targeting a specific style affecting a selected area.

The other timesaving action included in this step is the shortcut to typing a measurement unit. For many CSS properties requiring a measurement value, Dreamweaver 8 has two input fields: a text field for the number and a list for the measurement unit (pixels, percent, and so on). Although you could have typed 0.9 in the font-size text field and then chosen ems from the list, it's much faster to type 0.9em, press Enter (Windows) or Return (Mac), and let Dreamweaver 8 handle the rest.

---

5 Place your cursor anywhere in the unordered list, and from the **Tag Selector**, choose **<ul>**. In the **CSS Styles** panel, click **New CSS Rule**. In the **New CSS Rule** dialog box, delete everything except **#navbar ul** from the **Selector** pop-up menu, and click **OK**. In the **CSS Rule definition for #navbar ul** dialog box, click the **List** category, and choose **none** from the **Bullet image** list. Click **OK**.

When you create a new CSS rule, Dreamweaver 8 automatically includes the full selector identifying any selected item. Often, it's overkill, and you just need to remove a number of the initial items. Here, you want to affect just the unordered list within the **#navbar <div>** tag and remove any bullet symbols for the list items. Your unordered list has begun to metamorphose into a navigation bar! Next, you'll prepare the list items for displaying side-by-side.

6 Place your cursor in any list item, and from the **Tag Selector**, choose **<li>**. In the **CSS Styles** panel, click **New CSS Rule**. In the **New CSS Rule** dialog box, delete everything except **#navbar li** from the **Selector** pop-up menu, and click **OK**. In the **CSS Rule definition for #navbar li** dialog box, click the **Block** category, and choose **no-wrap** from the **Whitespace** list. Click the **Box** category, and choose **left** from the **Float** list. Click **OK**.

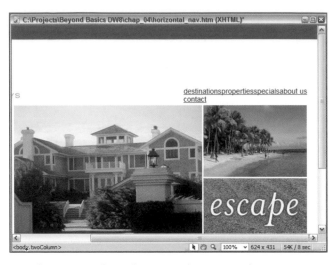

CSS at an intermediate stage isn't always pretty. Here, before you add any other styles, all the list items run together. You'll fix this design with the next applied style, but it's important to understand that sometimes you have to go through seemingly unwanted appearances to get the effect you want. The `whitespace: no-wrap` declaration ensures all navigation labels, including those with two or more words, appear in a single line.

The next step spaces out the individual links and adds the graphic button-like background—all by styling the **<a>** tags in the list.

---

7 Make sure your cursor is in the string of list items. From the **Tag Selector**, choose **<a>**. In the **CSS Styles** panel, click **New CSS Rule**. In the **New CSS Rule** dialog box, delete everything except **#navbar a** from the **Selector** pop-up menu. Click **OK**. In the **CSS Rule definition for #navbar a** dialog box, click the **Background** category, and click the **folder** icon for **Background image**. Navigate to the **assets/topNav** folder, and choose **main_short.gif**. From the **Repeat** pop-up menu, choose **no-repeat**. Keep the **CSS Rule definition for #navbar a** dialog box open.

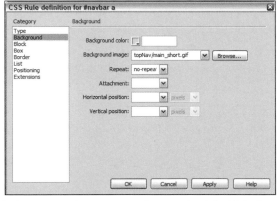

This is the heart of the technique for converting a text link to a graphic image with an embedded label. By adding a background image to the link selector, you begin to create the illusion of a button. However, you won't see any real change until you complete the styling of the **#navbar a** selector in the next step.

---

8 In the **CSS Rule definition for #navbar a** dialog box, click the **Block** category, and choose **center** from the **Text align** pop-up menu. From the **Display** list, choose **block**. Click the **Box** category, set **Width** to **110 pixels**, and set **Height** to **31 pixels**. Turn off the **Same for all** check box under **Padding**, and in the **Top** field, type **10 pixels**. Click **OK**.

Now you're cooking! The `display: block` declaration is key to achieving button-like behavior and actually separates the list items into individual entities. The remaining declarations (`width: 110px`, `height: 31px`, and `padding-top: 10px`) all serve to shape the button area. Next, you'll style the label text more appropriately.

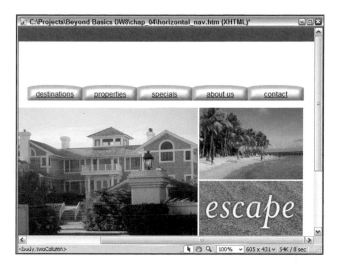

---

9 In the **CSS Styles** panel, click **New CSS Rule**. In the **New CSS Rule** dialog box, make sure **Selector Type** is set to **Advanced**. In the **Selector** field, type **#navbar a:link, #navbar a:visited**, and click **OK**. In the **CSS Rule definition #navbar a:link, #navbar a:visited** dialog box, click the **Type** category, set **color** to **#4b4b4b**, and turn on the **Decoration: none** check box. Click **OK**.

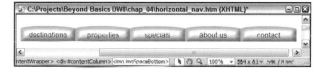

With the underline gone and the color adjusted for both the link and visited states, the navigation list is looking good. It's important that the styles for the various link states appear in a particular order: link, visited, hover, and active. (The standard mnemonic for remembering this order is the somewhat cynical LoVe, HA!) So, the next task is to set the values for the hover and active states.

---

10 In the **CSS Styles** panel, click **New CSS Rule**. In the **New CSS Rule** dialog box, type **#navbar a:hover, #navbar a:active** in the **Selector** field, and click **OK**. Click the **Type** category, set **color** to **#4b4b4b**, and turn on **Decoration: none**. Click the **Background** category, and click the **folder** icon for **Background image**. Navigate to the **assets/topNav** folder, and choose **main_short_f2.gif**. From the **Repeat** pop-up menu, choose **no-repeat**. Click **OK**.

This style combines the same color and text-declaration values applied to both the link and visited states while swapping a green-tinged background image for the gray version. Notice this CSS-based navigation bar uses only two graphic images: main_short.gif and main_short_f2.gif. A similar, purely graphic navigation bar would use ten images.

11 Press **Ctrl+S** (Windows) or **Cmd+S** (Mac) to save your file, and press **F12**. When your primary browser opens, move your cursor over the navigation "buttons" to see the hover effect.

In the next step, you'll use the same graphic, and in fact the same styles, as you applied for the hover and active states to indicate the current page.

12 In the **CSS Styles** panel, switch to **All** mode, and **right-click** (Windows) or **Ctrl+click** (Mac) the **#navbar a:hover, #navbar a:active** selector. Choose **Duplicate** from the contextual menu. In the **Duplicate CSS Rule** dialog box, type **#sellink a:link, #sellink a:visited, #sellink a:hover, #sellink a:active** in the **Selector** field. Click **OK**. To apply the style, place your cursor in the **specials** navigation link, and from the **Tag Selector**, **right-click** (Windows) or **Ctrl+click** (Mac) **<li>**, and choose **Set ID: sellink**.

The transformation from an unordered list to a fully graphical navigation bar is now complete. In this step, you created a style to indicate the current or selected navigation element. The style selector encompasses all the states of the navigation button to ensure the image does not change, regardless of the cursor position.

13 Choose **File > Save**, or press **Ctrl+S** (Windows) or **Cmd+S** (Mac). Press **F12** to preview the page in your browser. When your browser opens, move your cursor over the navigation to see the rollover effect. Close your browser; back in Dreamweaver 8, close **horizontal_nav.htm**.

In this exercise, you created a horizontal navigation bar by combining CSS styles and an unordered list. In the next exercise, you'll see how you can create tabbed navigation with CSS.

NOTE:

Creating Vertical CSS Navigation

You can convert an unordered list into a vertical CSS navigation bar in much the same manner as you create the horizontal navigation bar—in fact, it's even simpler. Because the unordered list is already in a vertical format, it requires less CSS styling. The key CSS selector to change is #container li, where #container is the ID of the enclosing style. In the horizontal navigation bar example, you styled the #navbar li selector like this:

```
#navbar li {
  float: left;
  white-space: nowrap;
}
```

You'll recall the float: left declaration brought all the list items onto a single, run-on line. The corresponding vertical navigation bar style is #navColumn li:

```
#navColumn li {
  margin-bottom: 10px;
  white-space: nowrap;
}
```

This replaces the float: left declaration with a bit of margin adjustment. If your vertical navigation bar uses background images, the rest of the CSS is basically the same—just substitute #navColumn for #navbar, and make whatever spacing adjustments (such as width) are necessary to fit the column.

Remember, you don't have to use graphics to indicate navigation—simple, clean text with highlighting borders can be just as effective. The vertical navigation bar shown in the illustration here uses an unordered list (with the bullets removed) with thin top and bottom borders to indicate the current link.

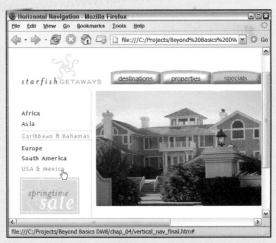

VIDEO:

vertical_nav.mov

To learn more about building your CSS vertical navigation from scratch, check out **vertical_nav.mov** in the **videos** folder on the **Dreamweaver 8 HOT CD-ROM**.

2 | Building Tabbed Navigation

You can extend CSS navigation bars to create another popular Web site look: tabs. Tabbed navigation gives the appearance of a single, unified file whose view switches whenever a site visitor selects a tab from those at the top of the page. To accomplish this effect, you'll need a different "current selection" image—one that appears to be open at the bottom. You'll also need to adjust your design to include borders around the content area. The combination of the two—the current selection image and the page design—gives the illusion of the current tab opening into the content. A bit of CSS positioning magic ties it all together. That's why a successful tabbed navigation design encompasses both the navigation (the images) and the page design (the CSS). In this exercise, you'll learn how to add the CSS to create a tabbed navigation effect.

1 In the **Files** panel, open **tab_specials.htm** from the **chap_04** folder you copied to your desktop.

To help you get started building a tabbed navigation, I have altered the horizontal navigation example file. First, I have moved the logo to the top of its **<div>** tag by changing the vertical positioning of this background graphic from 50 pixels to 10 pixels. Second, I have shifted the entire navigation bar (**#navbar**) to the left by dropping the **right** property entirely and setting **left: 0**.

Often you'll find you can adapt one design—such as this horizontal navigation example—to quickly build another just by changing a few simple CSS values.

Next, you'll make the most obviously needed change: the "current selection" link graphic.

2 Place your cursor in **specials**, the currently selected link. In the **CSS Styles** panel, switch to **Current** mode. In the **Properties** pane, select the **background-image** value, and click the **folder** icon. In the **Select Image Source** dialog box, navigate to the **chap_04/assets/topNav** folder, and select **main_tab.gif**. Click **OK**.

Rather than use a different color to indicate the current page, the tab graphic appears to remove the bottom portion of the image. One key point to remember is it's important to use the same color for the interior of the tab as the background color of the content area. In this example, both are white.

Although setting up the current selection creates the right look, you might notice the significant gap between the navigation bar and the top of the content area. In the next step, you'll modify the CSS styles to move them closer.

---

3 If your CSS layout outlines are not visible, in the **Document** toolbar, choose **Visual Aids > CSS Layout Outlines**. In the **CSS Styles** panel, switch to **All** mode, and select the **navbar a** selector. In the **Properties** pane, change the **height** value to **25px**. Click the **Add Property** link, type **margin-bottom**, press **Enter** (Windows) or **Return** (Mac), and type—**2px**.

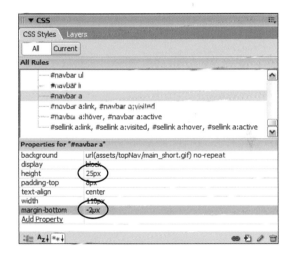

As you make the CSS adjustments, you can see the **#navbar <div>** moving closer to the content area. Although reducing the height of the style does the bulk of the work—effectively removing the unused whitespace below the images—it's often necessary to fine-tune your spacing with negative margins. Trial and error is the best way to find the precise desired value. Now, you're ready to add the first of your borders below the **#navbar <div>** and make sure it spans the page.

4 Place the cursor any-where in the navigation bar, and choose **<div#navbar>** from the **Tag Selector**. In the **CSS Styles** panel, switch to **Current** mode. In the **Properties** pane, click the **Add Property** link, type

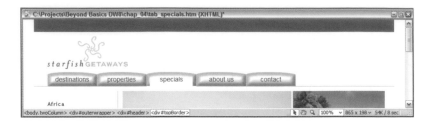

width, and press **Enter** (Windows) or **Return** (Mac). Type **100%**, and press **Enter** (Windows) or **Return** (Mac). Click the **Add Property** link again, type **border-bottom**, and press **Enter** (Windows) or **Return** (Mac). Type **solid 1px #CCC**, and press **Enter** (Windows) or **Return** (Mac).

To achieve the appearance of the border encompassing all the content, you set the width of the `#navbar` `<div>` to 100%. You typed the border itself in shorthand: solid 1px #CCC. Why didn't you have to use the full six-figure value, #CCCCCC? Full hexadecimal color numbers consist of three hexadecimal pairs. If both members of the pair are the same—such as CC—you can represent it with just a single letter. Thus, #FFF is the same as #FFFFFF.

Even with the `#navbar` border, the illusion is not complete. You'll add the missing side borders in the next step.

5 Place your cursor anywhere in the navigation column on the left side of the page. From the **Tag Selector**, choose **<div#content>**. In the **CSS Styles** panel, switch to **Current** mode, and click the **Add Property** link from the **Properties** pane. Type **border-left**, and press **Enter** (Windows) or **Return** (Mac). Type **solid 1px #CCC**, and press **Enter** (Windows) or **Return** (Mac). Before you confirm the entry, select it, and press **Ctrl+C** (Windows) or **Cmd+C** (Mac). Click the **Add Property** link again, and type **border-right**. Press **Enter** (Windows) or **Return** (Mac), and then press **Ctrl+V** (Windows) or **Cmd+V** (Mac) to paste **solid 1px #CCC** into the value field.

6 Place your cursor in the footer links, and choose **<div#footerText>** from the **Tag Selector**. In the **CSS Styles Properties** pane, click the **Add Property** link, and type **border-left**; press **Enter** (Windows) or **Return** (Mac), and then press **Ctrl+V** (Windows) or **Cmd+V** (Mac) to paste **solid 1px #CCC**. Click the **Add Property** link one last time, and type **border-right**. Press **Enter** (Windows) or **Return** (Mac), and then press **Ctrl+V** (Windows) or **Cmd+V** (Mac) to again paste **solid 1px #CCC**.

Although you might find the repetition a bit tedious, these steps add the necessary borders along the outer edges of the content area and the footer, which consolidates the page as a whole and completes the tabbed visual effect. Continuing the side borders from the content to the footer area has the added advantage of blurring the divisions the page is constructed from because it connects the content and footer areas.

Next, you'll see how to leverage all your work so far and begin building other pages in your tabbed set.

---

7 In the main navigation bar, select the **specials** navigation label. In the **Property Inspector**, type **tab_specials.htm** in the **Link** field. Select the **properties** label,

and in the **Link** field, type **tab_properties.htm**. Press **Ctrl+S** (Windows) or **Cmd+S** (Mac) to save your document. Choose **File > Save As**, and in the **Save As** dialog box, type **tab_properties.htm** in the **File name** field.

In a real-world situation, it's likely you would already have links set up for your primary navigation. To see the tabs in action, you'll need a minimum of two pages, each linked to the other.

---

8 In the main navigation bar, select the **specials** navigation label. From the **Tag Selector**, **right-click** (Windows) or **Ctrl+click** (Mac) **<li#sellink>**, and choose **Set ID > None** from the contextual menu. Select the **properties** navigation label, and **right-click** (Windows) or **Ctrl+click** (Mac) **<li>**, and choose **Set ID > sellink** from the contextual menu.

See how easy it is to switch from one indicated tab to another? In a production setting, you'd need to perform this operation for the major navigation items, each on their own page. You'll now see how it all works.

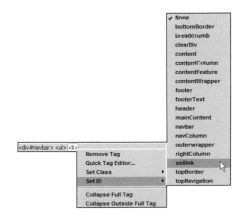

9 Press **Ctrl+S** (Windows) or **Cmd+S** (Mac), and then press **F12** to preview the page in your browser. Click from the **properties** page to the **specials** page to see the tabs move from one page to the other.

In a real-world situation, the content would change on each page, but you can see how the tabbed navigation is effective at simultaneously indicating the current page while retaining a connection to all the other navigation elements.

---

10 Close **tab_specials.htm**.

In this exercise, you learned how to create a tabbed navigation bar with CSS. Next, you'll learn how to combine JavaScript with CSS to create a sliding navigation panel.

---

3 | Sliding CSS Navigation Panels with JavaScript

Navigation, especially in a sidebar, can take up a lot of screen real estate. Sometimes the site design calls for more emphasis on content areas and less on always-visible secondary navigation. One solution is to put your side navigation on a separate panel, which a site visitor can display or hide with the click of a button. Although the panel simply repositions from offscreen to onscreen, the site visitor sees a sliding motion. In this exercise, you'll learn how to produce this action by combining JavaScript (to move the panel in and out) with CSS (to display the interactive area).

1 In the **Files** panel, open **sliding_nav.htm** from the **chap_04** folder you copied to your desktop.

For this starting point, I have replaced the usual series of side navigation links with additional content. A link at the bottom of the column (More Locations) indicates where first-time visitors can find additional choices. Whenever you expand your navigation into new—somewhat nonstandard—designs, it's always good to point the way for your site visitors.

In this example, the left-pointing angle bracket indicates where you can find the sliding panel control. The first step in creating the panel is to define a number of CSS styles that comprise the sliding panel; an outer wrapper is first necessary to contain the sliding panel's contents and its handles. As you'll see, you'll need two handles: one for when the sliding panel is on the screen (the **onHandle**) and another for when it is off (the **offHandle**).

2 In the **CSS Styles** panel, click **New CSS Rule**. In the **New CSS Rule** dialog box, set **Selector Type** to **Advanced**, and type **#navWrapper** in the **Selector** field. Click **OK**. In the **CSS Rule definition for #navWrapper** dialog box, click the **Background** category, and set **Background color** to **white**. Click the **Border** category, turn on all the **Same for all** check boxes, and then for **Top**, **Bottom**, and **Left**, set **Style** to **Solid**, **Width** to **1 pixel**, and **Color** to **#CCC**. Click the **Positioning** category, and set **Type** to **absolute**, **Width** to **186 pixels**, and **Z-Index** to **20**. Under **Placement**, set **Left** to **–176 pixels**. Click **OK**.

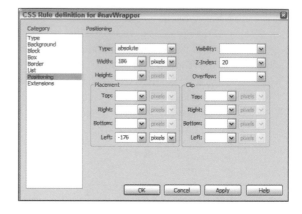

Obviously, a lot is going on with this rule. Although its main purpose is to hold together two other `<div>` tags, it also has some secondary functions. First, it must cover the existing side panel; this is why you explicitly set the background to white and assign a higher z-index value. Additionally, the `#navWrapper` controls the actual positioning of the sliding panel. Initially most of the panel—all but the handles—will be offscreen, which is why you set the Left value to a negative number.

Next, you'll define the style for the `#navColumn`.

---

3 In the **CSS Styles** panel, click **New CSS Rule**. In the **New CSS Rule** dialog box, set **Selector Type** to **Advanced**, and type **#navColumn** in the **Selector** field. Click **OK**. In the **CSS Rule definition for #navColumn** dialog box, click the **Type** category. Set **Line height** to **100%**. Click the **Block** category, and set **Letter spacing** to **.1em**. Click the **Box** category, set **Width** to **146 pixels**, and set **Float** to **left**. Turn off the **Same for all** check box under **Padding**, and type **30 pixels** for both **Top** and **Left**. Click **OK**.

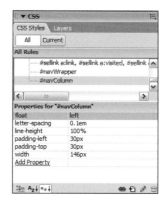

Aside from the `float: left` declaration, almost all the setup for this style concerns formatting and placing text. If you compare it to previous `#navColumn` rules, you'll notice it's a bit narrower. You do this to accommodate the two styles for the handle, defined in the next step.

---

4 In the **CSS Styles** panel, click **New CSS Rule**. In the **New CSS Rule** dialog box, set **Selector Type** to **Advanced**, and type **#onHandle** in the **Selector** field. Click **OK**. In the **CSS Rule definition for #onHandle** dialog box, click the **Background** category, and set **Background color** to **#CCC**. Click the **Block** category, and set **Display** to **none**. Click the **Box** category, and set **Width** to **8 pixels**, **Height** to **357 pixels**, and **Float** to **left**. Click **OK**.

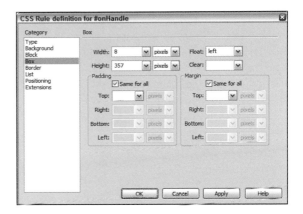

5 In the **CSS Styles** panel, **right-click** (Windows) or **Ctrl+click** (Mac) the just-created **#onHandle** style, and choose **Duplicate** from the contextual menu. In the **Duplicate CSS Rule** dialog box, change **Selector** to **#offHandle**, and click **OK**. In the **Properties** pane, select the value for **display**, and change it to **block**.

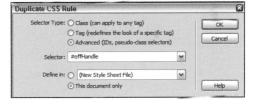

You're using two handles because you have two different actions: moving the panel on the screen and moving it off. As you can see, these two styles are the same except one (**#onHandle**) is set to **display: none** and the other (**#offHandle**) is styled with **display: block**. These reflect the default conditions. When the panel is offscreen, as it will be initially, the **#offHandle** appears, and the **#onHandle** is hidden. You can use JavaScript to dynamically switch these states. The final style, which you'll define next, controls the placement of the images for both handles.

6 In the **CSS Styles** panel, click **New CSS Rule**. In the **New CSS Rule** dialog box, type **#onHandle img, #offHandle img**, and click **OK**. In the **CSS Rule definition for #onHandle img, #offHandle img** dialog box, click the **Box** category, turn off the **Same for all** check box under **Margin**, and set **Top** to **125 pixels**. Click **OK**.

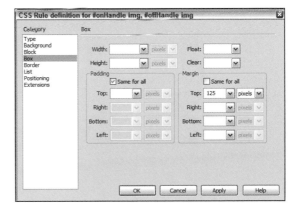

If you've gotten to the point where you can visualize CSS output based on the code, you may already be picturing the **#onHandle** and **#offHandle <div>** tags as long (357 pixels high) and narrow (8 pixels wide). This rule makes sure the clickable image is centered vertically in the styled handle areas.

With all the styles defined, you're ready to add the tags and content. In all, you need to insert four **<div>** tags. If you used the Insert Div Tag object, Dreamweaver 8 would automatically add placeholder content, which would be a hassle to remove. In this circumstance, it's quicker and easier to work in Code view.

7 If necessary, in the **Document** toolbar, choose **Visual Aids > CSS Layout Outlines**. In the **Document** window, select the **#leftColumn** outline, and switch to **Code** view. Press the **left arrow** key once, and then press **Enter** (Windows) or **Return** (Mac) to create a new line. Type the following code:

```
<div id="navWrapper">
   <div id="navColumn"></div>
   <div id="onHandle"></div>
   <div id="offHandle"></div>
</div>
```

The sliding panel is really a mini-version of the two-column layout used in Chapter 3, *"Creating CSS Column Layouts."* You insert the outer `<div>` tag to hold all the pieces together, and then you add the columns, each floated left. The wrinkle here, of course, is you actually have three side-by-side columns—`#navColumn`, `#onHandle`, and `#offHandle`—but JavaScript ensures only two are on the page at any one time. Now, you're ready to add content for the navigation column.

---

8 Place your cursor after the code **<div id="navColumn">**, press **Enter** (Windows) or **Return** (Mac), and then type the following code:

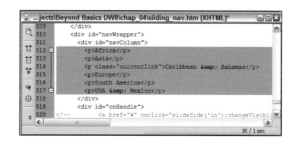

```
<p>Africa</p>
<p>Asia</p>
<p class="currentLink">Caribbean &amp;
Bahamas</p>
<p>Europe</p>
<p>South America</p>
<p>USA &amp; Mexico</p>
```

Although it's almost always easier to add text in Design view, in this situation it's not. As you'll remember, the `#navColumn` is currently hidden from view. Certain operations, however, are just as easy in Code view as in Design view—such as adding images, as you'll see in the next step when inserting the handle graphics.

---

9 Place your cursor after the code **<div id="onHandle">**, and in the **Insert** bar, click **Image**. In the **Select Image Source** dialog box, navigate to **chap04/assets/**, and select **handle.gif**. Place your cursor after the code **<div id="offHandle">**, and in the **Insert** bar, click **Image**. In the **Select Image Source** dialog box, select **handle_f2.gif**.

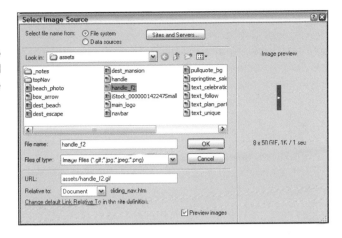

You can add almost all objects using the Insert bar in Code view; Dreamweaver 8 gives you the same convenience of point-and-click coding while allowing your positioning to be precise. You can even add a link, as you'll see next.

---

10 Select the code **<img src="assets/handle.gif" border ="0" />**, and then in the **Insert** bar, click **Hyperlink**. In the **Hyperlink** dialog box, type **javascript:;** in the **Link** field, and click **OK**. Select the code **<img src="assets/handle_f2.gif" border="0" />**. Again, in the **Insert** bar, click **Hyperlink**, and in the **Hyperlink** dialog box, type **javascript:;** in the **Link** field. Click **OK**.

Using the Hyperlink object gets around typing the full **<a>** tag; here, you're setting the link to a null value. Note this value—**javascript:;**—has both a colon and a semicolon. This is the code for invoking JavaScript but not calling any functions. Coincidentally, the next step is to call two JavaScript functions for each of the just-inserted links.

---

11 Press **F5** to refresh **Code** view, and place your cursor in the code **<img src="assets/handle.gif" border="0" />**. Choose **<a>** from the **Tag Selector**, and then choose **Window > Behaviors**. In the first column, choose **onClick**, and in the second column, type **slideSide('in')**. In the second row, choose **onClick** again, and in the second column, type **changeVisibility('offHandle')**.

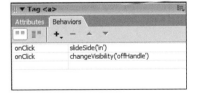

12 Place your cursor in the code **<img src="assets/handle_f2.gif" border="0" />**. Choose **<a>** from the **Tag Selector**, and then choose **Window > Behaviors**. In the first column, choose **onClick**, and in the second column, type **slideSide('out')**. In the second row, choose **onClick** again, and in the second column, type **changeVisibility('onHandle')**.

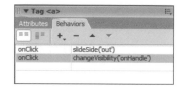

Although you may be more familiar with Dreamweaver 8's built-in JavaScript behaviors, such as Swap Image and Open Browser Window, you can also add calls to custom functions through the Behaviors panel. Two custom JavaScript functions power the sliding panel. The first, **slideSide()**, moves the panel back and forth. If the argument passed to the function is **in**, the panel moves offscreen; if it's **out**, the panel moves onscreen. The second function, **changeVisibility()**, swaps which handle **<div>** tag (**#offHandle** or **#onHandle**) displays.

The remaining elements to add to the page are the JavaScript functions themselves.

13 Switch to **Design** view, and choose **View > Head Content**. Select the head content area, and then choose **Insert > HTML > Script Objects > Script**. In the **Script** dialog box, make sure the **Language** pop-up menu is set to **JavaScript**, and click the **folder** icon for **Source**. In the **Select File** dialog box, navigate to the **chap_04/assets/** folder, and select **slideCSS.js**. Click **OK** to confirm your choice, and click **OK** again to close the **Script** dialog box.

Although you could include the JavaScript functions directly in the **<head>** tag, it's best to link to an external file whenever possible. This is especially important when you're using navigation functions that are likely to affect multiple pages.

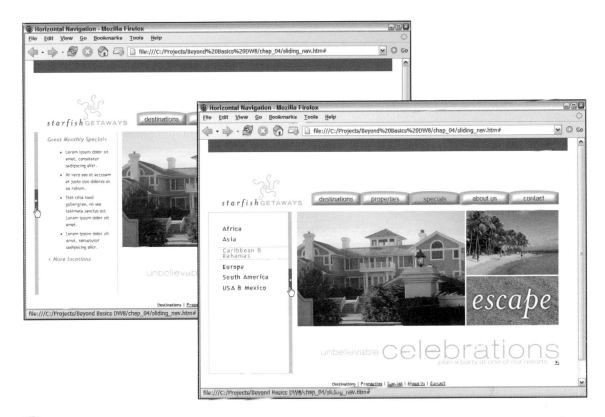

14 Press **Ctrl+S** (Windows) or **Cmd+S** (Mac) to save your page, and then press **F12** to preview it. When the page opens in your browser, click the button on the side navigation panel once. After the panel opens, click it again to close it.

With a few simple modifications to the CSS, you could easily set the sliding panel to be open by default. All you would need to do is change the **#navWrapper**'s `left` property and switch the initial values of the `display` property for both **#onHandle** and **#offHandle**.

In this exercise, you learned how to create a sliding navigation panel with CSS and JavaScript.

In this chapter, you learned how to use CSS to build several navigation systems, including both horizontal and vertical navigation bars, tabbed navigation, and sliding navigation panels. In the next chapter, you'll explore advanced CSS further and see how to integrate CSS in templates, highlight sections with nested templates, build a magazine-style layout, and integrate CSS hacks.

5

Taking CSS Further

Are you ready to take CSS to the next level? Then this is the chapter for you. As you've seen in previous chapters, CSS easily manipulates text and page content while simultaneously offering methods for structuring layouts. In this chapter, you'll learn how to exert more CSS control at the site level by integrating CSS and Dreamweaver 8 templates. You'll position CSS in your template structure so its effects ripple through the various branches of a site with finely tuned control.

You'll also learn how to overcome the rigid barriers of text blocks. You can use the technique described in this chapter, when combined with eye-catching large-scale graphics, to create true magazine-style layouts.

In addition, you'll explore the real-world side of CSS: CSS hacks. CSS hacks are the often-needed corrections so your page appears correctly in a wider range of browsers. In the final exercise in this chapter, you'll learn about two specific CSS hacks you can use with Dreamweaver 8.

1 | Integrating Templates and CSS

The combination of CSS and templates really illustrates the saying, "The sum is greater than its parts." Both CSS and Dreamweaver 8 templates are powerful Web technologies in their own rights. However, when used together, they give the word **powerful** a new meaning. In this exercise, you'll see how to apply CSS to templates for easy, one-step global changes.

1 Copy the **chap_05** folder from the **Dreamweaver 8 HOT CD-ROM** onto your desktop.

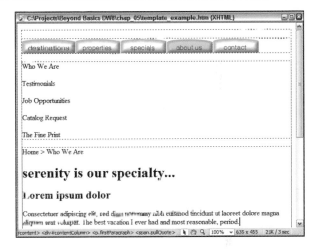

2 In the **Files** panel, open **template_example.htm** from the **chap_05** folder you copied to your desktop.

To illustrate how you properly apply external CSS style sheets when working with templates, I have removed all styling from the exercise file. The first task is to convert the file to a Dreamweaver 8 template.

3 Choose **File > Save as Template**. In the **Save As Template** dialog box, use the default name in the **Save as** field, and click **Save**. When Dreamweaver 8 prompts you to update the links, click **Yes**.

You'll see the Update Links dialog box whenever you save an existing file as a template, and you always want to opt to update the links. All templates reside in a site root-level folder cleverly named Templates. You want Dreamweaver 8 to modify any relative links—whether to another page, image source, or external file—so they point to the correct file from the Templates folder.

For example, for the first navigation graphic, the destination is assets/topNav/destinations.gif in the original template_example.htm file. However, when you create a template based on that file, you can have Dreamweaver 8 automatically change the links to .../chap_05/assets/topNav/destinations.gif. In fact, Dreamweaver 8 will automatically change the links again when you create a child page from the template.

Now you'll attach the external CSS file.

4 In the **CSS Styles** panel, click **Attach Style Sheet**. In the **Attach External Style Sheet** dialog box, click **Browse**. In the **Select Style Sheet File** dialog box, navigate to the **chap_05/assets/styles** folder, select **main.css**, and click **OK**. In the **Attach External Style Sheet** dialog box, leave all other settings at their defaults, and then click **OK**.

The key tenet to working with templates is to always let Dreamweaver 8 write the paths to any file you are linking to, regardless of whether the file is an image or an external style sheet. After you have attached the style sheet, you're ready to start creating editable regions, beginning with the primary navigation bar.

---

5 In **Design** view, select the **destinations** graphic, and from the **Tag Selector**, choose the **<a>** tag. Switch to **Code** view, press the **Shift** key, and select the closing **</a>** tag before the closing **</div>** tag.

This effectively selects all the images in the navigation bar and their anchor tags.

---

6 In the **Insert** bar, click the **Common** category, and choose the menu button **Templates: Editable Region**. In the **New Editable Region** dialog box, type **navBar** in the **Name** field, and click **OK**. Switch to **Design** view.

The goal when working with CSS layouts and templates is to choose the code within the layout tags, such as the **<div>** tags, that you want to maintain. The hardest part of achieving this goal is making sure you've selected just the right code to enclose in an editable region.

Unfortunately, Dreamweaver 8 doesn't always make this a Design view–friendly activity. If, for example, you tried to Shift+click the five graphic elements of the navigation bar, you'd find that the outer **<a>** tags were not selected. It's frequently necessary to go directly to the code to fine-tune your editable region selection, as is the case with the side navigation—your next candidate for an editable region.

---

7 In the side navigation area, select the first entry, and switch to **Code** view. Expand the selection to include all the content within the **#navColumn <div>** tag. In the **Insert** bar, click the **Common** category, and choose the menu button **Templates: Editable Region**. In the **New Editable Region** dialog box, type **sideNav** in the **Name** field, and click **OK**.

Now you have set all the content in the **#sideNav <div>** tag—but not the **<div>** tag itself—in an editable region. This procedure allows you to change any of the existing navigation links, whether the destination changes or the **.currentLink** class moves from one link to another. You can also easily add new links if needed.

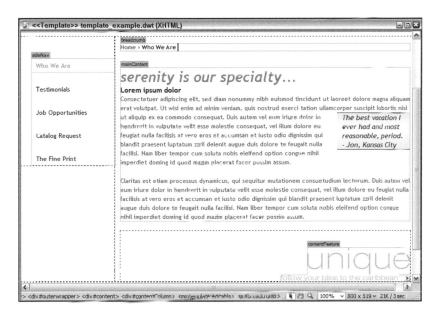

8 Switch to **Design** view, and select the entire breadcrumb: **Home > Who We Are**. Choose **Templates: Editable Region**. In the **New Editable Region** dialog box, type **breadcrumb** in the **Name** field, and click **OK**. Position your cursor in the heading, **serenity is our specialty**, and from the **Tag Selector**, click **<h1>**. Switch to **Code** view, and **Shift+click** all the content up to, but not including, the code **<div id="contentFeature">**. Choose **Templates: Editable Region**, and in the **New Editable Region** dialog box, type **mainContent** in the **Name** field. Click **OK**. Select all the code between **<div id="contentFeature">** and the next **</div>** tag. Again, choose **Templates: Editable Region**, and in the **New Editable Region** dialog box, type **contentFeature** in the **Name** field. Click **OK**, and switch to **Design** view.

When you want to create an editable region within a **<p>** or any heading tag, you can choose the content in Design view and apply the editable region object. To select the content within a **<div>** tag, however, you'll need to work in either Code view or Split view to make sure you preserve your CSS styles.

You've seen how to attach a basic CSS external style sheet to a template and how to properly set up editable regions while maintaining CSS styles. In the next part of this exercise, you'll learn how to use nested templates to create a specific look and feel for different sections of your site, without giving up the productivity boost of templates.

9 Press **Ctrl+S** (Windows) or **Cmd+S** (Mac) to save your page, and then choose **File > Close**. In the **Assets** panel, click the **Templates** category. **Right-click** (Windows) or **Ctrl+click** (Mac) **template_example**, and choose **New from Template**. After you've created the page, press **Ctrl+S** (Windows) or **Cmd+S** (Mac) again to save it with the name **testimonials.htm**.

Dreamweaver 8 provides a number of ways to create a page from a template. One way is to choose File > New to display the New Document dialog box. From there, you'll need to click the Template category, locate the current site in the left column, select your template, and then click Create. I prefer using the Assets panel, as detailed here, because it's much more direct and much faster.

With the child page created, you'll now modify the content and the CSS.

---

10 Place your cursor in the current side navigation link, **Who We Are**, and in the **Property Inspector**, choose **Style: none**. Place your cursor in the second side navigation link, **Testimonials**. From the **Tag Selector**, **right-click** (Windows) or **Ctrl+click** (Mac) the **<p>** tag, and choose **Set Class > CurrentLink**.

Because the `sideNav` editable region surrounds all the navigation links in this area, you can easily switch a CSS class from one link to another to indicate the current page. You'll remember that you selected just the content within the `<div id="navColumn">` tag for this editable region. This placement ensures you're applying the selector for this style (`#navColumn .currentLink`) properly. A common mistake designers make when setting up their CSS layouts as templates is to include the entire `<div>` tag within the editable region. All too often they accidentally delete or modify the `<div>` tag and thus lose the CSS formatting.

Next, you'll customize the main content area while retaining the same look and feel as the template.

---

11 In the **breadcrumb** editable region, select **Who We Are**, and change it to **Testimonials**. In the **mainContent** editable region, change **serenity is our specialty...** to **we're finally relaxed...**, and then change the placeholder subheading **Lorem ipsum dolor** to **One family's story**. Place your cursor anywhere in the pull quote section. From the **Tag Selector**, choose **<span .pullQuote>**, and press **Delete**. Leave the cursor where it is; in the **Insert** bar, click the **Common** category, and then choose **Image**. If the **Select Image Source** dialog box opens, navigate

to the **chap_05 / assets** folder, select **casa.jpg**, and then click **OK**. After you've inserted the image, choose **floatRight** from the **Property Inspector Class** list.

Again, you can see the advantages of keeping the editable regions within the CSS-designated layout tags. For the breadcrumb as well as the **<h1>** and **<h2>** tag content, the styles are immediately, properly applied. If you want your style sheets to be well designed, you can include a number of classes to apply as needed, such as the **floatRight** style. Because this style sheet is linked to the template, any child page of the template can use the included styles. Likewise, any changes made to the linked style sheet affect all the child pages and the template, as you'll see in the next step.

12 Place your cursor anywhere in the **<h1>** tag **we're finally relaxed**. In the **CSS Styles** panel, switch to **Current** mode. In the **Properties** pane, change the **color** value from **#609DC9** to **#76A406**. Choose **File > Save All**, and then in the **Files** panel, choose **Templates > template_example.dwt**. After you've confirmed the change in the **<h1>** tag, close the file.

Note: If you modify a style that is part of an external style sheet attached to a child page, you're altering that style for all associated documents, including the template. Moreover, the change takes place without any warning or ability to abort the operation.

13 Choose **File > Save**, or press **Ctrl+S** (Windows) or **Cmd+S** (Mac). Leave **testimonials.htm** open for the next exercise.

In this exercise, you learned how to apply editable regions to templates to get the most benefit out of CSS styles. In the next exercise, you'll learn how to create nested templates that extend the power of CSS throughout your site.

2 | Highlighting Sections with Nested Templates

Templates are best known for providing a consistent look and feel across a site. Unfortunately, with larger sites, that big plus can turn into a negative. It's not uncommon for Web sites with multiple divisions or sections to look for ways to highlight each section's individuality while maintaining an overall connection to the site.

Nested templates are one way to achieve an individualized appearance within a collective approach. After you've created a nested template and customized it, you can easily create child pages for a special section and, if necessary, update the master template to insert baseline changes across the site. In this exercise, you'll take the template you created in the previous exercise and convert it to a nested template for all the testimonial pages within the Starfish Getaways site.

1 If you followed the previous exercise, **testimonials.htm** should still be open in Dreamweaver 8. If it's not, complete Exercise 1, and then return to this exercise.

In Dreamweaver 8, you create a nested template by first building a child page from a template and then saving that child page as a different template. So the starting point for a nested template is, in fact, a page like testimonials.htm, which was itself derived from a template.

2 Choose **File > Save as Template**. In the **Save As Template** dialog box, type **testimonials** in the **Save as** field, and click **Save**. When Dreamweaver 8 prompts you to update the links, click **Yes**.

After you've created your new template, you'll want to begin the process of marking editable regions again. The main difference between working with basic templates and working with nested templates is where you place editable regions. With a basic template, you can mark any section of the page as editable; with a nested template, you can insert editable regions only inside editable regions created in the original template.

3 In **Design** view, select the current text of the **<h1>** tag **we're finally relaxed ...**. In the **Insert** bar, click the **Common** category, and choose **Templates: Editable Region**. In the **New Editable Region** dialog box, type **heading** in the **Name** field, and click **OK**. Select the text of the **<h2>** tag **One family's story**, and again choose **Templates: Editable Region**. In the dialog box, type **subheading** in the **Name** field, and click **OK**. Place your cursor at the start of the placeholder paragraph, and switch to **Code** view. Select the two full paragraphs of content between the closing **</h2>** tag and the **<!— InstanceEndEditable —>** code. Choose **Templates: Editable Region**; then in the dialog box, type **testimonial** in the **Name** field, and click **OK**. Switch to **Design** view.

An immediate and obvious change occurs when you insert your first new editable region: The outline and tab of the original editable region (in this case, `mainContent`) turn orange, and a new blue outline—signifying a new editable area—appears. The orange region indicates the area is still editable but only when the current template is open. In any child page derived from this nested template, the areas within the orange outline not specifically marked as editable regions will be locked. This is why the larger content area was set to be an editable region.

When you're designing nested templates for sections of a site, the pages mostly likely will have a structured layout. By surrounding the content of both the **<h1>** and **<h2>** tags with editable regions—and leaving the tags themselves outside the regions—you're forcing each child page to include both a heading and a subheading as well as primary content, all styled appropriately.

Next, you'll see how to lock other editable regions.

4 Place your cursor in the **bread-crumb** editable region, at the end of the text. Press **Ctrl+T** (Windows) or **Cmd+T** (Mac) to open the **Quick Tag Editor** in **Insert HTML** mode. Delete the two angle brackets, **<** and **>**, and then type **@@("")@@**. Press **Esc** to hide the **Code Hints** list, and press **Enter** (Windows) or **Return** (Mac).

If you have invisible elements turned on, you'll see a small symbol next to the code you just added to the page. You'll also note that the breadcrumb editable region turned orange, indicating it will be locked in any page derived from this template. The code you inserted indicates a template expression, an advanced feature in Dreamweaver 8 template architecture. You'll learn more about how to use template expressions in Chapter 6, *"Working with Advanced Templates,"* but for now, the key use is clear: When you add a template expression within a nested template's editable region, you lock the region. After you've added one, it's easy to add others.

5 If you don't see the code symbol for the template expression, choose **Visual Aids > Invisible Elements** in the **Document** toolbar. Select the just-inserted template expression symbol, and press **Ctrl+C** (Windows) or **Cmd+C** (Mac). Place your cursor after the first entry in the side navigation, **Who We Are**, and press **Ctrl+V** (Windows) or **Cmd+V** (Mac). Select the final navigation graphic, labeled **contact**, and press the **right arrow** key once. Press **Ctrl+V** (Windows) or **Cmd+V** (Mac) to paste another instance of the template expression.

Because you've created a nested template specifically to be used for testimonial pages, it's a good practice to lock all the other aspects of the page. All three regions where you inserted template expression code are concerned with navigation, and now all the navigational elements for the testimonial page are set.

Now you're ready to add some CSS styles specific to the testimonial page to give it a slightly distinctive appearance.

6 In the **CSS Styles** panel, click **Attach Style Sheet**. In the **Attach External Style Sheet** dialog box, click **Browse**. Navigate to the **chap_05/assets/styles** folder, select **testimonial.css**, and click **OK**. Leave the **Add as** option at the default setting, and click **OK**.

You won't see any differences after attaching this style sheet; it's a blank CSS file included for your convenience.

7 Place your cursor in the **subheading** editable region, and from the **Tag Selector**, choose **<h2>**. In the **CSS Styles** panel, click **New CSS Rule**. When the **New CSS Rule** dialog box appears, set **Type** to **Advanced**, and delete all but **#contentColumn h2** from the **Selector** field. Make sure **Define in** is set to **testimonial.css**, and click **OK**. In the **CSS Rule definition for #contentColumn h2 in testimonial.css** dialog box, click the **Border** category, and turn off all the **Same for all** check boxes. In the **Bottom** row, set **Style** to **solid**, **Width** to **1 pixel**, and **Color** to **#CCC**. Click **OK**.

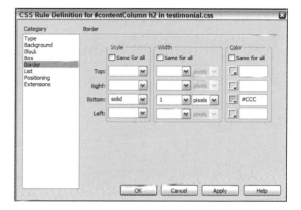

8 In the **CSS Styles** panel, click **New CSS Rule** to create another new style. In the **New CSS Rule** dialog box, type **#contentColumn**, and click **OK**. In the **CSS Rule definition for #contentColumn** dialog box, click the **Background** category, type **#EEE** in the **Color** field, and click **OK**. Choose **File > Save All**. When Dreamweaver 8 notifies you that you've created an editable region inside a block element, click **OK**.

9 Choose **File > Save**, or press **Ctrl+S** (Windows) or **Cmd+S** (Mac). Close **testimonials.htm**.

4 | Applying CSS Hacks

Although CSS is a major step forward in Web design flexibility and power, it's not perfect. To make matters worse, how various browsers interpret CSS styles varies wildly—making it extremely difficult for designers to create cross-browser Web sites without resorting to CSS hacks.

A **CSS hack** is a bit of code used in an unintended fashion to exclude one or more browsers from rendering a style. Some CSS hacks target specific browsers to exclude, whereas others exclude all but a specific browser. Dreamweaver 8 includes the capability to insert two CSS hacks: one to hide CSS from Microsoft Internet Explorer 5 for the Mac and the other to hide CSS from Netscape Navigator 4.x. In this exercise, you'll learn how to apply the backslash-comment hack, the CSS hack for Internet Explorer 5 for the Mac.

1 In the **Files** panel, open **backslash_comment_hack.htm** from the **chap_05** folder you copied to your desktop.

With the rising popularity of Safari, the market for Internet Explorer for the Mac is rapidly dwindling. However, it is still in use, particularly in schools using older Macs. To see whether you need to be concerned with this or any other older browser, be sure to check the site logs for any site on which you're working.

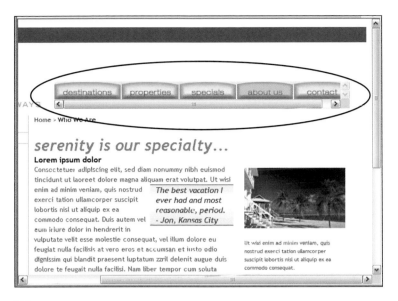

2 If possible, preview the file in Internet Explorer 5 for the Mac.

One of the CSS bugs in Internet Explorer 5 for the Mac concerns absolutely positioned **<div>** tags; the browser often improperly renders the widths, resulting in an unwanted scrollbar. One method of addressing this problem is to assign a larger width to the **<div>** tag style; however, once you fix that problem, you create another with other browsers. Instead, you can use the backslash-comment hack to hide the CSS from Internet Explorer 5 for the Mac. In this case, your first task is to adjust the CSS so the width is correct for that browser.

3 In Dreamweaver 8, select the graphic in the primary navigation, **navbar.jpg**. From the **Tag Selector**, choose **<div #navbar>**. In the **CSS Styles** panel, switch to **Current** mode. In the **Properties** pane, change the **width** value to **540px**.

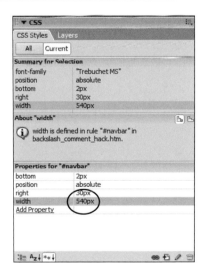

Next, you'll use the backslash-comment hack to mask the standard value for all other browsers.

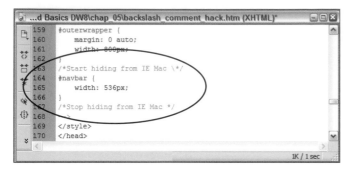

```
  ...d Basics DW8\chap_05\backslash_comment_hack.htm (XHTML)*
159   #outerwrapper {
160       margin: 0 auto;
161       width: 800px;
162   }
163   /*Start hiding from IE Mac \*/
164   #navbar {
165       width: 536px;
166   }
167   /*Stop hiding from IE Mac */
168
169   </style>
170   </head>
                                              1K / 1 sec
```

4 In the **CSS Styles** panel, switch to **All** mode. **Right-click** (Windows) or **Ctrl+click** (Mac) the final defined style, **#outerwrapper**, and choose **Go to Code** from the contextual menu. In **Code** view, add a new line after the final style, and type the following CSS code:

```
#navbar {
   width: 536px;
}
```

5 Select the code you just typed. **Right-click** (Windows) or **Ctrl+click** (Mac), and then choose **Selection > Apply Backslash-comment Hack**. Press **Ctrl+S** (Windows) or **Cmd+S** (Mac) to save your document. Preview the page again in Internet Explorer 5 for the Mac.

The backslash-comment hack works because Internet Explorer 5 for the Mac thinks the CSS comment, which starts with a slash and asterisk combination, ends later than it does. Take a close look at the code:

```
/*Start hiding from IE Mac \*/
#navbar {
   width: 536px;
}
/*Stop hiding from IE Mac */
```

Most browsers see two CSS comments, one on each side of the CSS declaration. Internet Explorer 5 for the Mac, however, misinterprets the backslash within the first comment as an escape character, which then nullifies the closing indicators at the end of the initial comment. To Internet Explorer 5 for the Mac, the comment doesn't end until the closing indicators in the second comment.

The other CSS hack accessible from Dreamweaver 8, the Caio hack (named after its discoverer, Caio Chassot), applies a similar concept but hides CSS from Netscape Navigator 4.x. The code inserted by Dreamweaver 8 is somewhat different:

```
/*/*/
#navbar {
   width: 536px;
}
/* */
```

Here, Netscape Navigator 4.x misinterprets a slash in the first CSS comment line as an escape character. All other browsers ignore it and can access whatever styles are enclosed.

6 Choose **File > Save**, or press **Ctrl+S** (Windows) or **Cmd+S** (Mac). Close **backslash_comment_hack.htm**.

In this exercise, you learned a bit about CSS hacks in general and how to apply a specific hack, the back-slash-comment hack, for fixing issues in Internet Explorer 5 for the Mac.

In this chapter, you learned a number of special ways of working in Dreamweaver 8 to get the most from CSS, including combining CSS with standard templates, working with nested templates, building magazine-style layouts, and applying CSS hacks. In the next chapter, you'll learn how to take templates to the next level by applying template expressions to automate repeating regions, build navigation, and customize CSS.

Working with
Advanced Templates

Many designers, if they use Dreamweaver 8 templates, stick with the basics. They might put a few editable regions on the page to lock down the header, navigation, and footer areas or, if they're more advanced, might even incorporate optional or repeating regions. If you use templates in these ways only, you're not taking advantage of the full power of templates.

A key but little-known component of Dreamweaver 8 templates is the template expression feature. In brief, a **template expression** is a variable, modified and evaluated at design time. Basically, template expressions display otherwise hidden areas of the page, called **optional regions**. However, with a little planning, template expressions can alter many design details with minimal action required by the designer.

In this chapter, you'll learn how to use template expressions to more effectively develop common Web elements. You'll build a FAQ (**F**requently **A**sked **Q**uestions) page complete with an automated design and internal linking. Next, you'll use template expressions to easily create links for navigating through a series of pages. Finally, you'll set up your CSS designs with template expressions so nondesigners can implement design changes you've specified—without touching the CSS. But first, let's spend a little time getting more familiar with template expressions and how they work.

Introducing Template Expressions

As mentioned, a template expression is a variable in a template that can have a different value in each page derived from that template. You can change the values for these variables, also called **parameters**, during the design process using the **Template Properties** dialog box. Once you modify the value of a template expression, Dreamweaver 8 instantly evaluates the template expression and rewrites the page, incorporating the results. For example, let's say you have a template expression that changes the `width` attribute of a specific `<table>` tag. After you have changed the template expression from a default value of, say, 400 to 500, the tag in the child page will read `<table width="500">` instead of `<table width="400">`. You won't see any indication a template expression is present in the child page; the code is just different.

Most template expressions are similar to the one just described and have two components. One part, called a **template parameter**, appears in the `<head>` section of the document and defines the template expression with a name, type, and default value, like this:

```
<!--TemplateParam name="tableWidth"
type="number" value="400">
```

In the `<body>` section of the template, you'll find the corresponding part in the affected `<table>` tag, either written as a parenthetical, like this:

```
<table width="@@(tableWidth)@@">
```

or written as a comment, like this:

```
<table width="<!--TemplateExpr:
expr="tableWidth"-->">
```

The primary difference between the two variations is the parenthetical version can display an icon—identified by double @ signs—in **Design** view, as shown in the illustration below, whereas the comment cannot. You'll see the icon only when the template expression is part of the page's content and not within a tag. As a rule, I prefer the parenthetical method, primarily because it is shorter and easier to write.

Some template expressions do not have a user-definable component. Instead, those template expressions rely on keywords in the defined template expression language developed for Dreamweaver 8. One of the most commonly used keywords in this language is `_index`, which, when evaluated at design time, displays the value of the current entry in a repeating region. You'll use this type of template expression in this chapter's first exercise.

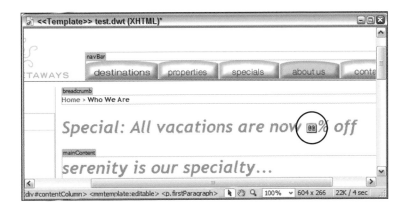

1 | Automating Repeating Regions

Repeating regions are the Dreamweaver 8 template version of a dynamic page's Repeat Region server behavior. Whereas Dreamweaver 8 increments whatever is enclosed in a repeating region automatically at run time—for example, the number of rows in a table increases to match the number of entries in the record set—you have to increase a template repeating region manually at design time. Repeating regions can replicate applied styles and both editable and locked regions. As you'll see in this exercise, they can, in combination with template expressions, even automatically number items and provide named anchor links within a page.

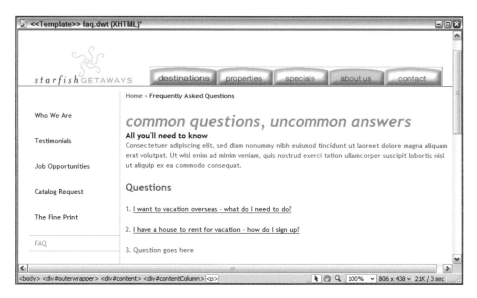

1 In the **Files** panel, open **faq.dwt** from the **Templates** folder you copied to your desktop.

You'll probably notice this template has almost no editable regions. You'll create only one page based on this template (the standard FAQ page), so you don't need a great deal of flexibility. In fact, you'll add only the questions and corresponding answers. The first step in the process is to set up the appropriate editable and repeating regions so you can add new questions.

2 Select the placeholder text in the **Questions** section, **Question goes here**. In the **Link** field in the **Property Inspector**, type **#a_**. Click anywhere to deselect, and then reselect the same placeholder text to ensure you've selected just the text within the **<a>** tag. In the **Insert** bar, click the **Common** category, and choose **Templates : Editable Region**. In the **New Editable Region** dialog box, type **Question** in the **Name** field, and click **OK**. From the **Tag Selector**, choose **<p>**, and in the **Insert** bar, choose **Templates : Repeating Region**. In the **Repeating Region** dialog box, type **Questions** in the **Name** field, and click **OK**.

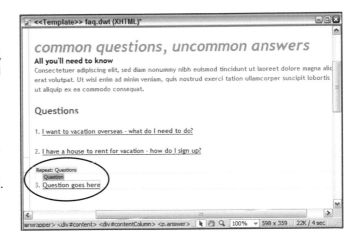

Remember, you are carefully placing the editable region on the page to make sure the text will be properly styled. It's important to note that although you can place editable regions within a repeating region, the reverse is not true. If you tried to add a repeating region inside an editable or optional region, Dreamweaver 8 would stop you with an alert.

With the template regions in place for the question, you're ready to add template expressions for both the question number and the named anchor link to the answer.

3 In the **Questions** section, select the placeholder **3**, and switch to **Code** view. Press **Delete** to remove the placeholder number, and type the following template expression code:

```
@@(_index + 3)@@
```

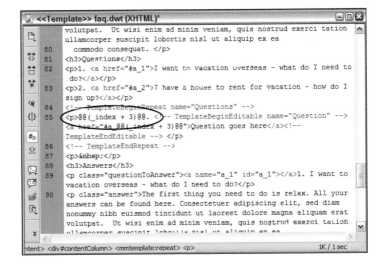

4 Select the just-typed code, and press **Ctrl+C** (Windows) or **Cmd+C** (Mac) to copy the selection. Follow the code with a period; you'll see the question number followed by a period. Locate the **<a>** tag on the same code line, and position your cursor after the code **href="#a_**; then press **Ctrl+V** (Windows) or **Cmd+V** (Mac) to paste the copied code. The entire code block you've worked on should look like this (I've added line returns and indentations to make the code easier to read):

```
<!-- TemplateBeginRepeat name="Questions" -->
  <p>@@(_index + 3)@@.
  <a href="#a_@@(_index + 3)@@">
  <!-- TemplateBeginEditable name="Question" -->
    Question goes here
  <!-- TemplateEndEditable -->
  </a>
  </p>
<!-- TemplateEndRepeat -->
```

5 Switch to **Design** view.

You'll use the same template expression throughout this template. Remember, **_index** is part of the Dreamweaver 8 template expression language, and it refers to the number of the current entry, beginning with 0. To display the correct number, you added 3 to the **_index** value. This means the first question in the repeating region will be 3 (**_index = 0 + 3**), and the next will be 4 (**_index = 1 + 3**). When you return to Design view, you'll see the template expression symbol for the question number if you have the Invisible Elements option turned on (in the Document toolbar, select Visual Aids > Invisible Elements).

Next, you'll apply the editable regions to the Answers section.

6 In the **Answers** section, select the placeholder heading, **Question**. In the **Insert** bar, click the **Common** category, and choose **Templates : Editable Region**. In the **New Editable Region** dialog box, type **Repeated Question** in the **Name** field, and click **OK**. Select the answer placeholder text, **Answer goes here**, and again choose **Templates : Editable Region**. In the **Editable Region** dialog box, type **Answer** in the **Name** field, and click **OK**.

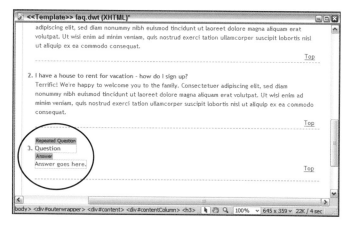

To maintain the different styles for the two parts of the answer, you are applying separate editable regions. In my experience, the more sophisticated your use of templates, the more editable regions you'll use. Although it takes a bit longer to set up the template, multiple editable regions make it much faster and less error prone when creating child pages because you're just adding or changing content—Dreamweaver 8 does all the styling for you. The next step in this process is to add the repeating region to the Answers section.

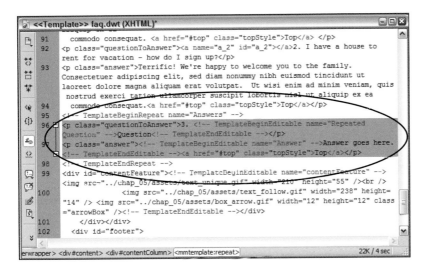

```
 91     commodo consequat. <a href="#top" class="topStyle">Top</a> </p>
 92     <p class="questionToAnswer"><a name="a_2" id="a_2"></a>2. I have a house to
        rent for vacation - how do I sign up?</p>
 93     <p class="answer">Terrific! We're happy to welcome you to the family.
        Consectetuer adipiscing elit, sed diam nonummy nibh euismod tincidunt ut
        laoreet dolore magna aliquam erat volutpat. Ut wisi enim ad minim veniam, quis
         nostrud exerci tation ullamcorper suscipit lobortis nisl ut aliquip ex ea
 94        commodo consequat.<a href="#top" class="topStyle">Top</a></p>
 95     <!-- TemplateBeginRepeat name="Answers" -->
 96     <p class="questionToAnswer">3. <!-- TemplateBeginEditable name="Repeated
        Question" -->Question<!-- TemplateEndEditable --></p>
 97     <p class="answer"><!-- TemplateBeginEditable name="Answer" -->Answer goes here.
        <!-- TemplateEndEditable --><a href="#top" class="topStyle">Top</a></p>
 98     <!-- TemplateEndRepeat -->
 99     <div id="contentFeature"><!-- TemplateBeginEditable name="contentFeature" -->
        <img src="../chap_05/assets/text_unique.gif" width="210" height="55" /><br />
100                <img src="../chap_05/assets/text_follow.gif" width="238" height=
        "14" /> <img src="../chap_05/assets/box_arrow.gif" width="12" height="12" class
        ="arrowBox" /><!-- TemplateEndEditable --></div>
101        </div></div>
102        <div id="footer">
```

7 Position your cursor in the **Repeated Question** editable region. From the **Tag Selector**, choose **<p.questionToAnswer>**. Switch to **Code** view. Press **Shift**, and click after the closing **</p>** tag to extend your selection to the following **<p>** tag. In the **Insert** bar, choose **Templates : Repeating Region**. In the dialog box, type **Answers** in the **Name** field, and click **OK**.

The Answers repeating region wraps around a number of elements: the numbered, repeated question; the answer; and the anchor link at the top of the page. Both the repeated question and the answer are styled with their own classes. Because the dashed bottom border is part of the **.answer** class style, it too is included and will be repeated with each iteration.

The next step is to include the template expressions for the Answers section.

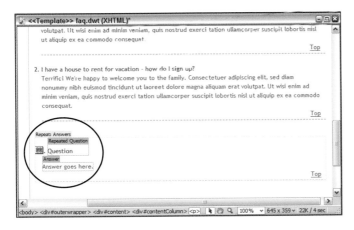

8 While in **Code** view, delete the placeholder number, **3** (but not the following period), and type this template expression:

```
@@(_index + 3)@@
```

9 Copy the code you just typed, and then position your cursor between the **<p class="questionToAnswer">** tag and the just-typed template expression. In the **Insert** bar, choose **Named Anchor**. In the dialog box, type **a_** in the **Anchor name** field, and click **OK**. Position your cursor in the inserted code just after **name="a_**, and press **Ctrl+V** (Windows) or **Cmd+V** (Mac). Move the cursor after **id="a_**, and press **Ctrl+V** (Windows) or **Cmd+V** (Mac) to paste the expression here as well. The code at this point will look like the following (I've added line returns and indentations to make the code easier to read):

```
<p class="questionToAnswer">
  <a name="a_@@(_index + 3)@@" id="a_@@(_index + 3)@@"></a>
  @@(_index + 3)@@.
  <!-- TemplateBeginEditable name="Repeated Question" -->
    Question
  <!-- TemplateEndEditable -->
</p>
```

10 Switch to **Design** view.

Because you're using the same template expression, the two sections (Questions and Answers) will have similar results. The one variation is the use of the named anchor. You'll notice you couldn't insert the template expression directly into the Named Anchor dialog box; if you had, Dreamweaver 8 would have noted the unallowed characters and inserted an incorrect tag. Instead, you used the initial portion of the named anchor (**a_**) and added the template expression in Code view. All that's left is to see how all your hard work comes together in a page derived from the template.

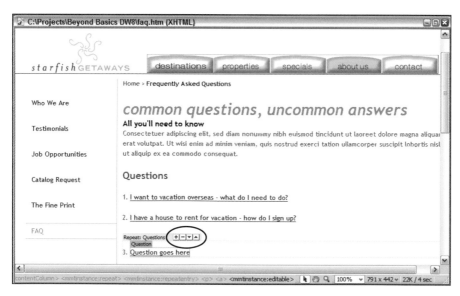

11 Press **Ctrl+S** (Windows) or **Cmd+S** (Mac) to save your template. Close **faq.dwt**. Press **F11** to open the **Assets** panel. Switch to the **Templates** category, **right-click** (Windows) or **Ctrl+click** (Mac) **faq**, and choose **New from Template**. After this creates the page, press **Ctrl+S** (Windows) or **Cmd+S** (Mac) again to save your new page with the name **faq.htm**.

You'll notice within each of the repeating regions, the proper number of the question appears. The other most noticeable aspects of the child page are the mini-toolbars on the top of each repeating region. These allow you to add or remove instances or move them up or down. You'll try them next to see how the template expressions work.

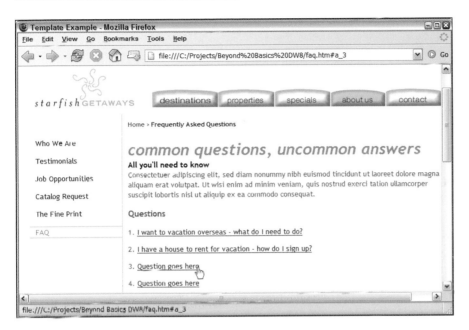

12 In the **Questions** repeating region, click **Add (+)** to insert another question. Move down to the **Answer** repeating region, and click **Add (+)** to include a corresponding answer.

13 To test the template expression–derived named anchors, preview the page in the browser by pressing **F12**. If Dreamweaver 8 asks you to save your page, click **Yes**. In the browser, click the **Question 3** link, and verify the page moves to just above the matching answer. Click **Top** to return to the top of the page, and repeat this test with the **Question 4** link.

You may need to resize your browser to see where precisely the linked questions are pointing.

Another way to verify the link is properly written is to look at the status bar at the bottom of the browser when you position your cursor over the linked question. The displayed link will include the named anchor, such as `faq.htm#a_3` or `faq.htm#a_4`.

14 Close your browser, and return to Dreamweaver 8. Close **faq.htm**.

In this exercise, you incorporated template expressions in a FAQ page to facilitate the rapid entry of questions and answers at design time. In the next exercise, you'll see how you can use template expressions to navigate from one page to another, as well as within a single page.

2 | Navigating with Template Expressions

Creating a link from one page to another in a site is typically a manual, one-link-at-a-time task. Certain types of Web pages, however, require a special type of navigation—Previous and Next links—that you can create automatically with template expressions. Specifically, sets of tutorial pages and any other content designed to be read in sequence benefit from links to the previous and next pages. Links like these allow page visitors to proceed through the material at their own pace and return to prior pages as necessary. After you've designed the proper template expression system, you need to change only one value in the **Template Properties** dialog box for each child page, which you'll learn to do in this exercise.

---

1 In the **Files** panel, open **list_steps.dwt** from the **Templates** folder you copied to your desktop.

I've already added the Previous and Next text to the page. You'll notice these text elements are outside any editable region and are therefore locked. This is because later in this exercise you'll add a template expression to the **<a>** tags around each word, which is not allowed in an editable region. In the next step, you'll add the code to define the template parameter.

---

2 Switch to **Code** view, and position your cursor between the closing **</style>** and **</head>** tags. Press **Enter** (Windows) or **Return** (Mac) to create a new line, and type the following comment:

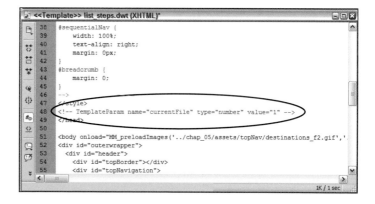

```
<!-- TemplateParam name="currentFile" type="number" value="1" -->
```

The template parameter is the Dreamweaver 8 syntax for establishing a template property. Dreamweaver 8 automatically adds this code when you create an optional region or make an attribute editable; however, because you'll be referring to the template parameter in a link, the fastest way to accomplish this goal is simply to type the code.

3 Switch to **Design** view. Select the text **< Previous**. In the **Link** field in the **Property Inspector**, type the following code, making sure to use single quotation marks:

```
@@('list_' + (currentFile - 1) + '.htm')@@
```

4 Select the text **Next >**. In the **Link** field in the **Property Inspector**, type the following code:

```
@@('list_' + (currentFile + 1) + '.htm')@@
```

This code represents a sophisticated use of template expressions. Essentially, you're using the power of template expressions to build a file name based on the value of the template parameter, `currentFile`.

Let's say the `currentFile` value is **3** and it's the third file in the series. In that case, the template expression you added to the Previous link would evaluate to `list_2.htm`, and the Next link would result in `list_4.htm`.

To make the navigation truly effective, you need to incorporate a couple of optional regions, as shown in the next step.

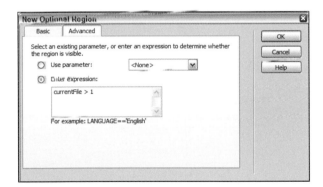

5 Position your cursor anywhere in the **< Previous** link. From the **Tag Selector**, choose **<a>**. In the **Insert** bar, click the **Common** category, and choose **Templates : Optional Region**. In the **New Optional Region** dialog box, select the **Advanced** tab. Click the **Enter expression** radio button to select it, and in the text area, type **currentFile > 1**, as shown in the illustration here. Click **OK**.

Optional regions appear whenever their associated parameter or expression is true. With the expression you typed in this optional region, the template parameter `currentFile` needs to be greater than 1 for the Previous link to appear. In other words, on the first page of the series, the Previous link will not display. A similar operation controls the Next link, as you'll see in the next step.

6 Position your cursor anywhere in the **Next >** link. From the **Tag Selector**, choose **<a>**. In the **Insert** bar, click the **Common** category, and choose **Templates : Optional Region**. In the **New Optional Region** dialog box, select the **Advanced** tab. Click the **Enter expression** radio button, and in the text area, type **currentFile < 4**. Click **OK**.

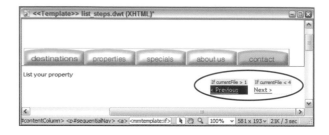

To successfully use this feature of the template, you'll need to know just how many pages are in the series. Here, you're assuming the series contains four pages. On the final page, you'll set the `currentFile` value to **4**, so the expression will no longer be true. Therefore, the Next link disappears.

The next step adds a simple indicator so you and your visitors will be able to locate where they are in the series.

---

7 In the phrase **Step 1**, select the placeholder number, **1**, and switch to **Code** view. Delete the placeholder number, and type the template expression **@@(currentFile)@@**. Switch to **Design** view. Press **Ctrl+S** (Windows) or **Cmd+S** (Mac).

Now the page displays the `currentFile` value, and you're ready to create a few child pages to see how it all comes together.

---

8 Press **F11** to open the **Assets** panel. Click the **Templates** category, **right-click** (Windows) or **Ctrl+click** (Mac) **list_steps**, and choose **New from Template**. After this creates the page, press **Ctrl+S** (Windows) or **Cmd+S** (Mac) again to save the new page with the name **list_1.htm**. Choose **Modify > Template Properties**. In the **Template Properties** dialog box, verify **currentFile** is set to **1**, and click **OK**.

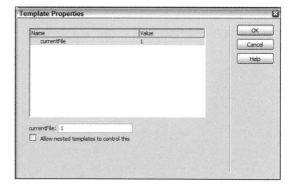

The first child page is easy, and you don't need to alter the `currentFile` value (by default, it's **1**). The other key action in this step is naming the file. For the template expression navigation to work, the files must have sequential names, starting with `list_1.htm`.

Next, you'll create a few more properly named files—with the correct `currentFile` values—so you can test the navigation.

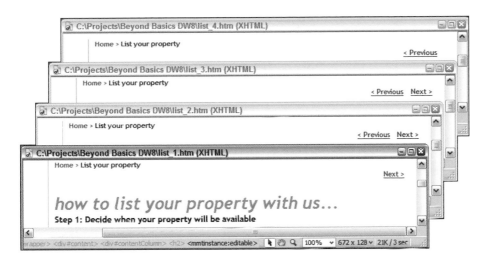

9 Repeat Step 8 three times. Save the first new page created as **list_2.htm**, and change the **currentFile** value to **2** in the **Template Properties** dialog box. Save the second new page as **list_3.htm** with a **currentFile** value of **3**. Save the third new page as **list_4.htm** with a **currentFile** value of **4**.

---

10 Select **list_1.htm**, and press **F12** to preview it. Click the **Next** links to move through the pages, and then click the **Previous** links to return.

If you're sharp, you'll notice you don't have to preview the pages in a browser to see the effect after changing the template properties. The number following the word *Step* updates immediately, and in the cases of `list_1.htm` and `list_4.htm`, the navigation links adjust as well, right in Dreamweaver 8.

---

11 Close your browser, and return to Dreamweaver 8. Choose **File > Close All**.

In this exercise, you created serial navigation with template expressions. In the next exercise, you'll extend your template expression prowess to CSS.

---

3 | Using Template Expressions with CSS

You've seen how you can use template expressions to enhance productivity by automatically creating navigational links between and within pages. You can benefit from template expressions in another way: By integrating template expressions into your CSS, you can offer creators of child pages a range of stylistic options. For example, if you are creating a site for a client, you can use template expressions in your CSS to allow the client to later change the look and feel of the site—without touching the CSS.

In this exercise, you'll see two examples of what template expressions—and the template language in Dreamweaver 8—can do in CSS. You'll first learn how to create a style sheet–switching mechanism, driven completely by values typed in the **Template Properties** dialog box. You'll then see how other values can trigger specific style changes.

1 In the **Files** panel, open **seasons.dwt** from the **Templates** folder you copied to your desktop.

This template currently links to a single CSS style sheet. During the course of this exercise, you'll add template language statements to allow the designers of child pages to switch between four style sheets: one for each season. The first step is to add the proper template parameter code to your page.

2 Switch to **Code** view, and locate the **<link>** tag near the closing **</head>** tag that references the **main.css** style sheet. Position your cursor in front of this line, and press **Enter** (Windows) or **Return** (Mac) to make a new line. Type the following code:

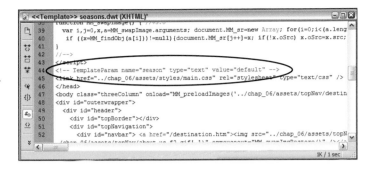

```
<!-- TemplateParam name="season" type="text" value="default" -->
```

This statement establishes a template parameter named **season** with an initial value of **default**. With any template conditional coding (also called **if clauses**) strategy—in which the designer has the option to choose from a number of options—it's a good idea to always have a default setting, in case the designer decides not to choose any of the available options.

Next, you'll add the template language to initialize the conditional code and establish the default condition.

3 Create a new line after the just-typed template parameter, and type the following code:

```
<!-- TemplateBeginMultipleIf -->
<!-- TemplateBeginIfClause cond="season == 'default'" -->
```

4 Position your cursor at the end of the style sheet **<link>** tag, and press **Enter** (Windows) or **Return** (Mac) to create another new line. When you're ready, type the following code:

```
<!-- TemplateEndIfClause -->
```

The opening code line starts the entire conditional block by beginning a **MultipleIf** statement. As the name implies, a **MultipleIf** statement allows you to test for numerous conditions and, if a condition is true, execute the specified code. In the Dreamweaver 8 template language, you can type as many **if-then** statements as you want, as long as you bracket them with **TemplateBeginMultipleIf** comments. The second two code lines form a complete, single **if** clause. In this case, if the template parameter named **season** is equal to the default value, then the condition is true and Dreamweaver 8 writes the code within the **if** clause into the HTML at design time. You'll follow this same structure—an opening **if** clause followed by the style sheet **<link>** tag and an ending **if** clause—for each style sheet option you'll create.

5 Select the three lines making up the complete **if** clause:

```
<!-- TemplateBeginIfClause cond="season == 'default'" -->
<link href="../chap_06/assets/styles/main.css" rel="stylesheet" type="text/css" />
<!-- TemplateEndIfClause -->
```

6 Press **Ctrl+C** (Windows) or **Cmd+C** (Mac) to copy the selected code, and then add a new line after the selected code. Press **Ctrl+V** (Windows) or **Cmd+V** (Mac) to paste the copied code. Modify the first line by changing **default** to **fall**. In the style sheet **<link>** tag, change **main.css** to **fall.css**.

As you can see, you're using the same structure for each **if** clause; only the key values—the season and the style sheet name—are different.

7 Paste the copied code three more times, one for each remaining season. In the first set of three lines, change **default** to **winter**, and change **main.css** to **winter.css**. In the second set, change **default** to **spring**, and change **main.css** to **spring.css**. In the final set, change **default** to **summer**, and change **main.css** to **summer.css**.

Although you can type all the code by hand, I'm a big believer in the copy-paste-modify school of coding—especially when you're changing only two values in each iteration. The final coding step is to finish the **MultipleIf** statement you inserted previously.

8 After the final **if** clause, create a new line, and type this code:

```
<!-- TemplateEndMultipleIf -->
```

9 Press **Ctrl+S** (Windows) or **Cmd+S** (Mac) to store your template. Should the Dreamweaver 8 alert appear regarding editable regions within a block element, click **OK**. Switch to **Code** view, and press **Shift+F11** to display the **CSS Styles** panel.

One of my least favorite features of Dreamweaver 8 is the way it treats template expressions when you're designing the templates: It basically ignores them. Dreamweaver 8 evaluates and displays template expressions properly at design time only in child pages derived from templates. This explains why you get a blend of styles and why all the inserted style sheets are visible in the CSS Styles panel. Although this can be disconcerting visually at design time, it has no effect at run time. Luckily, one Dreamweaver 8 feature is perfect for working around this unsettling effect: design-time style sheets.

10 In the **CSS Styles** panel, **right-click** (Windows) or **Ctrl+click** (Mac), and choose **Design-time** from the contextual menu. In the **Design Time Style Sheets** dialog box, click **Add (+)** in the **Hide at design time** section. In the **Select File** dialog box, navigate to the **chap_06/assets/styles** folder, and choose **fall.css**. Click **OK**. Repeat the process three times to add **spring.css**, **summer.css**, and **winter.css**. Click **OK**.

This returns you to the default setting for your style sheet at design time for both templates and child pages. Now you're ready to see how you can use template expressions to alter individual styles as well as style sheets by making the background image of one style optional.

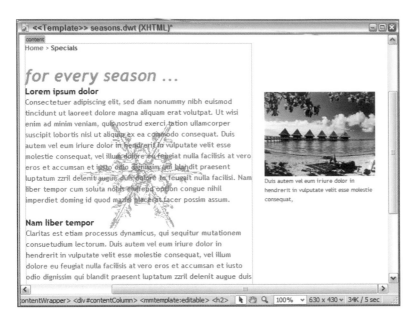

for every season ...

Lorem ipsum dolor
Consectetuer adipiscing elit, sed diam nonummy nibh euismod
tincidunt ut laoreet dolore magna aliquam erat volutpat. Ut wisi
enim ad minim veniam, quis nostrud exerci tation ullamcorper
suscipit lobortis nisl ut aliquip ex ea commodo consequat. Duis
autem vel eum iriure dolor in hendrerit in vulputate velit esse
molestie consequat, vel illum dolore eu feugiat nulla facilisis at vero
eros et accumsan et iusto odio dignissim qui blandit praesent
luptatum zzril delenit augue duis dolore te feugait nulla facilisi. Nam
liber tempor cum soluta nobis eleifend option congue nihil
imperdiet doming id quod mazim placerat facer possim assum.

Nam liber tempor
Claritas est etiam processus dynamicus, qui sequitur mutationem
consuetudium lectorum. Duis autem vel eum iriure dolor in
hendrerit in vulputate velit esse molestie consequat, vel illum
dolore eu feugiat nulla facilisis at vero eros et accumsan et iusto
odio dignissim qui blandit praesent luptatum zzril delenit augue duis

Duis autem vel eum iriure dolor in
hendrerit in vulputate velit esse molestie
consequat,

11 Position your cursor anywhere in the text content, and from the **Tag Selector**, choose
<div#contentColumn>. In the **CSS Styles** panel, click **New CSS Rule**. In the **New CSS Rule** dialog box,
delete all but **#contentColumn** from the **Selector** field. Change the **Define in** option to **This document
only**, and click **OK**. In the **CSS Definition** dialog box, switch to the **Background** category. Click **Background
Image Browse**, and navigate to the **chap_06/assets** folder; select **snowflake_dim.gif**, and click **OK**. Set
Repeat to **no-repeat**, **Horizontal position** to **center**, and **Vertical position** to **center**, and then click **OK**
to set the style.

It's important to note this creates the new CSS rule in the current document, not in an external style sheet.
Anytime you want to integrate template expressions with individual CSS rules, the CSS has to be within
the template; otherwise, the template expression will not be evaluated.

For this exercise, the goal is to make adding the snowflake background optional but restrict it to appear
only when it's winter, at least as far as the **season** template parameter is concerned. To do this, you'll need
to add a second template parameter to control the background.

---

12 Switch to **Code** view, and
locate the **season** template
parameter. Position your cursor in
front of this line, and press **Enter**
(Windows) or **Return** (Mac) to start
a new line. Type the following code:

```
<!-- TemplateParam name="bg" type="boolean" value="true" -->
```

You have a number of types of template parameters to use. The **boolean** template parameter is either true or false, and designers usually use it to set the state of optional regions.

With the template parameter defined, you're ready to include it in your template expression.

13 Locate the **<style>** tag containing the CSS rule defined in Step 11. Replace the **#contentColumn** declaration with the following code:

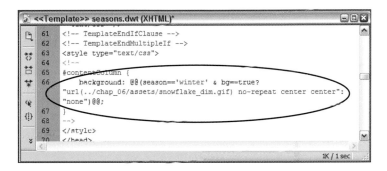

```
background: @@(season=='winter' & bg==true?"url(../chap_06/assets/snowflake_dim.gif) no-repeat
center center":"none")@@;
```

The type of template expression you're using here is known as a **ternary expression** because it has three parts: the condition, the **true** value, and the **false** value. If the condition evaluates to true, then the **true** value appears; otherwise, the **false** value appears. In this example, the condition is compound: sea-son=='winter' & bg==true. The condition reads as, "True only if both the **season** template parameter is **winter** and the **bg** template parameter is **true**. If so, then the snowflake background appears on the site; otherwise, the background is set to **none**."

Next you'll see how this all comes together.

14 Press **Ctrl+S** (Windows) or **Cmd+S** (Mac) to save the page. In the **Assets** panel, click the **Template** category, **right-click** (Windows) or **Ctrl+click** (Mac) **seasons**, and choose **New from Template**. When the page has been created, press **Ctrl+S** (Windows) or **Cmd+S** (Mac) again to save your new page with the name **seasons.htm** in the **chap_06** folder. Choose **Modify > Template Properties**. In the **Template Properties** dialog box, turn off the **Show bg** check box, and change **season** to **summer**. Click **OK**.

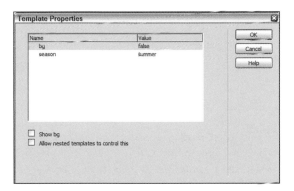

The background changes to a mellow yellow, and the text colors adjust for better contrast. Next, you'll try it with the winter scene.

15 Choose **Modify > Template Properties**. In the dialog box, turn on the **Show bg** check box, and change **season** to **winter**. Click **OK**.

Depending on the text content, you might decide to not use the snowflake background. With the flexibility you've built into the template expressions, you can easily dismiss the snowflake background by turning off the Show bg check box in the Template Properties dialog box.

---

16 Press **Ctrl+S** (Windows) or **Cmd+S** (Mac) to save your page. Close **seasons.dwt**.

In this chapter, you learned how to use template expressions to boost your productivity and design options. Template expressions are amazingly flexible, and as you've seen, you can use them to automate production, power navigation, and even systematically change style sheets. In the next chapter, you'll see how to get the most out of your coding environment.

Macromedia Dreamweaver 8 Beyond the Basics : H·O·T

7

Utilizing Rapid Coding Techniques

Even the most visually oriented designers need to touch the code sometimes. Although Design view in Dreamweaver 8 is capable of taking you to extraordinary places, familiarity with Code view is a must if you want to get the most from your Web page—you can make certain enhancements and tweaks only directly in the code.

In Dreamweaver 8, Code view enjoys somewhat of a renaissance: This release has more code-based features than in any previous version. A new Coding toolbar makes it easy to access all the new—and existing—features. In addition, new methods for selecting large, encompassing blocks of code complement one of the most fascinating new code innovations in Dreamweaver 8: code collapse. Dreamweaver 8 also now boasts commenting options for CSS, JavaScript, and all the supported server models, as well as for HTML. To help in the debugging process, Dreamweaver 8 works with your favorite file comparison program to highlight differences between files, whether they are on different computers or the same one.

In the exercises in this chapter, you will try all these features. You'll also see how you can set up the little-used Favorites category in the Insert bar to rapidly access common Dreamweaver 8 objects, in either Design view or Code view.

Introducing the New Coding Toolbar

Dreamweaver 8 offers a new point-and-click method for interacting with all kinds of code: the **Coding** toolbar. Unlike other toolbars in Dreamweaver 8, the **Coding** toolbar is vertical, not horizontal, and it hugs the left edge of the **Document** window.

Although you can't move the **Coding** toolbar to a different location or even detach it, you can hide it. The fastest way to hide (or reveal) the **Coding** toolbar is to **right-click** (Windows) or **Ctrl+click** (Mac) any visible toolbar and choose **Coding** from the contextual menu. You can also select **View > Toolbars > Coding**. The chart on the following page explains the tools in detail.

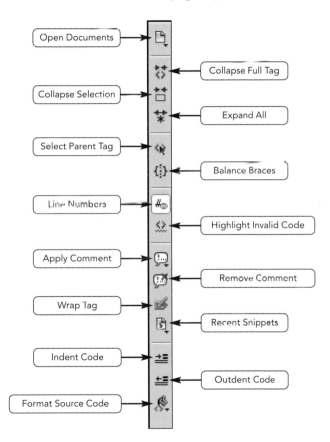

Coding Toolbar Tools

Button	Description
Open Documents	Lists all open documents, including the full path (for example, **C:\Projects\ DW 8 Beyond Basics\chap_07\coding_example.htm**). This functionality is a major plus when you're working on the main pages in four different folders and they're all labeled **index.htm**.
Collapse Full Tag	Selects and collapses the tag surrounding the current cursor placement. Press **Alt** (Windows) or **Opt** (Mac), and click to collapse all code outside the current tag. You'll learn more about this tool in Exercise 2.
Collapse Selection	Collapses the current selection of code. Press **Alt** (Windows) or **Opt** (Mac), and click to highlight all code outside the current selection. You'll learn more about this tool in Exercise 2.
Expand All	Expands all the collapsed code in the document.
Select Parent Tag	Highlights the tag surrounding the current selection or where the cursor is placed. Click again to select the next surrounding tag.
Balance Braces	Highlights any code within enclosing braces, brackets, or parentheses. Click again to expand the selection to the next set of braces, brackets, or parentheses.
Line Numbers	Toggles the line numbers in **Code** view on and off.
Highlight Invalid Code	Highlights any invalid HTML or XHTML (e**X**tensible **HTML**) with a yellow background.
Apply Comment	Displays a submenu of comment types. When you choose a comment type (such as **Apply HTML Comment**), Dreamweaver 8 inserts the full comment code at the cursor position; highlight some code and then pick this tool, Dreamweaver 8 wraps the current selection in the chosen comment style. You'll learn more about this tool in Exercise 3.
Remove Comment	Deletes comments from a selection.
Wrap Tag	Displays the **Quick Tag Editor** in **Wrap Tag** mode to allow you to surround a selection with a specific HTML tag.
Recent Snippets	Shows the last five snippets used.
Indent Code	Indents the selected code a single tab length, as defined in the **Code Format** category of **Preferences**.
Outdent Code	Outdents the selected code a single tab length.
Format Source Code	Applies the source-formatting options set in the **Code Format** category of **Preferences**; you can apply the source formatting to a selection or to the entire document.

1 | Applying Quick Tag Selection

In Design view, the first step to modifying something—whether it is a line of text, a table, or a single tag—is to select it. The same is true for modifying in Code view, although to a somewhat lesser extent. With direct access to the code, you're often best served by typing an attribute or value directly in an existing tag. However, many times you'll find you'll need to move, hide, or otherwise change one or more blocks of code—and Code view in Dreamweaver 8 has the tools to help you make the initial selection. You'll find selecting in Code view more precise and robust than in Design view; you can, for example, climb up the HTML tree by selecting the parent tag with the click of a button. In this exercise, you'll get some experience working with the selection options in the Coding toolbar, as well as learn other methods of rapidly selecting your code.

```
C:\Projects\Beyond Basics DW8\chap_07\coding_example.htm (XHTML)
158  #outerwrapper {
159       margin: 0 auto;
160       width: 800px;
161  }
162  -->
163  </style>
164  </head>
165  <body>
166  <div id="outerwrapper">
167    <div id="header">
168        <div id="topBorder"></div>
169        <div id="topNavigation"> <br /><img src="assets/navbar.jpg" id="navbar" /></
     div>
170    </div>
171    <div id="content">
172        <div id="navColumn">
173          <p class="currentLink">Who We Are</p>
174          <p> Testimonials</p>
175          <p> Job Opportunities</p>
176          <p> Catalog Request</p>
177          <p> The Fine Print</p>
178        </div>
179        <div id="mainContent">
180          <div id="contentColumn">
181            <p id="breadcrumb"><span class="currentSection">Home &gt;</span> Who We Are </p
       >
182            <h1>serenity is our specialty...</h1>
```

`<body> <div#outerwrapper>`   1K / 1 sec

1 In the **Files** panel, open **coding_example.htm** from the **chap_07** folder you copied to your desktop. Switch to **Code** view. If necessary, **right-click** (Windows) or **Ctrl+click** (Mac) any toolbar, and choose **Coding** to display the **Coding** toolbar.

```
C:\Projects\Beyond Basics DW8\chap_07\coding_example.htm (XHTML)
158  #outerwrapper {
159      margin: 0 auto;
160      width: 800px;
161  }
162  -->
163  </style>
164  </head>
165  <body>
166  <div id="outerwrapper">
167    <div id="header">
168      <div id="topBorder"></div>
169      <div id="topNavigation"> <br /><img src="assets/navbar.jpg" id="navbar" /></
     div>
170    </div>
171    <div id="content">
172      <div id="navColumn">
173        <p class="currentLink">Who We Are</p>
174        <p> Testimonials</p>
175        <p> Job Opportunities</p>
176        <p> Catalog Request</p>
177        <p> The Fine Print</p>
178      </div>
179      <div id="mainContent">
180        <div id="contentColumn">
181          <p id="breadcrumb"><span class="currentSection">Home &gt;</span> Who We Are </p
     >
182          <h1>serenity is our specialty...</h1>
```
`<body> <div#outerwrapper> <div#content> <div#navColumn> <p.currentLink>`   `1K / 1 sec`

2 Position your cursor within the first side navigation text, **Who We Are**. In the **Coding** toolbar, click **Select Parent Tag**, as shown in the illustration here.

When you click Select Parent Tag, you're selecting the tag surrounding the text. This is functionally the same as choosing <p.currentLink> from the Tag Selector, which you'll notice is also available in Code view. The handle you see next to the line numbers is for collapsing the code, discussed in Exercise 2.

```
C:\Projects\Beyond Basics DW8\chap_07\coding_example.htm (XHTML)
158  #outerwrapper {
159      margin: 0 auto;
160      width: 800px;
161  }
162  -->
163  </style>
164  </head>
165  <body>
166  <div id="outerwrapper">
167    <div id="header">
168      <div id="topBorder"></div>
169      <div id="topNavigation"> <br /><img src="assets/navbar.jpg" id="navbar" /></
     div>
170    </div>
171    <div id="content">
172      <div id="navColumn">
173        <p class="currentLink">Who We Are</p>
174        <p> Testimonials</p>
175        <p> Job Opportunities</p>
176        <p> Catalog Request</p>
177        <p> The Fine Print</p>
178      </div>
179      <div id="mainContent">
180        <div id="contentColumn">
181          <p id="breadcrumb"><span class="currentSection">Home &gt;</span> Who We Are </p
     >
182          <h1>serenity is our specialty...</h1>
```
`<body> <div#outerwrapper> <div#content>`   `1K / 1 sec`

3 In the **Coding** toolbar, click **Select Parent Tag** again to expand the selection to the surrounding navColumn **<div>** tag. Click **Select Parent Tag** once more to expand the selection to the **content <div>** tag.

The Select Parent Tag command is a great way to crawl up the HTML structure, and it becomes especially useful in CSS layouts with nested **<div>** tags.

Tip: If you prefer keyboard shortcuts, you can press Ctrl+[(Windows) or Cmd+[(Mac) to achieve the same effect.

The Select Parent Tag command works only on HTML tags; if you want to quickly select the content of a CSS declaration or JavaScript function, you'll need to use Balance Braces, as demonstrated in the next step.

4 Click anywhere to clear the selection. In the **<head>** section of the document, locate the **.pullQuote** style rule, and position your cursor next to any of the properties. In the **Coding** toolbar, click **Balance Braces**.

The selection expands to include all the content between the opening and closing braces for the **.pullQuote** class. Balance Braces is a good selection tool to use with complex CSS, especially in conjunction with the code collapse feature.

Note: If you were to click Balance Braces again, the selection would *not* expand. This is because no other set of braces, brackets, or parentheses surrounds the current selection—only HTML tags and Balance Braces do not look for HTML tags.

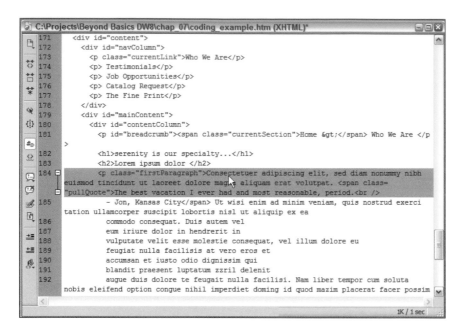

5 Click anywhere to clear the selection. In the **Document** toolbar, choose **View Options**, and then choose **Word Wrap** to turn it on, if necessary. Move your cursor to the **<body>** section of the document. Locate a line that wraps to a second line in the **Document** window, and triple-click any word or tag in that line, even if it wraps, to select the entire line. Press the **Shift** key, and click further down the page to expand the selection. Position your cursor in the line number column, and drag down the page to select a range of code lines.

The Coding toolbar isn't the only way to make selections in Code view. Use the triple-click method whenever you need to select a line of code. Alternatively, you can click once when your cursor is in the line number column, but I think the first method is faster. I'm also a fan of dragging down the line number column to choose a section of code; this works best when you need to select a number of paragraph tags not contained within a surrounding tag. For these situations, use Select Parent Tag for the fastest results.

---

6 Leave **coding_example.htm** open for the next exercise.

You've seen in this exercise how powerful the selection tools are in the Coding toolbar. In the next exercise, you'll get a chance to explore a useful new function in Dreamweaver 8: code collapse.

---

2 | Collapsing Code

You've probably heard the expression "You can't see the forest for the trees." The first time you look at a page of pure code, you may feel like you're looking at a giant forest, unable to discern any details. Dreamweaver 8 provides **code collapse** to temporarily hide code you don't need to see so you can focus on other, important code. This ability helps you pinpoint specific issues in your code. The code collapse feature is robust: You can collapse a tag or a selection—or everything *but* a tag or selection.

1 If you followed the previous exercise, **coding_example.htm** should still be open in Dreamweaver 8. If it's not, open it from the **chap_07** folder you copied to your desktop. Make sure you're in **Code** view, and if necessary, click anywhere to clear any highlighted code.

2 Place your cursor just after the side navigation **<div>** tag, **<div id="navColumn">**. In the **Coding** toolbar, click **Collapse Parent Tag**. Click the **collapse** button in the gutter (shown as a plus sign in Windows and a triangle on the Mac) next to the line numbers to expand the collapsed tag. Click the **collapse** button again to hide it. Move your cursor over the collapsed tag to reveal the hidden code.

Collapse Parent Tag is effective when you're debugging or otherwise working with specific code and you don't need to see a particular code block. Position your cursor over the collapsed tag to temporarily reveal the hidden code. If a large section of code is collapsed, Dreamweaver 8 displays only the first 10 lines in the pop-up window.

Note: By the way, Dreamweaver 8 will save the state of the collapsed code even if you close and reopen the document, so you can stretch out your debugging sessions if necessary.

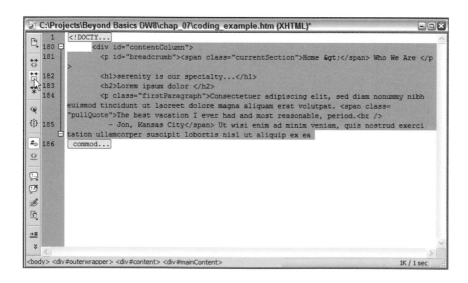

3 Drag to select any amount of code below the currently collapsed tag. Click either **collapse** button in the gutter next to the line numbers. Click the **collapse** button again to expand the selection. With the code still selected, press **Alt** (Windows) or **Opt** (Mac), and click **Collapse Selection** in the **Coding** toolbar.

When collapsing a section of code, I find it much faster to use the collapse buttons next to the code rather than the Collapse Selection tool in the Coding toolbar. However, the only way to collapse all but the selected code is to press Alt (Windows) or Opt (Mac) while clicking Collapse Selection.

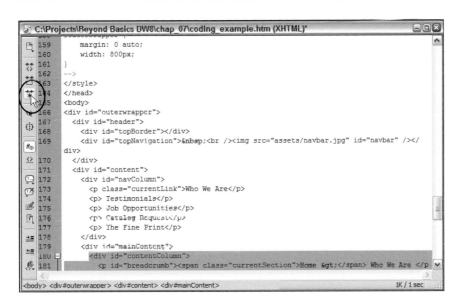

4 In the **Coding** toolbar, click **Expand All**.

As the name implies, Expand All expands all your previously collapsed code at once. If you prefer to use keyboard shortcuts, you can press Ctrl+Alt+F (Windows) or Cmd+Opt+E (Mac).

5 Press **Ctrl+S** (Windows) or **Cmd+S** (Mac) to save the page. Leave **coding_example.htm** open for the next exercise.

In this exercise, you worked with Dreamweaver's new code collapse feature; the more digging in the code you do, the more useful you'll find this feature. Next, you'll see how you can make your code more understandable by inserting comments.

3 | Commenting Code

Commenting your code is considered a best practice, whether you're developing a site for yourself, for a client, or for your boss. With complex pages, it's far easier to modify sections later if they are identified with HTML comments. The advent of CSS, with increasingly lengthy and sophisticated style rules, makes commenting even more important. Many Web designers use comments both to divide their CSS into sections and to annotate specific CSS rules. The new **Coding** toolbar in Dreamweaver 8 provides quick and easy commenting for HTML, CSS, JavaScript, and all the supported server models. In this exercise, you'll learn how to manage both HTML and CSS comments.

1 If you followed the previous exercise, **coding_example.htm** should still be open in Dreamweaver 8. If it's not, open it from the **chap_07** folder you copied to your desktop. Make sure you're in **Code** view, and if necessary, click anywhere to clear any highlighted code.

2 Select all the **<p>** tags within the **navColumn <div>**. In the **Coding** toolbar, click **Apply Comment**, and then choose **Apply HTML Comment**. Switch to **Design** view to verify the side navigation column is empty, and then return to **Code** view. In the **Coding** toolbar, click **Remove Comment**.

When you select code and then issue the Apply HTML Comment command, the selection is enclosed and "commented out." I often use commenting within the HTML body to temporarily hide sections of my page or to try different scenarios. Dreamweaver 8 makes it as easy to remove comments as to insert them. The comment does not have to be perfectly selected for you to use the Remove Comment feature; your selection can run over into the regular code. But as long as both the starting and ending part of the comment are within the selection, you can delete the comment with a single click. Working with CSS comments is just as straightforward, as you'll see in the next step.

3 Move to the top of the document, and locate the first CSS style, **#outerWrapper**. Create a new line before this style, and in the **Coding** toolbar, click **Apply Comment**. Then choose **Apply /* */ Comment**. After this inserts the **/* */** code, leave your cursor where it is positioned, and type **Main layout styles**. Locate the CSS style **#topBorder**, and create a new line before this style. Click **Apply Comment**, choose **Apply /* */ Comment**, and type **Minor layout styles**.

If you apply any comment without making a selection, Dreamweaver 8 inserts the code for the chosen comment and positions your cursor in the right place to begin entering your comment. You can use the Apply /* */ Comment command for CSS or for JavaScript.

Windows users can typically look in the folder containing the executable, which will either be the name of the program itself or the software company. Unfortunately, Mac users do not have the luxury of the folders having related names; all the tools and scripts reside in the usr/bin folder. If you're using BBEdit, look for bbdiff; if you're using TextWrangler, locate twdiff.

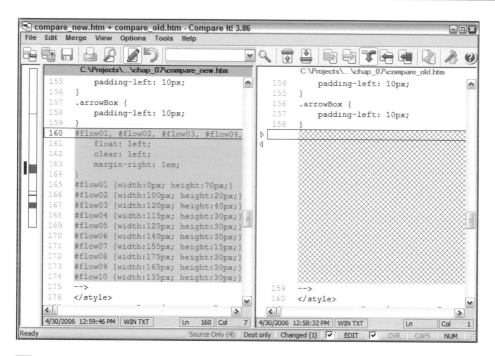

2 In the **Files** panel, expand the **chap_07** folder, if necessary. Select **compare_old.htm**, hold down the **Shift** key, and then select **compare_new.htm** to multiple-select the files. **Right-click** (Windows) or **Ctrl+click** (Mac) the selected files, and choose **Compare Local Files**. When your file comparison tool launches, verify the differences between the two files. When you're finished, close your comparison tool, and return to Dreamweaver 8.

Dreamweaver 8 provides several ways to take advantage of the file comparison tool. In addition to comparing two local files, you can also compare a local file and a remote file to make sure you're not overwriting desired changes. Almost all comparison tools include the capability to selectively merge changes from one document to another; you can use this functionality to make sure the file you're publishing or uploading to the remote site is complete.

If you've defined a comparison tool as you did in this exercise, Dreamweaver 8 offers a Compare option when you're publishing a file to the server and the remote file is newer than the local one in a pop-up dialog box; you'll also see a Compare button when synchronizing a site in the Synchronize dialog box.

In this exercise, you learned how Dreamweaver can work with a file comparison utility to compare the source code of two files. Next, you'll see how you can group your most commonly used tools in a single category in the Insert bar.

5 | Customizing Dreamweaver 8 Toolbars

Although it may not be obvious, you can use the **Insert** bar just as easily in Code view as in Design view. To really take advantage of this feature, you can group your most commonly used objects and commands in the **Favorites** category in the **Insert** bar. As any carpenter or gardener can tell you, keeping your most frequently accessed tools at hand is a terrific time-saver and productivity enhancer.

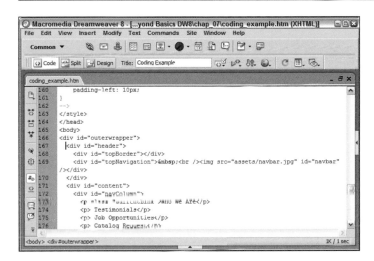

1 From the **chap_07** folder you copied to your desktop, open **coding_example.htm**, which you saved and closed at the end of Exercise 3. Make sure you're in **Code** view, and if necessary, click anywhere to clear any highlighted code.

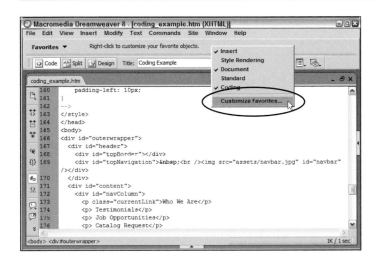

2 In the **Insert** bar, click the **Favorites** category. **Right-click** (Windows) or **Ctrl+click** (Mac) the toolbar, and choose **Customize Favorites**.

This particular feature can be a bit hard to find in Dreamweaver, which could be why so few people take advantage of its flexibility. As you'll see in the following steps, you can put any object from any other Insert bar category in the Favorites category, group the objects however you want, and even add separators.

3 In the **Customize Favorite Objects** dialog box, leave the **All** option chosen in the **Available objects** pop-up menu. Select **Table** from the **Available objects** list, and click the **Add (>>)** button. Repeat the process twice to add **Insert Div Tag** and **Image**.

Initially, Dreamweaver 8 shows you all the available objects from all the Insert bar categories. You can choose objects to add from this list if you like, but I find it a bit overwhelming to add more than the first few objects.

Note: You can add only one object at a time. In addition, you can't use Shift to multiple-select objects or insert entire categories.

Let's limit the available options to include some other favorites.

4 From the **Available objects** pop-up menu, choose **Common**. Using the method from Step 3, add **Flash**, **Editable Region**, **Optional Region**, and **Repeating Region** to the **Favorite objects** list. From the **Available objects** pop-up menu, select **Text**, and then add **Other Characters** to the **Favorite objects** list.

Limiting the selection of available objects to a single category makes it easier to find the ones you want. However, choosing your objects is only half the customization possible with the Favorites category in the Insert bar. As you'll see in the next step, you can also set the order and group the objects.

5 In the **Favorite objects** list, select **Image**, and click the **Up** button repeatedly to move it until it becomes the first object in the list. Repeat this process to move **Flash** to the second position. With the **Flash** item still selected, click the **Add separator** button. Select **Insert Div Tag**, click the **Add separator** button once, select **Repeating Region**, and then click the **Add separator** button one last time to group the template objects. Click **OK**.

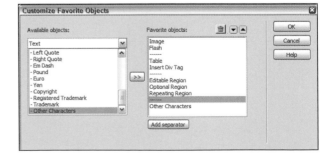

You can move any entry to a new position by using the Up and Down buttons. Likewise, you can insert a separator in any location to group your objects; the separator is always added below the currently selected object. Grouping objects helps you find the tool you're looking for more quickly. If you add an object in error or just want to delete one from your list, select its entry, and click the Trashcan button.

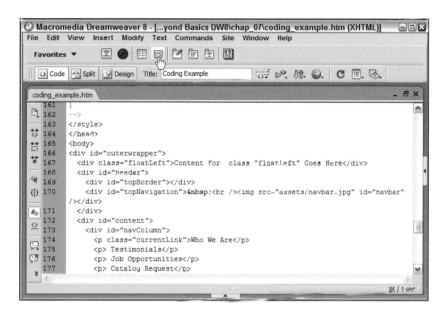

6 To verify your new custom toolbar is working as expected, place your cursor after **<div id="outerwrapper">**. From the **Favorites** category, choose the **Insert Div Tag** object. In the **Insert Div Tag** dialog box, set **Class** to **floatLeft**, and click **OK**.

Naturally, you're not stuck with whatever favorites you've chosen—or their configurations. You can alter the Favorites category in the Insert bar at any time. Simply right-click (Windows) or Ctrl+click (Mac) any toolbar, and choose Customize Favorites again.

7 Confirm the code was inserted as expected, and then close the file without saving it.

In this chapter, you learned how to take advantage of features in Dreamweaver 8 to work more effectively in Code view, including the selecting, coding, and commenting tools in the new Coding toolbar. In the next chapter, you'll see how you can use XML (e**X**tensible **M**arkup **L**anguage) to set up an RSS (**R**eally **S**imple **S**yndication) feed.

8

Setting Up an XML Feed

The Web thrives on information—the more current, the better. Until recently, if you wanted to post information, you needed to type it in your pages manually or insert it in a database. The plethora of RSS (**R**eally **S**imple **S**yndication) feeds now available has expanded the possibilities for publishing Web information.

RSS is just one use of XML (e**X**tensible **M**arkup **L**anguage). Although some Web professionals had the tools and skills to work with XML-based pages, XML was alien to most designers—until the release of Dreamweaver 8. With Dreamweaver 8, you can display XML data as styled HTML via a related technology: XSLT (e**X**tensible **S**tylesheet **L**anguage **T**ransformations). As the full name implies, XSLT transforms XML data into another format. The Dreamweaver 8 implementation of XML and XSLT permits client-side and server-side transformations. In other words, you can display XML data, such as RSS feeds, on both static and dynamic pages.

In this chapter, you'll explore RSS, XML, and XSLT, beginning with overviews of each. Next, you'll use Dreamweaver 8 to help you quickly write XML files. You'll then learn how to transform that data into presentable information with XSLT. Finally, you'll apply client-side and server-side transformations to your data.

Understanding XML, XSLT, and RSS Feeds

At its most basic, XML is a method of storing data. What gives XML its power is the X factor in its name: **eXtensible**. Because it's an extensible language, you can customize XML to fit any sort of data. Like HTML, XML is a tag-based language. Unlike HTML however, XML can use a different set of tags for every document. For example, let's say you want to create a document describing several vacation properties, including details about where the property is located and when it is available. A sample XML document might look like this:

```
<?xml version="1.0" encoding="iso-8859-1"?>
<vacations>
<property>
  <name>Vista Hills</name>
  <location>Florida</location>
  <available>October through May</available>
</property>
<property>
  <name>Northern Palace</name>
  <location>Vancouver</location>
  <available>June through September</available>
</property>
</vacations>
```

The first line of the XML file is similar to the opening **<html>** tag in a standard HTML file; it tells the browser what kind of page to expect. You'll notice the remaining tags are extremely specific to the data they are describing. You always need an outer, containing tag within XML. Here, the **<vacations>** tag serves that purpose. The document has two properties, each within the **<property>** tag pair. In XML, each of these tags containing additional information is referred to as a **node**. Each node uses the same tag structure: Each **<property>** tag contains **<name>**, **<location>**, and **<available>** tags.

Although XML is great for maintaining data, it's not so great at conveying that data in an easily readable format. That's where XSLT comes in. When properly set up, an XSLT file extracts the data from an XML file and—with the help of a browser or server—transforms the data into another format, which is HTML for our purposes. Because often similar data is repeated in an XML document, such as the two **<property>** tags in this example, XSLT has the ability to loop through the repeating information and display each detail separately, if desired. Here's a simple example of XSLT code displaying repetitive XML data:

```
<xsl:for-each select="vacations/property">
  <p><xsl:value-of select="name"/> in
<xsl:value-of select="location"/> is available
from <xsl:value-of select="available"/></p>
</xsl:for-each>
```

The **<xsl:for-each>** tag pair causes the data it contains (within the **<p>** tag) to appear once for each time the XML tag **<property>** exists. When associated with the XML example and translated into HTML, the viewer will see the following:

Vista Hills in Florida is available from May through October.
Northern Palace in Vancouver is available from June through September.

RSS is a specific form of XML in which tag names have been already agreed upon, so the data can be read and presented by a wide range of Web applications and devices.

In this chapter's first exercise, you'll see how easy it is to write your own XML file, thanks to dynamic code hinting in Dreamweaver 8.

N O T E :

Importing XML Schemas with Tag Libraries

Although customized tags are a hallmark of XML, at a certain point standardization becomes important. For you to use any set of tags for an Internet technology or across an industry, it's important the tags be standard within that industry. A collection of standard tags is called a DTD (**D**ocument **T**ype **D**efinition). You can find DTDs for everything from SMIL (**S**ynchronized **M**ultimedia **I**ntegration **L**anguage) to those in the healthcare industry. If you work in a field that routinely creates XML files based on a DTD, Dreamweaver 8 can make your life much easier by importing the DTD and incorporating all the tags, complete with tag and attribute hinting.

You import DTDs using the **Tag Library Editor**. To add a new set of tags to Dreamweaver 8, follow these steps:

1. Choose **Edit > Tag Libraries**.

2. When the **Tag Library Editor** opens, choose **Add (+)**, and from the list, choose **DTDSchema > Import XML DTD or Schema File**.

3. In the **Import XML DTD or Schema File** dialog box, click **Browse** to locate a DTD file on your system, or type an absolute URL (**U**niform **R**esource **L**ocator) pointing to a DTD. Click **OK**.

4. Verify the expected tags and attributes have been imported, and in the **Tag Library Editor** dialog box, click **OK**.

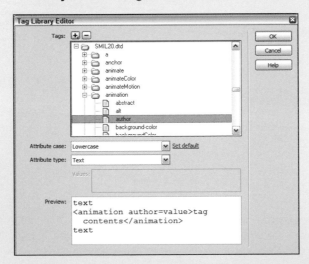

The next time you create a blank XML file in Dreamweaver 8, you'll find all your new tags available via code hinting. For example, after adding the SMIL 2.0 DTD, you will be able to quickly add an **<animation>** tag and choose any of its non-HTML attributes, including **author**, **clip-begin**, and **clip-end**.

1 Creating an XML File

Although numerous tools are available for exporting data from databases to the XML format, one of the most common ways to create an XML document is to simply code it by hand. Dreamweaver 8 offers several features to ease the tedium of manually creating an XML file. If you've done any hand-coding in Dreamweaver 8, you're probably familiar with code hinting. You simply type an opening code bracket (<), and Dreamweaver 8 instantly presents an alphabetical list of available tags from which to choose. Then, when you type the first letter of the tag, the list displays the tags beginning with that letter. At any point, you can press **Enter** (Windows) or **Return** (Mac) to insert the selected tag. Moreover, when you want to close the tag, all you need do is type the first two characters of any closing tag (</), and Dreamweaver 8 writes the rest of the expected tag.

As you'll see in this exercise, Dreamweaver 8 also automatically brings code hinting to customized XML documents. You'll create an XML listing of a variety of vacation spots for the example site, Starfish Getaways. Code hinting will save you time and help prevent errors caused by manually typing code.

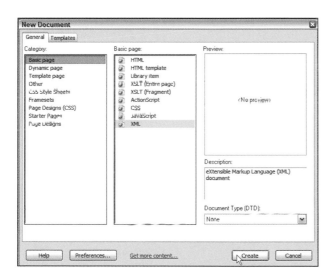

1 Choose **File > New**. In the **New Document** dialog box, select the **General** tab if necessary. In the **Category** list, select **Basic page**, and in the **Basic page** list, select **XML**. (Leave the **Document Type (DTD)** setting at the default, **None**.) Click the **Create** button. After this creates the XML page, press **Ctrl+S** (Windows) or **Cmd+S** (Mac) to save your page. In the **Save As** dialog box, navigate to the **chap_08** folder you copied to your desktop, type **vacations.xml** in the **File name** field, and then click **Save**.

The XML file created by Dreamweaver 8 is intentionally basic. It has only one line of code: `<?xml version="1.0" encoding="iso-8859-1"?>`. This code, similar to a document type declaration in HTML, identifies the page to browsers as written in XML 1.0 with the standard Latin-1 character set encoding. You add all custom tags to the page after this initial line.

2 Position your cursor after the opening code line, and press **Enter** (Windows) or **Return** (Mac). On the new line, type **<vacations>**; press **Enter** (Windows) or **Return** (Mac) twice more, and type **</vacations>**. Move your cursor to the line between the opening and closing tags.

As mentioned previously, every XML file needs to have a single tag encompassing all the other tags. In this example, **<vacations>** serves that purpose and, in essence, becomes this page's **<html>** tag.

Thanks to the autocompletion feature in Dreamweaver 8, you probably didn't need to type the closing tag; after typing just the first two characters (**</**), Dreamweaver 8 added the balance of the tag faster than you could probably type. Although you could wait until later to add the closing tag, the initial containing tag is so important it's best to type the complete pair.

Next, you'll add a tag to identify the general area for the vacation listing.

---

3 With your cursor between the opening and closing **<vacations>** tags, type **<location>**, and then press **Enter** (Windows) or **Return** (Mac). Press the **Tab** key to indent the next code line, type **<place>U.S.</place>**, and press **Enter** (Windows) or **Return** (Mac). Type **<property>**, and press **Enter** (Windows) or **Return** (Mac). Press the **Tab** key, and type the following code:

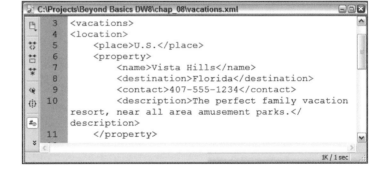

```
<name>Vista Hills</name>
<destination>Florida</destination>
<contact>407-555-1234</contact>
<description>The perfect family vacation resort, near all area amusement parks.</description>
```

---

4 If necessary, press **Enter** (Windows) or **Return** (Mac) after the closing **</description>** tag, and type **</property>**.

You'll notice autocompletion takes effect for each set of closing characters typed. The code typed in this step sets up the first **<location>** tag—the United States—and the first **<property>** tag in that location.

A major benefit of XML is the capability to nest one element inside another. To demonstrate this concept, this XML file will include two properties in the United States, each with its own characteristics, and another property in Mexico.

5 Press **Enter** (Windows) or **Return** (Mac), and type the following code:

```
<property>
  <name>Northern Palace</name>
  <destination>Vancouver</destination>
  <contact>407-555-5678</contact>
  <description>Enjoy great shopping and whale watching in the ultimate stylish setting.</description>
</property>
</location>
```

As you begin typing the second set of **<property>** data, you'll notice Dreamweaver 8 is there to help. Right after you type the initial opening character (<), the code-hinting list appears with the available tags. After typing the first couple of letters, you'll see the desired tag highlighted in the list; press Enter (Windows) or Return (Mac) to accept the selected tag. Once you get in the rhythm of working with code hinting and code completion, you'll find your coding moving much faster.

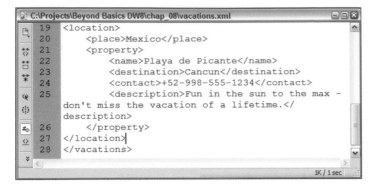

```
19  <location>
20      <place>Mexico</place>
21      <property>
22          <name>Playa de Picante</name>
23          <destination>Cancun</destination>
24          <contact>+52-998-555-1234</contact>
25          <description>Fun in the sun to the max -
    don't miss the vacation of a lifetime.</
    description>
26      </property>
27  </location>
28  </vacations>
```

6 Press **Enter** (Windows) or **Return** (Mac), and type the following code:

```
<location>
  <place>Mexico</place>
  <property>
    <name>Playa de Picante</name>
    <destination>Cancun</destination>
    <contact>+52-998-555-1234</contact>
    <description>Fun in the sun to the max - don't miss the vacation of a lifetime.</description>
  </property>
</location>
```

7 Press **Ctrl+S** (Windows) or **Cmd+S** (Mac). Close **vacations.xml**.

In this exercise, you developed an XML file to better understand how one is typically structured and see how Dreamweaver aids you in this chore with code hinting and code completion. Now you're ready to bring the data into an HTML page through the transformational magic of XSLT. The next exercise demonstrates how to accomplish this goal on the client side.

2 | Integrating an XML Feed

When you first work your way through the process of displaying XML data—like the file completed in the previous exercise—through an XSLT file, you might find the concepts difficult to grasp. One way to think of the process is to compare it with building a template.

In this exercise, you'll start with a basic HTML page—complete with placeholder content. You'll convert this page into the XSLT format using a procedure similar to saving a page as a template. Next, you'll mark areas of the page to serve a special function; with the XSLT page, you'll create repeating regions, which are displayed in Design view in the same manner as editable regions are in templates. Then, you'll insert special code to be replaced by data at run time, much like using template parameters to substitute values at design time. Finally, you'll tie your XSLT page to the XML page and preview, just as you'd create a page based on a template for previewing and publishing. Both approaches are highly productive and, in the end, technologically magical.

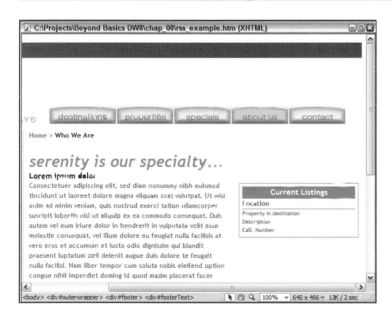

1 In the **Files** panel, open **rss_example.htm** from the **chap_08** folder you copied to your desktop.

In this standard HTML page, we have already included a placeholder section to handle the XML data. Dreamweaver 8 has the capability to convert an HTML page to the XSLT format in a single, simple operation. This conversion feature allows you to easily design the layout for your data with placeholder content. Such a design should include only a single instance of the data; you will add all the code for repeating the data on the XSLT page.

2 Choose **File > Convert > XSLT 1.0**.

Dreamweaver 8 converts the page, opens it, and saves it to the current folder, all in one smooth operation. In Design view, you won't see any apparent change. However, if you switch to Code view, you'll see an entirely new header:

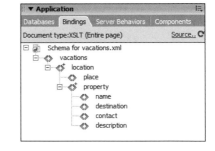

```
<?xml version="1.0" encoding="iso-8859-1"?>
<!DOCTYPE xsl:stylesheet  [
  <!ENTITY nbsp    " ">
  <!ENTITY copy    "&#169;">
  <!ENTITY reg     "&#174;">
  <!ENTITY trade   "&#8482;">
  <!ENTITY mdash   "&#8212;">
  <!ENTITY ldquo   "&#8220;">
  <!ENTITY rdquo   "&#8221;">
  <!ENTITY pound   "&#163;">
  <!ENTITY yen     "&#165;">
  <!ENTITY euro    "&#8364;">
]>
<xsl:stylesheet version="1.0" xmlns:xsl="http://www.w3.org/1999/XSL/Transform">
<xsl:output method="html" encoding="iso-8859-1" doctype-public="-//W3C//DTD XHTML 1.0
Transitional//EN" doctype-system="http://www.w3.org/TR/xhtml1/DTD/xhtml1-transitional.dtd"/>
<xsl:template match="/">
```

The opening code line establishing the XML page will look familiar; however, the rest is new. After declaring a number of character entities, the code includes a series of XSL (e**X**tensible **S**tylesheet **L**anguage) statements. Dreamweaver 8 handles all this coding for you automatically. As you might suspect, XSL is the language used to create XSLT files. The next step is to apply the repeat regions so you are presenting all the XML data.

---

3 Choose **Window > Bindings**, and in the **Bindings** panel, click the **XML** link. In the **Locate XML Source** dialog box, make sure the **Attach a local file on my computer or local area network** radio button is selected, and click **Browse**. In the **Locate Source XML for XSL Template** dialog box, navigate to the **chap_08** folder, click **vacations.xml** to select it, and click **OK**. In the **Locate XML Source** dialog box, click **OK**.

To bind XML data to the XSLT page, you first need to connect the two. You have the option of selecting either a local XML file accessible on your system or one stored on a remote server. If your choice is the latter, you'll need to type a fully qualified URL, starting with **http://**. In either case, if you've chosen a valid XML file, the XML schema then appears in the Bindings panel.

---

4 Place your cursor in the **<h3>** tag, **Location**, and switch to **Code** view. Select the **<h3>** tag and the next three **<p>** tags, up to but not including the closing **</<div>** tag as follows:

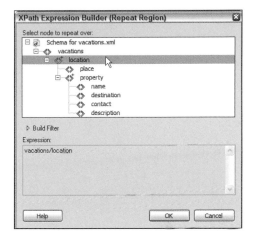

```
<h3>Location</h3>
<p class="firstProperty">Property in destination</p>
<p>Description</p>
<p><strong>Call</strong>: Number</p>
```

In the **Insert** bar, click the **XSLT Objects** category, and click **Repeat Region**. In the **XPath Expression Builder (Repeat Region)** dialog box, select the **location** entry. Click **OK**.

The repeat region signifies the area containing data from the specified XML node, in this case, `location`. Dreamweaver 8 indicates the area in Design view with a thin border and a tab labeled `xsl: for-each`, which is the XSLT code for looping through data. Before you return to Design view, however, you'll add a second repeat region, inside the first.

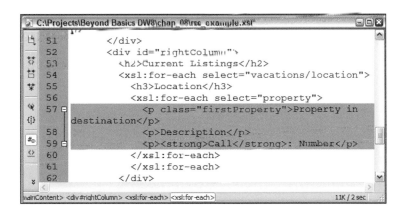

5 Select the three **<p>** tags included in the previous selection as follows:

```
<p class="firstProperty">Property in destination</p>
<p>Description</p>
<p><strong>Call</strong>: Number</p>
```

In the **Insert** bar, click the **XSLT Objects** category, and click **Repeat Region**. In the **XPath Expression Builder (Repeat Region)** dialog box, select the **property** entry. Click **OK**.

You've now nested one XSL repeat region inside another. This has the effect of listing every property within a given location before listing the next location and its properties. The next step is to bind the data to the page, replacing the placeholder text. Because of the precise nature of this task, we prefer to use Code view.

6 Select the placeholder text in the **<h3>** tag, **Location**, and delete it. In the **Insert** bar, click the **XSLT Objects** category, and click **Dynamic Text**. In the **XPath Expression Builder (Dynamic Text)** dialog box, select the **place** entry. Click **OK**.

Dreamweaver 8 has a minor bug preventing you from replacing selected text with XSLT dynamic text; Dreamweaver 8 expands the selection and mistakenly replaces both the text and the surrounding tag. The workaround is to remove the placeholder text before inserting the XSLT dynamic text. With this technique in hand, you're ready to replace the rest of the placeholder text. In all, you have four placeholder terms to replace.

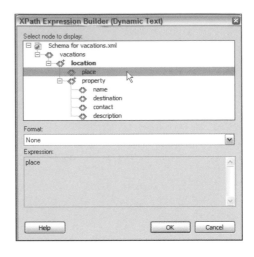

7 Select the placeholder text **Property**, and delete it. In the **Insert** bar, click the **XSLT Objects** category, and click **Dynamic Text**. In the **XPath Expression Builder (Dynamic Text)** dialog box, select the **name** entry, and click **OK**. Next, repeat the process to replace the placeholder text **destination** with the XSLT dynamic text, **destination**. Repeat the process again to replace the placeholder text **description** with the XSLT dynamic text, **description**. Finally, perform the process one last time to replace the placeholder text **Number** with the XSLT dynamic text, **contact**.

You'll notice that although in many cases the placeholder text is the same as the dynamic text, it doesn't have to be—as in the case of the final operation. The XSL page is now complete but not quite ready for preview; one final step remains. Although the XSL page is connected to the XML file, the reverse is not yet true and is a necessary step to complete the XML integration.

8 Switch to **Design** view, and press **Ctrl+S** (Windows) or **Cmd+S** (Mac).

9 In the **Files** panel, double-click the **vacations.xml** file created in Exercise 1. Choose **Commands > Attach an XSLT Stylesheet**. In the **Attach an XSLT Stylesheet** dialog box, click **Browse**. In the **Select XSLT File** dialog box, navigate to the **chap_08** folder, click **rss_example.xsl** to select it, and click **OK**. In the **Attach an XSLT Stylesheet** dialog box, click **OK**.

---

10 Press **Ctrl+S** (Windows) or **Cmd+S** (Mac), and then press **F12** to preview the page in your primary browser. After you've finished previewing the page, return to Dreamweaver, and close **vacations.xml**.

Note: To see the transformed XML file, you'll need a fairly modern browser, such as any Mozilla-based browser (including Firefox and Netscape 8+), Internet Explorer 6 or newer, Opera 8, or Safari 1.3 or newer.

When you preview the XML file, you'll see the fully translated XSL file presents a perfectly readable HTML page, complete with all the data. Notice how the major location category is offset stylistically with the top and bottom borders and how the individual property listings appear within each major section.

If you wanted to post these files to the Web for viewing, you'd need to publish both the XML and the XSLT file; make sure they are both in the same folder so dependent files appear correctly. Although you can preview either the XML file or the XSLT file in Dreamweaver 8, you should link to the XML file when publishing the pages.

---

11 Switch to Dreamweaver 8, and close **vacations.xml** but leave **rss_example.xsl** open for the next exercise.

This exercise took you through the steps of combining XML and XSLT files to display XML data in a styled format on the client side. First you converted the HTML page to an XSL page. Then you attached an XML file and used XSLT code to set up repeat regions and dynamic text. Finally, you linked the XML file to the XSL file. In the next exercise, you'll achieve the same basic results but work with server-side applications.

---

3 | Transforming XML on the Server

As powerful as the client-side XSLT method demonstrated in Exercise 2 is, it does have some serious limitations. As mentioned, XSLT transformations work only in a specific set of browsers. More critically, the technique depends on being able to access and modify the XML file in order to connect it to the XSLT page. Such access is not always available, especially when trying to connect to an RSS feed. Dreamweaver 8 is quite prepared to deal with such circumstances when you use server behaviors. In this exercise, you'll use Dreamweaver's advanced XSLT server behaviors to convert XML data to a more presentable form.

Note: This exercise assumes you're familiar with creating server-side pages in Dreamweaver 8; the steps reference the Adobe ColdFusion server model, but all the actions are the same for all the supported server models in Dreamweaver 8, including ASP (**A**ctive **S**erver **P**ages), PHP (**P**HP **H**ypertext **P**reprocessor), and Microsoft .NET. If the dynamic side of Dreamweaver 8 is new to you, hold off on completing this exercise until after you've worked through Chapter 15, *"Integrating Multimedia Content."*

1 If you followed the previous exercise, **rss_example.xsl** should still be open. If it's not, complete Exercise 2, and return to this exercise. Alternatively, you can open it in the **Files** panel.

With a few slight modifications, you can use the same XML and XSLT files in this server-side application as in the previous exercise. We've taken the liberty of modifying this XML file by removing the connection to the XSL page and posting it to the Web to better simulate working with an external file. In the next step, you'll update the XSLT page and save it with a different name.

2 Choose **Window > Bindings**. In the **Bindings** panel, click the **Source** link. In the **Locate XML Source** dialog box, click the **Attach a remote file on the Internet** radio button, and type the following URL in the text field:

```
http://www.idest.com/dw8beyond/chap_08/
vacations_server.xml
```

Click **OK**.

---

3 Choose **File > Save As**, and save the file as **rss_example_server.xsl**. Close the file when you're done.

Rather than work with a local file, you have set up this XSLT page to pull its data from a file on a Web server. As mentioned, this XML file is the same as the one you used locally, except we've removed the connection to the XSLT page. Now you're ready to build your dynamic page.

TIP:

Attaching an RSS Feed

To connect to an RSS feed, you'd follow step 2 above, opt to attach a remote file on the Internet, and then type the full URL of the RSS file. On most sites, you can easily find the RSS file by clicking the small orange RSS logo. The RSS XML file then appears in your browser; simply copy the Web address from the **Location** field, and paste it in the **Locate XML Source** dialog box.

---

4 Choose **File > New**. In the **New Document** dialog box, click **Dynamic page** in the **Category** list. Then click the dynamic page for your server model (ASP, ASP.NET, ColdFusion, or PHP). When the page opens, switch to **Code** view. Select all the HTML code, and delete it. Choose **File > Save As**, and save the page as **vacations.ext** using your server model extension (for example, **vacations.asp**, **vacations.aspx**, **vacations.cfm**, or **vacations.php**).

Why remove all the HTML code? All this dynamic page will contain is server-side code that will combine the XML and XSLT and then inject HTML code into the page. Because the XSLT page already contains the core HTML tags, such as **<html>** and **<body>**, you need to remove them from the dynamic page.

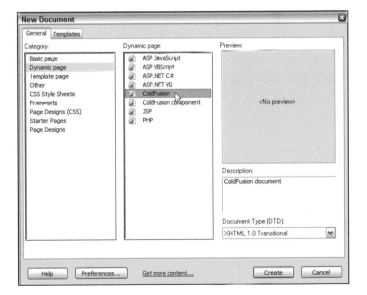

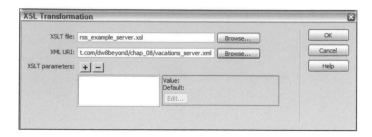

5 Choose **Window > Server Behaviors**. In the **Server Behaviors** panel, click **Add (+)**, and select **XSL Transformation**. In the **XSL Transformation** dialog box, click the XSLT file **Browse** button. In the **Select XSLT File** dialog box, select **rss_example_server.xsl**, and click **OK**. This automatically populates the **XML URI** field.

The code inserted by the XSL Transformation server behavior varies according to the chosen server model. In addition, this step creates an includes folder in the site root with the necessary support files. In all cases, your work on this page is now completed, and it's ready to be published and tested.

---

6 Press **Ctrl+S** (Windows) or **Cmd+S** (Mac), and then close the page.

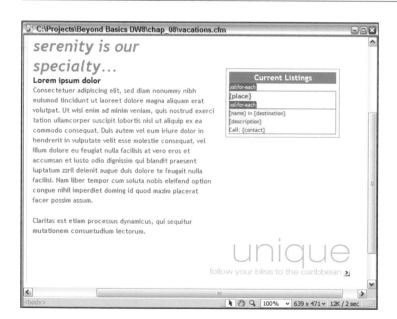

7 In the **Files** panel, select your dynamic page, **rss_examples_server.xsl**, and the **includes** folder in the site root, and click **Put**. If the **Put Dependent Files** dialog box appears, click **Yes**. After this publishes the files, open your browser, and navigate to the dynamic page on your server.

If you examine the source code for your page in the browser, you'll see a complete HTML page. Unlike the client-side XSLT transformation, the server-side XSLT transformation outputs standard HTML readable by any browser.

---

8 Switch to Dreamweaver 8. Close your dynamic page.

VIDEO: | **attach_rss.mov**

To learn how to attach an RSS feed directly to an XSLT file, check out **attach_rss.mov** in the **videos** folder on the **Dreamweaver 8 HOT CD-ROM**.

In this chapter, you learned about the XML, XSLT, and RSS technologies. You also explored the Dreamweaver 8 implementation of XML transformations on the client and on the server. In the next chapter, you'll examine a Web 2.0 mainstay, Ajax.

Implementing Ajax in Dreamweaver 8

Recently, a new technology has swept the Web promising a better user experience and advanced functionality. Ajax (originally an acronym for **A**synchronous **Java**Script and **XML**) can present data to users more smoothly and more like desktop applications do. One of the best examples of an Ajax-powered application is Google Maps (**http://maps.google.com**), which allows seamless scrolling, zooming, and map refreshing, even when presenting satellite imagery. Other Ajax-enabled sites include Flickr (**www.flickr.com**), the photo-sharing site, and Yahoo! Tech (**http://tech.yahoo.com**).

Although Ajax balances several complex technologies, you don't need a master's degree in computer science to incorporate these advances into your pages. Adobe is on the cutting edge of making Ajax more approachable to everyday designers. They recently released Spry— a set of Ajax libraries, demos, and documentation—via Adobe Labs (**http://labs.adobe.com**). Although integrating Spry into Dreamweaver 8 requires a bit of hand-coding, intermediate Web designers can easily do it. You'll even be able to add some advanced effects—such as data sorting— to your Ajax-powered page. Before you dive into the code, you'll get a better sense of what Ajax is and what it can do. Then you'll explore the brave new world of the Ajax implementation for Dreamweaver 8, Spry.

Understanding How Ajax Works

Ajax weaves together a number of Web technologies—JavaScript, XML (e**X**tensible **M**arkup **L**anguage), XSLT (e**X**tensible **S**tylesheet **L**anguage **T**ransformations), the DOM (**D**ocument **O**bject **M**odel), and CSS (**C**ascading **S**tyle **S**heets)—to present a truly different interactive experience. Although the core technology allowing Web pages to read XML documents has been around since 1995, it wasn't until a decade later that all the pieces of Ajax were firmly in place. In some respects, the naming of the technology by Jesse James Garrett (from the interactive design firm Adaptive Path) in 2005 consolidated the approach and helped popularize Ajax.

As noted earlier, Ajax originally stood for Asynchronous JavaScript and XML. Although each term is vital to the concept, the first—**asynchronous**—is the least understood and arguably the most important. Standard Web communication is a serial, or **synchronous**, operation:

1. A page is loaded in the browser (also called the **client**).

2. The user clicks a link on the Web page to display additional data.

3. The browser sends a request to the Web server.

4. The Web server responds with the new data in a new page.

5. The browser then renders the new page.

Ajax sits between the browser and the Web server and, effectively, acts like a middleman. Here's how an Ajax-powered page works:

1. The page is loaded in the browser, which simultaneously loads the data into the Ajax engine.

2. The user clicks a link on the Web page to display additional data.

3. The Ajax engine intercepts the request for new data and responds with just the relevant data.

4. The browser integrates the new data into the existing page, changing only the related portion of the page.

If more data is required than was previously loaded, the Ajax engine requests and receives the data from the Web server in the background, or **asynchronously**

Ajax is still a relatively new technology, and it has numerous issues. For instance, only the more recent browsers are Ajax compatible; these include Mozilla and its derivatives (including Firefox), Safari, and Internet Explorer 6 or newer. However, Ajax's primary drawback is accessibility. What happens, for example, when a user has disabled JavaScript ? The answer depends on how you construct the structure surrounding Ajax. If no additional strategy is in place, the page is likely to appear broken and incomplete. A more complete implementation serves alternative page content but may require an application server.

The tremendous interest in Ajax and the wide range of technologies involved have given rise to a great number—more than 200 currently—of Ajax implementations. Next, you'll look at Adobe's entry in the world of Ajax, Spry.

Introducing Spry

First posted on Adobe Labs (**http://labs.adobe.com**) in the spring of 2006, Spry is a freely distributable Ajax implementation, or **framework**, developed by the Dreamweaver 8 engineers. Spry was created to make it easy for everyday designers and developers—not just those using Dreamweaver 8—to incorporate Ajax into their pages. At its core, Spry is a series of JavaScript files allowing Web professionals to rely on standard HTML techniques, such as adding attributes and values to existing tags, for added Ajax power.

The initial Spry setup on a Web page involves two key steps. First, you'll need to include the required JavaScript libraries; a basic Spry project requires two files, which you can include with code like this:

```
<script type="text/javascript" src="includes/xpath.js"></script>
<script type="text/javascript" src="includes/SpryData.js"></script>
```

Second, you'll need to establish a JavaScript variable to hold the XML data. This process is referred to as **creating a data set**. To create a data set, you'd use code like this:

```
var dsVacations = new Spry.Data.XMLDataSet("vacations.xml", "vacations/location/property");
```

The function `Spry.Data.XMLDataSet()` takes two arguments: the XML file to be read and the path to the node of data in the XML file you want to use. The latter argument is actually an XPath expression—part of the language driving XSL transformations, covered in Chapter 8, *"Setting Up an XML Feed"*—that makes more advanced functionality, such as filtering the data, possible. You can incorporate multiple data sets on the same page.

In the **<body>** portion of the document, Spry uses a combination of tag attributes and dynamic data placeholders. For example, to identify an area on the page that incorporates Spry-based Ajax functionality, you can add a **spryregion** attribute to the containing tag, like this:

```
<div id="contentColumn" spryregion="dsVacations">
```

The **spryregion** attribute indicates which data set is to be applied in the area.

Inserting dynamic data into the page is just as straightforward. All dynamic data is indicated by a set of curly braces surrounding the XML node name. So, to display the dynamic data from the `description` node in a table cell, your code will look like this:

```
<td>{description}</td>
```

If you're using multiple data sets and you want to display data from a different data set (say, **dsRegions**) in the same Spry dynamic region, you use this syntax:

```
<td>{dsRegions::place}</td>
```

Even in its earliest release, Spry appears to be quite robust and easy to apply. In the following exercise, you'll get a chance to create a simple Spry Ajax page and see firsthand how it all works.

1 | Integrating Ajax Code

In this exercise, you'll create a basic Ajax-driven master-detail page displaying data from a provided XML file. When completed, you'll be able to select an entry from a master list of all vacation spots to view additional details, including a description and picture. If you were to create a similar application without Ajax, you'd need to either generate a large number of static pages, which would load when a user clicked a linked entry, or work with a server model and database. Your finished Ajax page refreshes only a small section of the page—the detail area—and requires no application server.

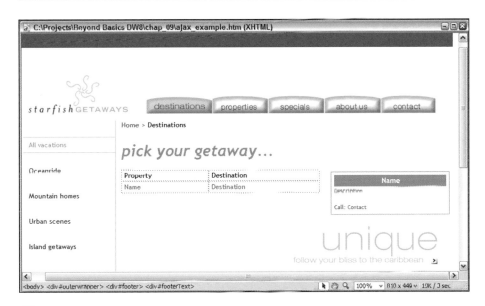

1 In the **Files** panel, open **ajax_example.htm** from the **chap_09** folder you copied to your desktop.

To help you focus on the task at hand—integrating Ajax into your page—this starter page already contains several placeholder areas. The table in the main content area will contain the master list of available properties. The bordered box in the right column will display the details—including a description, image, and contact information—for any selected item from the master list. The first step in the process of adding Ajax functionality is to establish an XML namespace for Spry. **Namespaces** are publicly available files defining the XML tags used in a particular document.

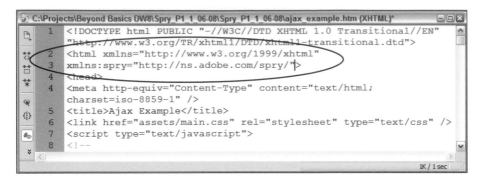

2 Switch to **Code** view. Locate the opening **<html>** tag, and add the following attribute to the tag: **xmlns:spry="http://ns.adobe.com/spry/"**.

The Spry namespace defines all the proprietary tags used in the framework, all of which begin with the term **spry** followed by a colon, for example, `spry:region`. Once the opening **<html>** tag references a namespace document, any XHTML (e**X**tensible **HTML**) validator will check unrecognized tags it finds against that document. Without a namespace declaration, the page will not validate.

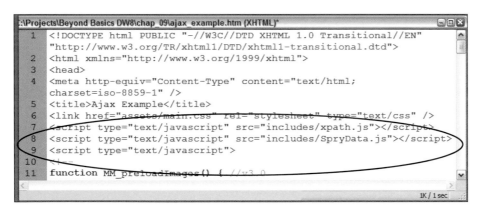

3 Near the top of the document, locate the **<link>** tag attaching the **main.css** file; place your cursor at the end of the code line, and press **Enter** (Windows) or **Return** (Mac). Type the following code:

```
<script type="text/javascript" src="includes/xpath.js"></script>
<script type="text/javascript" src="includes/SpryData.js"></script>
```

The Spry framework has two primary JavaScript files: xpath.js and SpryData.js. The former includes functions to parse and evaluate XPath expressions. **XPath** is a language used to traverse an XML document to locate specified data. Much of the work of Ajax is reading an XML document file and interpreting its structure correctly.

The second document, SpryData.js, relies on the functionality found in xpath.js to create JavaScript functions, which are, in turn, added to the HTML page. Because xpath.js contains functions used by SpryData.js, you must include xpath.js before SpryData.js.

```
 C:\Projects\Beyond Basics DW8\chap_09\ajax_example.htm (XHTML)*
  5   <title>Ajax Example</title>
  6   <link href="assets/main.css" rel="stylesheet" type="text/css" />
  7   <script type="text/javascript" src="includes/xpath.js"></script>
  8   <script type="text/javascript" src="includes/SpryData.js"></script>
  9   <script type="text/javascript">
 10
 11   var dsVacations = new Spry.Data.XMLDataSet("vacations.xml",
      "vacations/location/property");
 12   function MM_preloadImages() { //v3.0
 13     var d=document; if(d.images){ if(!d.MM_p) d.MM_p=new Array();
 14       var i,j=d.MM_p.length,a=MM_preloadImages.arguments; for(i=0; i<
      a.length; i++)
 15         if (a[i].indexOf("#")!=0){ d.MM_p[j]=new Image; d.MM_p[j++].src
<head> <meta>                                                      171K / 25 sec
```

4 After the opening HTML comment tag, place your cursor within the **<script>** tag following the code with **SpryData.js** in it. Press **Enter** (Windows) or **Return** (Mac) to create a new line, and type the following code:

```
var dsVacations = new Spry.Data.XMLDataSet("vacations.xml", "vacations/location/property");
```

This code line essentially creates a variable called **dsVacations** with all the requested data from the associated XML file; in other words, this creates the data set. You'll find yourself using this variable name repeatedly while creating your Ajax page.

You'll recall the **Spry.Data.XMLDataSet()** method uses two arguments. The first is an XML data source, such as **vacations.xml**. The second argument is the XPath expression that points to the node containing the desired data. In this example, the expression is **vacations/location/property**, which identifies the **property** node of the XML file. The XML file used here is an extended version of the one created in Chapter 8, *"Setting Up an XML Feed."*

Note: Your XML file should be in the same folder as your HTML file, especially if the XML file contains references to dependent files such as images. If the HTML and XML files are in different folders, the browser will incorrectly interpret the paths to dependent files.

These three code blocks—the two including the JavaScript library files and the one creating the data set variable—are all you need to lay the foundation for your Spry-based Ajax coding. The following steps require adding code to the **<body>** section of the HTML page, starting with setting up the master data region.

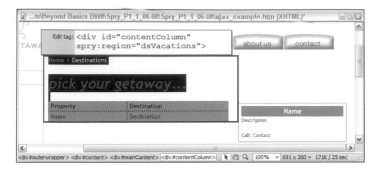

5 Switch to **Design** view, and place your cursor in the **pick your getaway** heading. From the **Tag Selector**, choose **<div #contentColumn>**, and press **Ctrl+T** (Windows) or **Cmd+T** (Mac). In the **Quick Tag Editor**'s **Edit Tag** mode, move your cursor to the end of the tag, and type **spry:region="dsVacations"**. Press **Enter** (Windows) or **Return** (Mac).

The main content area, the `#contentColumn` `<div>` tag, will hold the master data region listing all the available properties in the XML file. To identify this Spry dynamic area properly, you add a `spry:region` attribute pointing to the desired data set, `dsVacations`. You can apply the `spry:region` attribute to most block element tags, such as `<div>`, `<p>`, and `<ul>`.

Note: Several tags are not suitable as the containing element for a Spry dynamic area: `col`, `colgroup`, `frameset`, `html`, `iframe`, `style`, `table`, `tbody`, `tfoot`, `thead`, `title`, and `tr`.

6 Under the **Property** column, select the **Name** placeholder text, and replace it with **{name}**. Select the **Destination** placeholder text, and replace it with **{destination}**.

Spry uses a simple method to represent data on an HTML page. In fact, it's so simple you can enter the values directly in Design view. You just enclose the name of each desired XML node in curly braces and insert it on the page where the data will appear.

Next, you'll add the syntax to repeat the data until all is displayed; you'll also add the link to display each listing's details.

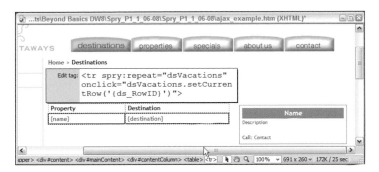

7 With your cursor adjacent to the data placeholder, **{destination}**, from the **Tag Selector**, choose **<tr>**. Press **Ctrl+T** (Windows) or **Cmd+T** (Mac) to open the **Quick Tag Editor** in **Edit Tag** mode. Add a space, and type the following code:

```
spry:repeat="dsVacations" onclick="dsVacations.setCurrentRow('{ds_RowID}')"
```

As you probably suspected, the attribute `spry:repeat` is responsible for establishing a repeat region for the selected **<tr>** tag; the value, `dsVacations`, tells Spry which data set to use. The second bit of code sets up the trigger to display the detail data by establishing an `onclick()` event. Translated into English, this code says, "When an item is clicked, make this row of data the current one." You'll establish the Spry dynamic detail region, which uses this information, next.

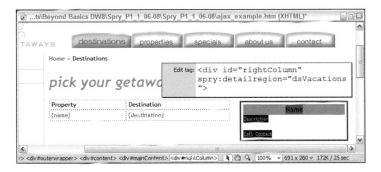

8 Place your cursor in the right text column, and from the **Tag Selector**, choose **<div #rightColumn>**. Press **Ctrl+T** (Windows) or **Cmd+T** (Mac) to open the **Quick Tag Editor** in **Edit Tag** mode. Move your cursor to the end of the tag, and type **spry:detailregion="dsVacations"**. Press **Enter** (Windows) or **Return** (Mac).

Like with the master region, you add the Spry detail region to the tag slated to contain all the dynamic data. Again, the value of the attribute points to the desired data set, `dsVacations`. All that's left is to insert the dynamic data placeholders, including one for an image.

9 Select the **Name** placeholder text, and replace it with **{name}**. Select the **Description** placeholder text, and replace it with **{description}**. Select the **Contact** placeholder text, and replace it with **{contact}**. Place your cursor in the **<p>** tag below the **{description}** data, and press **Ctrl+T** (Windows) or **Cmd+T** (Mac) to open the **Quick Tag Editor** in **Insert HTML** mode. Type the code **<img src="assets/{image}" />**, and press **Enter** (Windows) or **Return** (Mac).

Although you've encountered dynamic text entries, using a dynamic image is new. The XML data includes a node, `image`, with the file name of a graphic for each property, such as `vista_hills.jpg`. To take advantage of this data, you need to insert an `img` tag and set the `src` attribute dynamically. Because the XML data file contains only the name of the actual file and not the path, you must provide the path to the folder where the images are stored.

Tip: It's always best to store just the file names of images in your data source, whether it's a database table or an XML file. By including only the file names, you're free to put the images in any location and add the path at design time, as in this example.

---

10 Press **Ctrl+S** (Windows) or **Cmd+S** (Mac), and then press **F12**. When the page opens in your primary browser, click any of the listed properties to view the details for that property. Notice only the detail section of the page changes.

The benefits of an Ajax page like this are immediately noticeable. The data loads and displays quickly, and you do not need to refresh the entire page. However, certain visual cues—such as alternating colored rows for the data—are not currently present. You'll add those effects, and more, in the next exercise.

---

11 Close your browser, and return to Dreamweaver 8. Leave the page open for the next exercise.

In this exercise, you learned how to set up a basic Ajax-driven master-detail page in Dreamweaver 8 using the Spry framework. In the next exercise, you'll enhance the usability of the Ajax page by adding key effects.

---

2 | Adding Ajax Effects

Although the page constructed in Exercise 1 exhibits Ajax functionality, it's not user-friendly. Listings of data in table rows are often hard to read if they're left undifferentiated; alternating row colors can help the site visitor peruse the data. Moreover, no visual cues indicate which entry the user is considering, much less which one has been selected. You'll add all these effects to your Ajax page in this exercise and even incorporate some advanced sorting functionality to columns. However, you'll first need to include a library of Spry JavaScript effects.

1 If you followed the previous exercise, **ajax_example.htm** should still be open in Dreamweaver 8. If it's not, complete Exercise 1, and then return to this exercise.

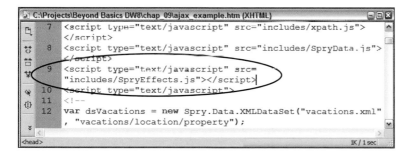

2 Switch to **Code** view. In the **<head>** section of the document, locate the two **<script>** tags you inserted in the previous exercise that include the two JavaScript files from the Spry framework. Place your cursor at the end of the second **<script>** tag, and press **Enter** (Windows) or **Return** (Mac) to create a new line. Type the following code:

```
<script type="text/javascript" src="includes/SpryEffects.js"></script>
```

This Spry library extends the core functionality to a variety of DHTML (**D**ynamic **HTML**) effects such as moving **<div>** tags, resizing images, and even changing opacity. It's a necessary addition to the page to show the selected and hover states of the dynamic data. Next, you'll add a sorting ability to your Ajax application.

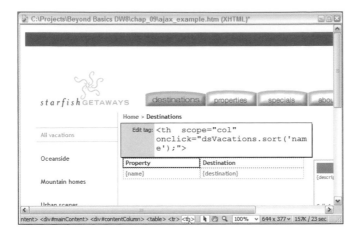

3 Return to **Design** view. In the main content area, select the **Property** table header. From the **Tag Selector**, choose **<th>**, and press **Ctrl+T** (Windows) or **Cmd+T** (Mac) to open the **Quick Tag Editor** in **Edit Tag** mode. Type the code **scope="col" onclick="dsVacations.sort('name');"**, and press **Enter** (Windows) or **Return** (Mac) to close the **Quick Tag Editor**.

---

4 Repeat the process with the **Destination** table header, and choose **<th>** from the **Tag Selector**. Press **Ctrl+T** (Windows) or **Cmd+T** (Mac) to open the **Quick Tag Editor** in **Edit Tag** mode, and type the following code: **scope="col" onclick="dsVacations.sort('destination');"**. Press **Enter** (Windows) or **Return** (Mac) to close the **Quick Tag Editor**.

Spry has a built-in sorting routine to rearrange the data in the `spryregion` attribute. Spry sorts the data according to the provided parameter, which corresponds to the XML node, in ascending order. For example, when you preview this page in the browser and click Destination, you'll see the listings in alphabetical order, by destination.

In the next step, you'll set up the dynamic data so it will be able to show alternating row colors.

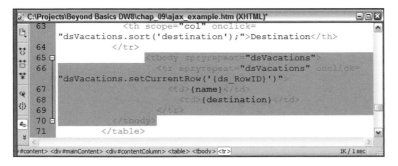

5 Place your cursor in the same data row with **{name}** and **{destination}**. From the **Tag Selector**, choose **<tr>**. Press **Ctrl+T** (Windows) or **Cmd+T** (Mac) twice to open the **Quick Tag Editor** in **Wrap Tag** mode. Type **<tbody spry:repeat="dsVacations">**, and press **Enter** (Windows) or **Return** (Mac). Switch to **Code** view to verify the addition.

To make the alternating row color technique work, you'll eventually need to add dynamic data table rows, one for each color. To make sure they repeat correctly, you have to enclose them with a surrounding tag—such as **<tbody>**—and apply the **spry:repeat** attribute.

In the next step, you'll add the second table row and adjust the code for both.

```
...ts\Beyond Basics DW8\Spry_P1_1_06-08\Spry_P1_1_06-08\ajax_example.htm (XHTML)*
67              </tbody>
68                      <tr spry:if="({ds_RowNumber} % 2) == 0"
    class="even" onclick=
    "dsVacations.setCurrentRow('{ds_RowID}');" >
69                          <td>{name}</td>
70                          <td>{destination}</td>
71                      </tr>
72                      <tr spry:if="({ds_RowNumber} % 2) != 0"
    onclick="dsVacations.setCurrentRow('{ds_RowID}');" >
73                          <td>{name}</td>
74                          <td>{destination}</td>
75                      </tr>
76              </table>
                                                              1K / 1 sec
```

6 Change the opening **<tr>** tag following the opening **<tbody>** tag from this:

```
<tr spry:repeat="dsVacations" onclick="dsVacations.setCurrentRow('{ds_RowID}');" >
```

to this:

```
<tr spry:if="({ds_RowNumber} % 2) == 0" class="even"
onclick="dsVacations.setCurrentRow('{ds_RowID}');" >
```

7 Place your cursor after the **<tr>** tag, and from the **Coding** toolbar, click **Select Parent Tag**. Press **Ctrl+C** (Windows) or **Cmd+C** (Mac) to copy the selection, and then press the **right arrow** key to move the cursor past the selection. Press **Ctrl+V** (Windows) or **Cmd+V** (Mac) to paste the copied code block. Change the pasted **<tr>** tag to the following:

```
<tr spry:if="({ds_RowNumber} % 2) != 0" onclick="dsVacations.setCurrentRow('{ds_RowID}')" >
```

Change the equality sign (**==**) to an unequal sign (**!=**), and delete the **class="even"** attribute.

This step introduces a new Spry attribute, **spry:if**. As you might expect, **spry:if** is a conditional attribute. Here, you are performing an operation to determine whether the row number modulo 2 is or isn't equal to zero. **Modulo** is a mathematical operation similar to division that returns just the remainder; any even number when divided by 2 returns a remainder of 0. If the condition is true in the first **<tr>** tag, the even class is applied; in the second **<tr>**, the odd row, the default styling takes effect. Next you'll see how the page is progressing.

8 Press **Ctrl+S** (Windows) or **Cmd+S** (Mac); then press **F12** to preview the page in your browser. Note the alternating row styles. To verify the sort-by-column feature is working, click the **Property** heading first, and then click the **Destination** heading. When you're done testing, close the browser, and return to Dreamweaver 8.

The user experience is getting better with every step! It is, however, still a bit difficult to tell which data entry the user is considering or has selected. Next, you'll add functions to address these problems.

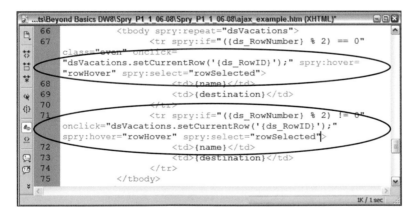

9 In Dreamweaver 8, add the following attributes and values to both **\<tr>** tags in the **\<tbody>** section:

```
spry:hover="rowHover" spry:select="rowSelected"
```

These two Spry attributes handle the hover and selected states, or the dynamic data. To be effective, you'll need CSS classes with the names **.rowHover** and **.rowSelected**. We have created these styles for you to save you a little grunt work and keep you focused on the Spry and Ajax code. Ready to see how they look? Continue to the next step.

10 Press **Ctrl+S** (Windows) or **Cmd+S** (Mac). Press **F12** to preview the page in your primary browser. Position your cursor over each of the data rows to see the hover effect. Click any entry to view the style for a selected item.

Even with adding the various effects in this exercise—sorting, alternating row styles, and hover and selected states—you've truly just scratched the surface of what's possible with Ajax and Adobe's Spry framework. We encourage you to visit Adobe Labs and explore Spry more deeply.

VIDEO: **spry_widget.mov**

To learn how to add a set of collapsible panels called an Accordian widget to your Spry page, check out **spry_widget.mov** in the **videos** folder on the **Dreamweaver 8 HOT CD-ROM**.

11 When you're done testing, close your browser, and return to Dreamweaver. Close **ajax_example.htm**.

In this chapter, you began exploring the possibilities of integrating Ajax into your Web pages. You learned about Ajax and about Adobe's implementation of Ajax and Spry, and you had an opportunity to build an Ajax-powered page to display data with numerous visual effects without reloading. In the next chapter, you'll learn how to incorporate custom typography for your headings with Macromedia Flash, CSS, and JavaScript.

10

Incorporating sIFR Text

Let's say a group of leading print designers were swooped up by aliens in 1990, just before the Internet became mainstream. If they returned 16 years later, what do you think their reaction would be to the wonder of the Web? I bet their first words would be, "Why are the fonts the same?"

The Web relies on the lowest common denominator when it comes to typefaces. To ensure everyone can view headlines and other text, Web designers use only those fonts everyone has. This practice results in a maddening limitation on designers—imagine if Web professionals could use their favorite fonts without sacrificing readability or accessibility!

Fortunately, a new Macromedia Flash–based technique brings the wide world of fonts to the Web. The somewhat unusually named sIFR (**s**calable **I**nman **F**lash **R**eplacement) technique uses CSS and JavaScript to replace headlines and short bits of text with Flash text when a page loads. The result is designer-specified typography that remains searchable and degrades gracefully if necessary.

In this chapter, you'll dive behind the scenes of sIFR to help you better understand the theory and practice. Naturally, you'll get an opportunity to implement sIFR in a Dreamweaver 8 page—and experience the magic for yourself.

Understanding sIFR

Simply put, **sIFR**—pronounced "siff-er"—is a technique for displaying design-time typography at run time. In other words, by incorporating sIFR code on your Web pages, you can display fonts found only on your machine in any Flash-enabled browser, regardless of whether viewers have the same fonts on their systems. sIFR combines JavaScript, Flash, and CSS to unobtrusively substitute Flash text in the typefaces of your choice.

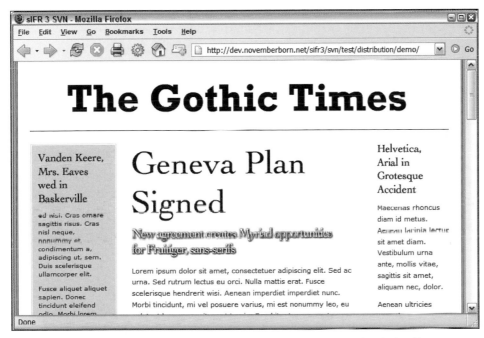

This sIFR-enabled page shows a number of designer-owned fonts, as well as the Flash 8 shadow filter

sIFR is the product of an ongoing effort by a number of developers. Originally developed by Mike Davidson for ESPN.com, Shaun Inman generalized the concept and released the technology under the name Inman Flash Replacement. Davidson worked with the advanced methods Inman provided and advanced the technique to another level to make replacing Flash text more adaptable, creating the scalable Inman Flash Replacement technique. Most recently, Mark Wubben, who was responsible for much of sIFR's JavaScript engine in sIFR 2.0, took on the project under Davidson's guidance and released sIFR 3.0. You can find out more about the current state of sIFR at **http://novemberborn.net/sifr3/**.

This technique overcomes the lowest common denominator aspect of font usage on the Web in a novel way. Here's how it works:

1. When a browser loads the requested page, a JavaScript function checks to see whether the proper version of Flash (7 or newer) is available. If the browser doesn't detect Flash, it renders the page, including all the headings, with CSS-styled text.

2. If the correct version of Flash is present, the browser dynamically assigns a CSS class, `sIFR-hasFlash`, to the HTML tag via DOM (**D**ocument **O**bject **M**odel) manipulation. A CSS style sheet includes rules that affect headings for children of this class, for example, `sIFR-hasFlash h1`. These style rules hide these headings through the `visibility:hidden` property.

3. JavaScript functions then traverse the page's DOM to find elements styled with the `sIFR-hasFlash` class. Once they find an element, a sIFR Flash movie with the design-time font replaces it, using the actual `<h1>`, or other heading, text.

Although this technique has many moving parts, it all happens very quickly when the page loads. In most cases, you won't be able to discern a delay.

Note: Keep in mind that sIFR is really intended to replace only short text phrases, such as headings or pull quotes. If you attempt to replace large text blocks, you'll experience a significant increase in time for the page to load.

In many ways, the best part of the sIFR technique is what happens when it fails. Because all the CSS-styled headings are already part of the page, if the visitor's browser has JavaScript disabled or if the browser doesn't find the proper Flash version, the page degrades gracefully and displays the text with the CSS styles intact. Even better, because the Flash replacement is layered on top of the existing text, the technique remains accessible to screen readers and other assistive devices.

In the following exercise, you'll learn how to integrate sIFR fonts in Dreamweaver 8. As you'll see, Dreamweaver 8 consistently displays the standard CSS designs—until you preview the page in a browser.

1 | Implementing sIFR Components

As noted previously, sIFR uses several technologies—CSS, JavaScript, and Flash—that work together. In the process of building your Web page, you'll incorporate references to each of these technologies. JavaScript functions perform most of the heavy lifting in an external file, so your first task is to include that file. Then, you'll insert a few JavaScript function calls in your code to initialize sIFR and preload the Flash font files for quicker start-up. The final task is to add the necessary CSS style rules so sIFR knows which headings to replace.

1 In the **Files** panel, open **sifr_example.htm** from the **chap_10** folder you copied to your desktop.

In this exercise, you'll replace the **<h1>** heading—Serenity is our Specialty—and the **<h2>** heading just below it. First, you'll lay the foundation by including the sIFR JavaScript file.

2 Choose **View > Head Content**. At the top of the **Document** window, click in the **Head Content area** (circled in the illustration here). In the **Insert bar**, click the **HTML** category, and click the menu button **Script: Script**. In the **Script** dialog box, click the **folder** icon next to **Source**. In the **Select File** dialog box, navigate to **chap_10/js**, and select **sifr.js**. Click **OK** once to close the **Select File** dialog box, and click **OK** again to close the **Script** dialog box.

The sifr.js file contains a wealth of functionality in sophisticated JavaScript coding, and it's important to place the file in the **<head>** of the document because several actions, such as preloading the .swf files, need to take place before the browser displays the page. You'll next need to add several JavaScript function calls that reference code in this file.

3 With the **Script** icon in the **Head Content area** still selected, switch to **Code** view. Your cursor should be at the end of the **<script>** tag. Press **Enter** (Windows) or **Return** (Mac) to create a new line. In the **Insert** bar, click **Script** to open the **Script** dialog box. Without typing any additional code, click **OK** to insert an empty **<script>** tag. Place your cursor in the new **<script>** tag, and type the following code:

```
//<![CDATA[
//]]>
```

The **<CDATA>** (**C**haracter **DATA**) tag allows you to include JavaScript functions in your code while maintaining a valid XHTML (**E**xtensible **HTML**) page. When the browser parses the page, it ignores all the code within the **<CDATA>** tag, so it overlooks functions that would otherwise throw an error when validated.

Unfortunately, some older browsers don't understand the **<CDATA>** tag, which causes the JavaScript code to break. The double slashes at the beginning of each line effectively comment out the **<CDATA>** tag for those older browsers while retaining validation.

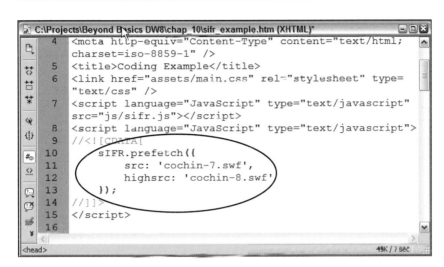

4 Place your cursor on the blank line between the two code lines you typed in the previous step. Press the **Tab** key, and type the following code:

```
sIFR.prefetch({
  src: 'cochin-7.swf',
  highsrc: 'cochin-8.swf'
});
```

The first JavaScript routine preloads the .swf files containing the necessary font information. sIFR 3.0 uses two files: one for Flash 7 and another for Flash 8. The Flash 8 file allows sIFR to take advantage of some advanced features such as filters.

NOTE:

Creating Flash sIFR Files

Although you need a fair degree of JavaScript and CSS to implement the sIFR technique, the secret ingredients are the Flash movies themselves. Each Flash movie contains all the characters in the chosen embedded fonts; the file size is small because the character information is stored in vector rather than bitmap format.

The core sIFR files include a basic Flash source file, **sifr.fla**, that you can easily adapt to produce the required files for the fonts you want to use. Using the file shown in this exercise, here's how you do this:

1. In Flash 8, choose **File > Open**.

2. Locate **sifr.fla** in the **Flash** directory of the **chap_10** folder, and click Open.

3. Double-click the movie clip holder spanning the entire **Stage**. Three words—**Bold Normal Italic**—appear, each in its respective style.

4. From the **Font** pop-up menu in the **Property inspector**, choose the desired typeface.

5. Choose **File > Publish Settings**.

For wider compatibility, you'll need to publish two versions of the same file: one for Flash 7 and another for Flash 8.

6. In the **Publish Settings** dialog box, turn off the **HTML** check box in the **Formats** category, and change the **.swf** file name to *fontname*-8.swf—for example, **book_antiqua-8.swf**.

continues on next page

NOTE:

Creating Flash sIFR Files *continued*

7. In the Flash category, set the following options: Set **Version** to **Flash Player 8**, set **Load Order** to **Bottom Up**, set **ActionScript Version** to **Version 2.0**, turn on **Protect from Import**, and turn on **Compress Movie**.

8. Click **Publish**.

9. Repeat Steps 6–8, but change the **.swf** file name to *fontname-7.swf* (for example, **book_antiqua-7.swf**) in the **Formats** category, and set **Version** to **Flash Player 7** in the **Flash** category.

10. Click **OK**.

Over time, you can build up a solid library of typefaces and apply them when appropriate by copying instances into the desired sites.

```
C:\Projects\Beyond Basics DW8\chap_10\sifr_example.htm (XHTML)*
 5  <title>Coding Example</title>
 6  <link href="assets/main.css" rel="stylesheet" type=
    "text/css" />
 7  <script language="JavaScript" type="text/javascript"
    src="js/sifr.js"></script>
 8  <script language="JavaScript" type="text/javascript">
 9  //<![CDATA[
10      sIFR.prefetch({
11          src: 'cochin-7.swf',
12          highsrc: 'cochin-8.swf'
13      });
14  sIFR.compatMode = true;
15  sIFR.activate();
16  //]]>
17  </script>
18
<head>                                              49K / 7 sec
```

5 If necessary, after the code you typed in the previous step, press **Enter** (Windows) or **Return** (Mac). Type the following code:

```
sIFR.compatMode = true;
sIFR.activate();
```

The first of these two lines of code sets up sIFR to be compatible with older browsers. If you do not want to support older versions of Mozilla, Safari, and Opera, set `sIFR.compatMode` to `false`.

With the `sIFR.activate()` function call, the sIFR engine is in motion. This function establishes a listening event in Flash. What is Flash listening for? It's listening for the next JavaScript function, which dynamically replaces the chosen CSS selectors with the corresponding Flash text.

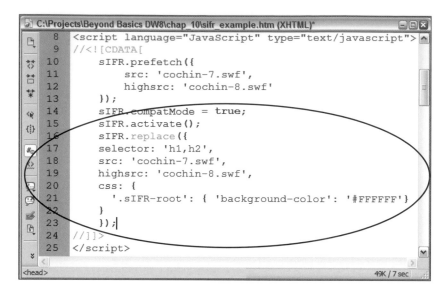

```
C:\Projects\Beyond Basics DW8\chap_10\sifr_example.htm (XHTML)*
8   <script language="JavaScript" type="text/javascript">
9   //<![CDATA[
10      sIFR.prefetch({
11          src: 'cochin-7.swf',
12          highsrc: 'cochin-8.swf'
13      });
14      sIFR.compatMode = true;
15      sIFR.activate();
16      sIFR.replace({
17      selector: 'h1,h2',
18      src: 'cochin-7.swf',
19      highsrc: 'cochin-8.swf',
20      css: {
21        '.sIFR-root': { 'background-color': '#FFFFFF'}
22      }
23      });
24   //]]>
25   </script>
<head>                                            49K / 7 sec
```

6 Press **Enter** (Windows) or **Return** (Mac), and type the following code:

```
sIFR.replace({
selector: 'h1,h2',
src: 'cochin-7.swf',
highsrc: 'cochin-8.swf',
css: {
  '.sIFR-root': { 'background-color': '#FFFFFF'}
}
});
```

The `sIFR.replace()` function is the real workhorse of the included JavaScript code. The first parameter, `selector`, establishes which CSS selectors will be replaced. As the example code shows, you can group two or more selectors in a comma-separated list.

Next, you specified the Flash files to use, in both the Flash 7 and Flash 8 varieties.

Finally, you specified the CSS you want to apply for the `sIFR-root` selector. You can specify properties and their values in a comma-separated list. For example, if you want to change the color of the text in the Flash movie as well as set the `background-color` property to `white`, you use code like this:

```
'.sIFR-root': { 'background-color': '#FFFFFF', 'color': '#FF0000'}
```

Note: When specifying color values in sIFR, you must use hexadecimal values rather than color names.

You have just one more JavaScript function to add—which you'll insert in the **<body>** tag of the document rather than in the **<head>** tag.

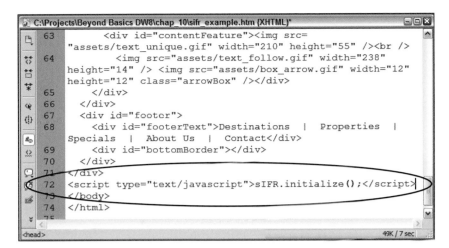

```
63          <div id="contentFeature"><img src=
    "assets/text_unique.gif" width="210" height="55" /><br />
64          <img src="assets/text_follow.gif" width="238"
    height="14" /> <img src="assets/box_arrow.gif" width="12"
    height="12" class="arrowBox" /></div>
65          </div>
66      </div>
67      <div id="footer">
68          <div id="footerText">Destinations  |   Properties   |
    Specials   |   About Us   |   Contact</div>
69          <div id="bottomBorder"></div>
70      </div>
71  </div>
72  <script type="text/javascript">sIFR.initialize();</script>
73  </body>
74  </html>
```

7 In **Code** view, scroll to the bottom of the page, and place your cursor between the final closing **</div>** tag and the closing **</body>** tag. Press **Enter** (Windows) or **Return** (Mac) to create a new line, and type the following code:

```
<script type="text/javascript">sIFR.initialize();</script>
```

By placing the code that initializes sIFR at the bottom of the document, you ensure the entire page will load and be ready to be displayed. The JavaScript portion of the sIFR technique is now complete.

Next, you'll bring CSS into the sIFR mix.

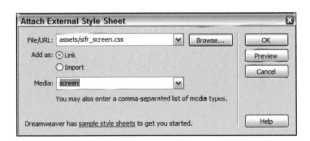

8 Switch to **Design** view. In the **CSS Styles** panel, click **Attach Style Sheet**. In the **Attach External Style Sheet** dialog box, click the **Browse** button. In the **Select File** dialog box, navigate to the **chap_10/assets** folder, select **sifr_screen.css**, and click **OK**. Make sure **Link** is selected for the **Add as:** option. From the **Media** pop-up menu, choose **screen**, and click **OK**.

The sifr_screen.css file already includes the core sIFR declarations: **sIFR-Flash**, **sIFR-replaced**, and **sIFR-alternate**. The first two styles set the **visibility** property to visible, whereas the third establishes the style used for a dummy **<div>** tag to hold the regular typefaces, should sIFR not be available.

The only other style rule handles AdBlock, a popular Flash blocker utility for Firefox and Mozilla browsers, to make sure the text displays without an overlaying tab.

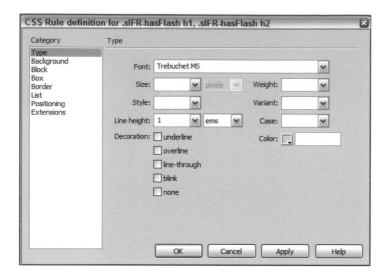

9 In the **CSS Styles** panel, make sure **All** mode is displayed. From the list of attached style sheets, select **sifr_screen.css**, and then click **New CSS Rule**. In the **New CSS Rule** dialog box, set **Selector Type** to **Advanced**. In the **Selector** field, type **.sIFR-hasFlash h1, .sIFR-hasFlash h2**, and click **OK**. In the **CSS Rule definition for .sIFR-hasFlash h1, .sIFR-hasFlash h2** dialog box, stay in the **Type** category. In the **Font** pop-up menu, type **Trebuchet MS**, and set **Line height** to **1 ems**. Click the **Positioning** category, and choose **hidden** from the **Visibility** pop-up menu. Click **OK**.

This step establishes how sIFR should generally handle the selectors that will be replaced in your page. The font chosen is the same one used in the CSS rule for the body. It's important to use the same font so Dreamweaver 8 can calculate the height of the Flash movie properly.

Tip: By the way, we slipped a slightly advanced use of Dreamweaver 8 in here: It's not generally known that the Font list is editable, meaning you can type your desired font directly in the pop-up list, without choosing it from the list.

The `line-height: 1ems` declaration is also necessary to make sure the height of the Flash replacement matches that of the standard font. Finally, the `visibility: hidden` declaration makes sure this style— applied only if sIFR has detected the correct version of Flash is available—does not appear.

All that's left to do is set the individual sizes for each selector.

10 In the **CSS Styles** panel, click **New CSS Rule**. In the **New CSS Rule** dialog box, make sure **Selector Type** is set to **Advanced**. In the **Selector** field, type **.sIFR-hasFlash h1**, and click **OK**. In the **CSS Rule definition for .sIFR-hasFlash h1** dialog box, stay in the **Type** category. Set **Size** to **28 pixels**. Click **OK**.

The chosen size matches that of the standard CSS style for the **<h1>** tag. The final action is to set the size for the **<h2>** tag.

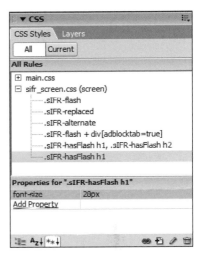

11 In the **CSS Styles** panel, click **New CSS Rule**. In the **New CSS Rule** dialog box, make sure **Selector Type** is set to **Advanced**. In the **Selector** field, type **.sIFR-hasFlash h2**, and click **OK**. In the **CSS Rule definition for .sIFR-hasFlash h2** dialog box, stay in the **Type** category. Set **Size** to **14 pixels**. Click **OK**.

With all the JavaScript and CSS complete, you're ready to see the results of your hard work.

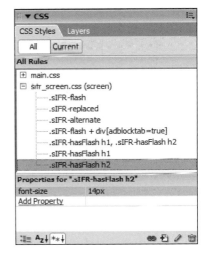

12 Choose **File > Save All**, and then press **F12** to preview the page in your primary browser. After you've noticed the replaced headings, close your browser, and return to Dreamweaver 8. Close **sifr_example.htm**.

Note: If you're using Internet Explorer 6 or newer, you might need to click the message bar at the top of the browser to allow the blocked active content.

What's really amazing about the sIFR-replaced headings is that it's almost impossible to tell they're Flash. Select a heading like you would any text. If you right-click the selection, you'll see the standard set of Select/Copy/Paste menu options. You can copy the heading and paste it elsewhere you like. Choose View > Page Source (or your browser's equivalent) in your browser, and you won't see any code for a Flash movie—just the **<h1>** tag.

In this chapter, you learned all about the sIFR technology for replacing headings with Flash text to achieve a more professional typographic look and feel for your site. In the next chapter, you'll learn how to develop Dreamweaver 8 sites when working in a team environment.

11

Working in Groups

Movies featuring Web designers always seem to cast the role as a young, totally hip artist, working alone to create edgy sites. Well, that's Hollywood, and this is the real world. Although solo, freelance Web designers do exist, many Web professionals work together. Fortunately, Dreamweaver 8 is effective in both scenarios. This chapter explores the Dreamweaver 8 features that make it a terrific tool for teams, whether the team members are working in a corporate or design studio environment.

The number-one priority for groups is simple: Don't overwrite someone else's work. Dreamweaver 8 has the answer to this concern: the check-in/check-out system. This feature is quite robust and effective, as long as everyone plays by the rules described in this chapter. Communication is another key component of any design team; in this chapter, you'll see how you can use Dreamweaver 8 Design Notes to convey information about any part of a Web page from one person to another. Finally, this chapter examines another communication tool in Dreamweaver 8: reports. Dreamweaver 8 reports are great for detailing potential bottlenecks in production and verifying certain aspects of the site are shipshape and ready to go live.

EXERCISE

1

Using the Check-in/Check-out System Effectively

Whenever a number of people have design-level access to a Web site, you need some sort of access control. The danger is two or more people might be working on the same file at the same time—and inevitably, someone's work will be lost. Dreamweaver 8 uses a check-in/check-out system to prevent this type of mishap. When the check-in/check-out system is turned on for a site, a file that has been published to the site (or staging server) must be checked out before it can be modified. Once one person has checked it out, no one else can work on it until that person has checked in the file. For the check-in/check-out system to work, everyone with access to the site files must have it turned on in their Dreamweaver 8 site definition. In this exercise, you'll set up Dreamweaver 8 to turn on the check-in/check-out system and try it for yourself.

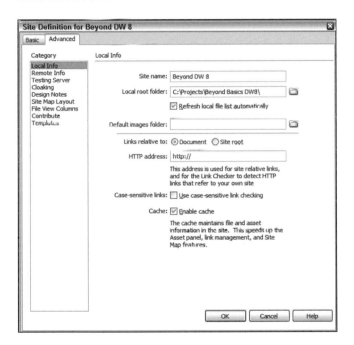

1 While you're in the Dreamweaver 8 site established for this book's exercises, choose **Site > Manage Sites**. In the **Manage Site** dialog box, click **Edit**. In the **Site Definition for Beyond DW 8** dialog box, switch to **Advanced** mode, if necessary.

The check-in/check-out system requires both a local site and a remote site. Usually, you would access your remote site via FTP (**F**ile **T**ransfer **P**rotocol), via a version control system such as Microsoft Visual SourceSafe, or via the network to a staging server. As you'll see in the next step, you can simulate the needed connection by choosing a separate folder on your system as your remote folder.

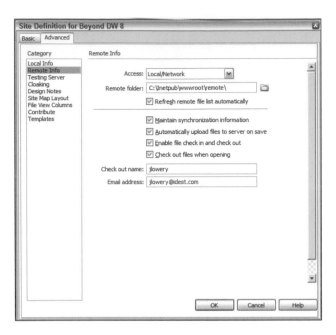

2 In the **Site Definition for Beyond DW 8** dialog box, click the **Remote Info** category. If you have an FTP site you can use, choose **FTP** from the **Access** pop-up menu, and type the necessary information including your username and password. If you don't have an FTP site, choose **Local/Network** from the **Access** pop-up menu. Click the **folder** icon for **Remote folder**, and in the **Choose Remote Root Folder** dialog box, navigate to your **C:\Inetpub\wwwroot** folder (Windows) or **Sites** folder (Mac). Create a new folder called **remote**, and select it as your remote folder. Once you have typed your FTP or local/network information, turn on the **Refresh remote file list automatically** check box, and leave **Maintain synchronization information** turned on. Turn on the **Enable file check in and check out** check box, and when available, turn on the **Check out files when opening** check box. In the **Check out name** field, type your username, and in the **Email address** field, type your e-mail address.

Once you've identified a remote folder, turning on the various available options smoothes your workflow. The username you typed appears as a mailto: link—using the e-mail address you typed—next to any files you've checked out in the Site panel's Remote pane. However, to see these username links, you'll need to first turn on the column displaying them.

3 Click the **File View Columns** category. Select the **Checked Out By** entry, and turn on the **Show** check box. When Dreamweaver 8 alerts you that showing the **Checked Out By** column will affect performance, click **OK**. Click **OK** again to close the **Site Definition for Beyond DW 8** dialog box, and click **Done** to close the **Manage Sites** dialog box.

Because Dreamweaver 8 has to gather information regarding checked-out files to show the Checked Out By entries, this selection can slow down the initial connection between local and remote sites. Although this is not noticeable on small to medium sites, it can affect larger sites. As an alternative to displaying all the files and who checked them out all the time, you can hide this column and use the Dreamweaver 8 report system to view all the files checked out by a specific individual.

---

4 In the **Files** panel, click the **chap_11** folder in the site to expand the list, and select the **check_in_out_example.htm** file. In the **Files** panel, click **Check In**. If Dreamweaver 8 asks whether you'd like to also check in dependent files, click **Yes**.

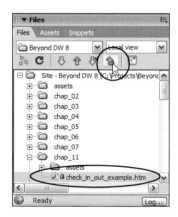

Dreamweaver 8 prompts you regarding a page's dependent files according to the Dependent Files settings in the Site category of Preferences. It's a bit of a judgment call as to whether you should check in your dependent files. Some designers think checking in all the dependent files has too comprehensive an effect, especially because they use many such files, such as logo graphics, throughout their sites. We tend to err on the side of caution and check in these files as well as the primary HTML file.

You'll now learn how the remote site represents checked-in files. By the way, you'll notice Dreamweaver 8 adds a small, closed padlock icon to identify all checked-in files because these files are now locked until checked out.

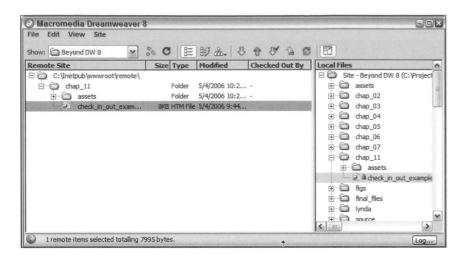

5 In the **Files** panel, choose **Expand/Collapse**. When the **Site** panel displays, drag the divider between the **Remote** and **Local** panes to show the **Checked Out By** column in the **Remote** pane. Expand the **chap_11** folder to show the **check_in_out_example.htm** file.

From a remote file perspective, you'll notice the checked-in file is not marked in any way. When the check-in/check-out system is turned on, all files on the remote site are considered to have been checked in. You will, however, see a difference when a file is checked out.

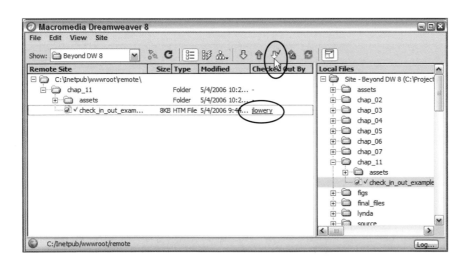

6 In the **Remote** pane, select the **check_in_out_example.htm** file, and in the toolbar, click **Check Out**. When Dreamweaver 8 asks whether you'd like to check out the dependent files, click **Yes**.

Now, Dreamweaver 8 is marking the changes in a number of ways. You'll note a green check mark next to the file name in both the Remote and Local panes. The checked-out check mark is green for files you've checked out and red for files others have checked out. Additionally, the Checked Out By column has a new entry: a linked username. Next, you'll see how that is used.

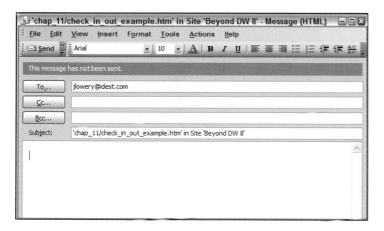

7 In the **Checked Out By** column, click the username.

This opens an e-mail message in your default e-mail client, if available. Dreamweaver 8 automatically sets the To field of the e-mail to match the e-mail address you typed in the Site Definition for Beyond DW 8 dialog box. It also enters the file name and site name as the suggested subject. The idea is that you have an easy and immediate method of communicating with whomever checked out the file in question. If you need to work on a file and you see it is checked out by someone else in your organization, just click the Checked Out By link, and drop a quick note asking when it will be available again. Slick, eh?

8 Leave Dreamweaver 8 open for the next exercise.

In this exercise, you learned how to set up and use the check-in/check-out system. Next, you'll explore another team-building component, Design Notes.

2 | Applying Design Notes

When two or more people are working on a product, whether it's a single Web page or an entire site, ongoing communication is essential. Dreamweaver 8 includes a terrific tool for exchanging information among team members on the page level: **Design Notes**. Design Notes are great for tracking progress and detailing problems as different people work on a specific page; it's also an excellent management instrument for reviewing submitted work and noting required corrections. In this exercise, you'll learn how to turn on Design Notes, how to add a note to a page, and how to make it easy for fellow team members to track a site's progress with Design Notes and custom file-viewing columns.

1 In the **Files** panel, open **design_notes.htm** from the **chap_11** folder.

2 In the **Files** panel, double-click the name of the site in the pop-up menu. In the **Site Definition for Beyond DW 8** dialog box, click the **Design Notes** category. Verify the **Maintain Design Notes** check box is turned on, and turn on the **Upload Design Notes for sharing** check box. Click **OK**.

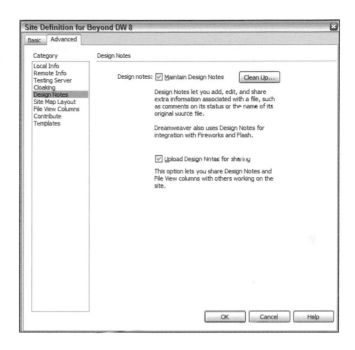

Before you can use the Design Notes feature, you must turn it on in the Site Definition for X dialog box. The Maintain Design Notes check box is turned on by default, but it's always good practice to make sure the check box is turned on before you attempt to use it. If you've followed the exercises in this chapter in order, you're probably ready to go with Design Notes because they are a requirement for the check-in/check-out functionality covered in Exercise 1.

By turning on Upload Design Notes for sharing, you're setting up your system so it will work well with your team members. Everyone on your team should select this option so everyone can see everyone else's Design Notes. If you're working by yourself on a single machine, you wouldn't have to turn on this check box; however, if you're a solo worker and you're designing a page both from a desktop system at the office and from a laptop at home or on the road, you should turn on the Upload Design Notes for sharing check box.

Now, you're ready to add a note to the page.

---

3 Choose **File > Design Notes**. In the **Design Notes** dialog box, from the **Status** pop-up menu, choose **needs attention**. Click the **Calendar** icon to include a date and in the **Notes** field, type **Big Ben picture needs caption.** Turn on the **Show when file is opened** check box to display comments, and click **OK**. Close **design_notes.htm**.

You may notice the Design Notes dialog box has two tabs: Basic info and All info. The dialog box always opens with the Basic info tab displayed. On this tab,

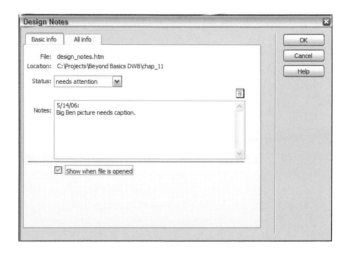

you'll find a single Design Notes category: Status. The status of a Web page in development is the primary concern for team management, so it is the focus of the Basic info Design Notes tab.

Dreamweaver 8 makes it easy for you to date-stamp your entry; one click of the calendar icon inserts the current system date. You can type as much detail as desired in the Notes field and ensure your message is seen by selecting the option that shows the file when the page is next opened—no matter who opens it.

Next, you'll set up your Site panel so you can view your page's status at a glance.

4 In the **Files** panel, double-click the name of the site in the pop-up menu. In the **Site Definition for Beyond DW 8** dialog box, click the **File View Column** category. Click **Add (+)**, and in the **Column name** field, type **Status**. From the **Associate with design note** pop-up menu, choose **Status**. Leave the **Show** check box turned on, and turn on the **Share with all users of this site** check box. Click the **Up** button several times to move the **Status** column above **Size** and below **Notes**. Finally, select the **Notes** entry, and turn on the **Show** check box. Click **OK**.

The file view of the Site panel contains a series of columns. It has a series of default columns, such as Name, Size, and Type, among others. Dreamweaver 8 gives you the power to create custom columns as well. If you name your custom column the same as an entry in your Design Notes—for example, Status—Dreamweaver 8 will display the corresponding Design Notes values in the custom column of the Site Definition for X dialog box. The Up and Down arrows in the File View Column category of the Site Definition for X dialog box allow you to reposition a column; the closer it is to the top, the further left the column appears. You cannot, however, place your custom (or any other) column to the left of the Name column.

Another Dreamweaver 8 file-viewing feature is the capability to share custom columns with other members of the site. Again, this is a key feature for those working in teams. You'll now learn what your team members might see.

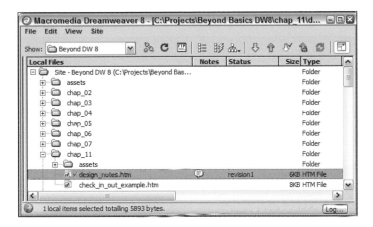

5 In the **Files** panel, click the **Expand/Collapse** button to expand the **Files** panel in the **Site** panel. If necessary, drag the separators between the **Notes** and **Status** column headers to display the symbol in the **Notes** column and the text in the **Status** column. Double-click the **Notes** symbol to open the Design Notes for the page. In the **Design Notes** dialog box, choose **revision1** from the **Status** list. Click the **calendar** icon, and type **Caption added**. Press **Enter** (Windows) or **Return** (Mac) to create a separating line, and click **OK**.

The Notes column not only gives you a clear indicator of which files have Design Notes attached but also provides an easy way to update a note. Anytime you change the status, the new choice instantly appears in the Status file view column.

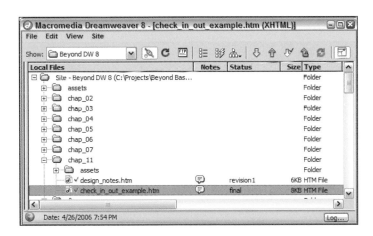

6 Under the **Notes** column, double-click the white space next to **check_in_out_example.htm**. In the **Design Notes** dialog box, choose **final** from the **Status** list. Click the **calendar** icon, and in the **Notes** area, type **All done!** Turn on the **Show when file is opened** check box, and click **OK**.

You can see how Design Notes and the custom file-viewing columns work together. Team members can use the Site panel to manage their Design Notes, revising existing notes and even creating new ones.

The final step is to understand what happens when you open a page with a note attached.

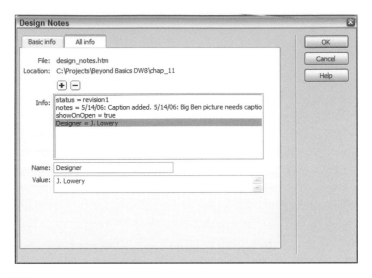

7 In the **Files** panel, double-click **design_notes.htm** to open the page. In the **Design Notes** dialog box, select the **All info** tab. Click **Add (+)**, and in the **Name** field, type **Designer**. In the **Value** field, type your name, and press the **Tab** key. When you're ready, click **OK**.

As expected, the note immediately appears when you opened the file. This feature makes sure the information in the note always displays for the person who opens the file. If you're working with other team members, the page would naturally be checked in after you completed your tasks. Because you elected to share Design Notes in the Site Definition for *X* dialog box, others will see your notes as well.

Tip: Additionally, you can create custom notes using the All info tab. With this option, you can type the name of the designer, as you did in this step, or any other details associated with the page, such as the due date or the client contact.

---

8 Close **design_notes.htm** without saving.

This exercise demonstrated how Design Notes work by themselves and in conjunction with the Site panel's file-viewing columns. With Design Notes, you can add information to share with your team members or reminders to yourself for work yet to be done. In the next exercise, you'll learn how you can create reports based on your site information.

---

3 | Generating Reports

In Dreamweaver 8, **reports** give you an objective view of a Web site's status. The nine available reports cover both team-oriented topics, such as who has what files checked out, and HTML-level details, such as untitled documents.

Reports are primarily output in an interactive format visible in the **Results** panel. Each entry in the report links to the page and, often, the exact line of the flagged code. Dreamweaver 8 includes a vital report for anyone concerned with accessibility requirements; you'll get a chance to generate an accessibility report later in this exercise, complete with a hard copy. In this exercise, you will start with a simpler report detailing which pages in your site have recently changed. This is handy information for the solo designer or any member working on a team.

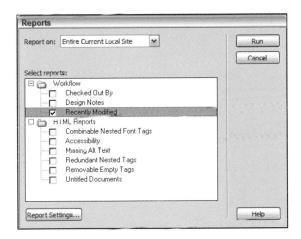

1 Choose **Sites > Reports** to display the **Reports** dialog box. From the **Report on** pop-up menu, choose **Entire Current Local Site**. In the **Select reports** area, turn on the **Recently Modified** check box. Leave the dialog box open.

The Reports dialog box has three main sections: the Report on pop-up menu, the Select reports area, and the Report Settings button. When you choose an option from the Report on pop-up menu, you can change the scope of the report from the current document to the entire site. In the Select reports area, you can choose which report you'd like to run. The Reports dialog box allows you to run multiple reports in one operation. (You could, in fact, run them all at once. However, this option is not practical: All the results from the reports you run will appear mixed together in the Results panel.) The final element of the dialog box, the Report Settings button, becomes active only when user-definable options are available for the selected report.

The first report you'll run, Recently Modified, offers such options.

2 In the **Reports** dialog box, click **Report Settings**. In the **Recently Modified** dialog box, make sure the **Files Created or Modified in the Last** radio button is selected, and in the **Days** field, type **21**. Leave the other settings at their defaults, and click **OK**.

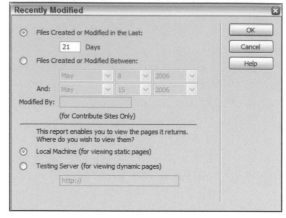

You can view which files have been changed over the past user-set number of days or in a specific date range. If you're working within a Contribute site, you can also limit your search to a specific user. (We discuss Contribute in Chapter 12, *"Designing for Contribute."*) The lower section of the dialog box specifies where you will view the final report; the Recently Modified report is the only one that displays the formatted report in the browser when it is completed. If you're working with a dynamic site, you'll need to select the Tester Server radio button and type the URL for the server; you can, if developing on your own system, use a **http://localhost/** address.

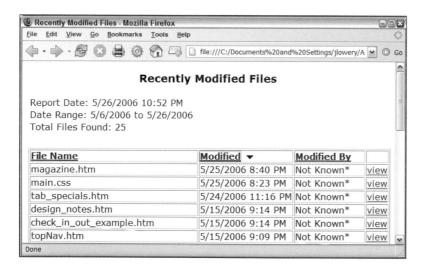

3 In the **Reports** dialog box, click **Run**. After the report runs, your system browser displays the results in HTML format, sorted by the modified date in ascending order. Click the **Modified** link once to re-sort the results and view the changed files in descending order. Click the **view** link associated with any file to open it in the browser (use your browser's **Back** button to return to the report). Close your browser when you're finished viewing the report.

Although it may take place too quickly to see what's happening, Dreamweaver 8 initially outputs the results from the report in the Results panel. Once that operation is complete, it creates a simple HTML page with a table of data based on those results and opens the page in the browser. Each of the column headers (File Name, Modified, and Modified By) acts as a trigger for re-sorting the table data. Click one of these links to sort by the chosen category in ascending order; click again for descending order.

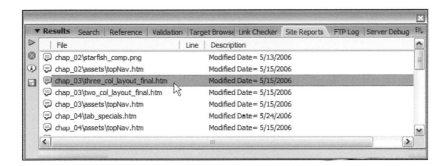

4 In Dreamweaver 8, double-click any HTML file in the **Results** panel. After you've finished viewing the file in the **Document** window, close the HTML file. From the **Panel options** menu (located in the upper-left corner of the panel), choose **Clear Results**.

The output results vary with each report. For the Recently Modified report, the file opens at the top of the page in Split view when you double-click the entry. For other, more detailed reports, Dreamweaver 8 places the cursor on the precise line of code noted in the report detail, as you'll see in the next report you'll run on your site's accessibility.

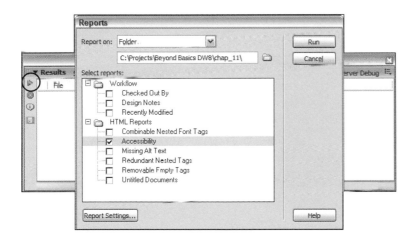

5 On the **Site Reports** tab in the **Results** panel, click the **green triangle** on the left of the panel. In the **Reports** dialog box, choose **Folder** from the **Report on** pop-up menu, and then click the **folder** icon to select the **chap_11** folder you copied to your desktop. In the **Select reports** section, turn on the **Accessibility** check box. Leave the dialog box open.

When available, the green triangle accesses the primary commands and interfaces for each tab in the Results panel. On the Site Reports tab, it reopens the Reports dialog box. For this report, you'll target a specific folder against which to run the report.

Tip: If you want to inspect specific files in one or more folders, you need to select them in the Files panel prior to opening the Reports dialog box. Once opened, you then choose Selected Files in Site from the Report on pop-up menu.

With the Accessibility report selected, you're ready to define the parameters for the report.

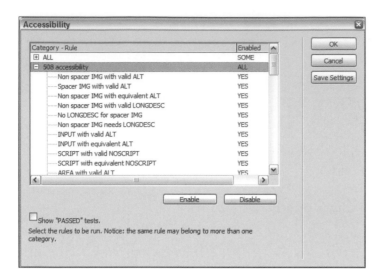

6 In the **Reports** dialog box, click the **Report Settings** button. In the **Accessibility** dialog box, make sure **All** is selected in the **Category – Rule** area, and click **Disable** (the terms in the **Enabled** column display **None** for all entries). Select **508 accessibility**, and click the **Enable** button (the **Enabled** values change to **All** for 508 accessibility). Expand **508 accessibility** to view all the accessibility requirements reviewed when this report is run. Click **Save Settings**, and then click **OK**.

Several accessibility standards, including Section 508 (U.S. federal law) and W3C/WCAG (World Wide Web Consortium), exist. The Accessibility dialog box gives you the power to choose the accessibility requirements you'd like to check. For maximum compliance, leave the All entry set to All. To focus on a specific set of guidelines, such as Section 508, you need to disable the All setting and then turn on the set you'd like to use. Similarly, you can check for specific requirements, but this is overkill. Selecting a general set of guidelines is a better course.

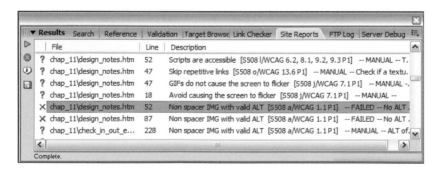

7 In the **Reports** dialog box, click the **Run** button. When the report has finished, click the blank column header above the first column of symbols (mostly question marks) until you see the red *X*s.

Some accessibility requirements are less subjective than others. For example, the Section 508 guidelines dictate every foreground image include an `alt` attribute with a valid value. Hard-and-fast requirements such as this are marked with red Xs in the report results. Those accessibility issues requiring a visual check, such as the screen-flicker requirement, are noted with a gray question mark.

Note: If you're unsure about how to check a flagged accessibility problem, select the entry in the Results panel, and click the More Info icon on the left side of the panel. The Reference panel displays the relevant details, including information about how to check and correct the accessibility entry.

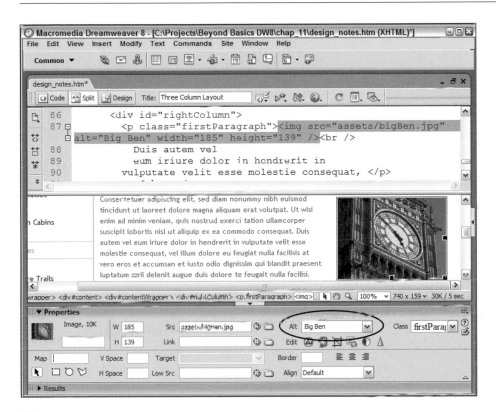

8 In the report results, double-click the first of the two red *X*s. When the associated page (**design_notes.htm**) opens in Dreamweaver 8 in **Split** view, the offending tag (the **Contact** image) is highlighted. In the **Property Inspector**, type **Contact** in the **Alt** field. In the **Results** panel, double-click the second red *X* to select the **Big Ben** image. In the **Alt** field of the **Property Inspector**, type **Big Ben**.

Dreamweaver 8 gives you a direct connection to accessibility issues. Just double-click the entry in the Results panel to pinpoint the problematic tag. The page opens in Split view so you can make the correction either in the code or in Design view. Notice that although you've addressed the problems, the report still displays them. You need to rerun the report to verify you've fixed this error.

Unlike the Recently Modified report, the Accessibility report does not automatically display an HTML version of the report. Although you can store the results in XML format, to really use this data, you'll need to transform the XML file to an HTML-viewable file. In the next part of this exercise, you'll apply lessons learned in Chapter 8, *"Setting Up an XML Feed,"* to accomplish this goal.

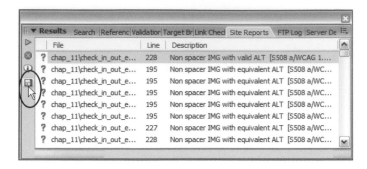

9 On the left side of the **Results** panel, click **Save Report**. In the **Save As** dialog box, navigate to the **chap_11** folder, and click **Open**. Type **accessibility_report.xml** in the **File name** field, and click **Save**. In the **Results** panel, click **Results** to collapse the panel.

Until the release of Dreamweaver 8, the XML report file output was pretty much a dead end. As you've seen in the exercises of Chapter 8, *"Setting Up an XML Feed,"* you can now easily transform XML into a much more accessible, styled HTML format. To save you some steps in the process, we have included a premade XSL (e**X**tensible **S**tyle **L**anguage) style sheet, ready for the XML data to be bound to it.

10 In the **Files** panel, navigate to the **chap_11** folder, and double-click the file **report.xsl**. Once the file opens in Dreamweaver 8, choose **Window > Bindings** to open the **Behaviors panel**, and click the **XML** link. In the **Locate XML Source** dialog box, make sure the **Attach a local file on my computer or local area network** radio button is selected, and click **Browse**. In the **Locate Source XML for XSL Template** dialog box, navigate to the **chap_11** folder, select **accessibility_report.xml**, and click **OK**. In the **Locate XML Source** dialog box, click **OK**.

In this step, you connected the XSL file just opened to the XML report previously stored. The XML schema appears in the Bindings panel after you close the Locate XML Source dialog box.

Macromedia Dreamweaver 8 Beyond the Basics : H•O•T

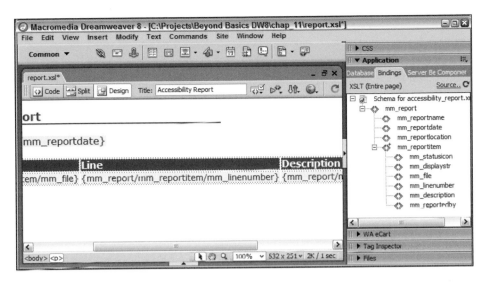

11 In the **Behaviors** panel, drag the **mm_reportdate** entry to the page, and drop it after **Created:**. Drag the **mm_file** entry to the cell beneath **File**, drag **mm_linenumber** under **Line**, and drag **mm_description** under **Description**.

The report now displays the date it was run, as well as the most important data: the file containing the error, the line number of the problem, and the description. The final action on the XSLT page is to apply a repeat region.

12 Select the **mm_file** dynamic text, and from the **Tag Selector**, choose **<tr>**. Choose **Insert > XSLT Objects > Repeat Region**. In the **XPath Expression Builder (Repeat Region)** dialog box, select the **mm_reportitem** entry, and click **OK**. Press **Ctrl+S** (Windows) or **Cmd+S** (Mac) to save your page.

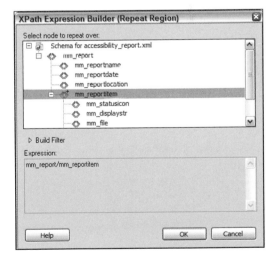

As with dynamic applications, a repeat region loops over the available data, outputting each record of information in the specified format, most frequently a table row. With the XSLT (**XSL T**ransformations) repeat region, you need to identify the XML node containing the repeated data—which, in this instance, is mm_reportitem. After you close the dialog box, you'll notice a border surrounding the **<tr>** tag and a small label identifying the region. Your work on this page is now complete, and the remaining task is to attach this XSL page to the XML file.

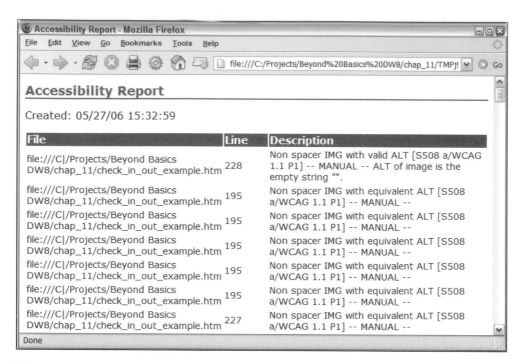

13 In the **Files** panel, double-click **accessibility_report.xml** to open the file. Choose **Commands > Attach an XSLT Stylesheet**. In the **Attach an XSLT Stylesheet** dialog box, click **Browse**. In the **Select XSLT File** dialog box, locate the **report.xsl** file in the **chap_11** folder, and click **OK**. In the **Attach an XSLT Stylesheet** dialog box, click **OK**.

---

14 Press **Ctrl+S** (Window) or **Cmd+S** (Mac) to save the page, and then switch to **report.xsl** in Dreamweaver 8. Press **F12** to preview the page in your primary browser.

With a minimum of hassle, you now have a browser-compatible accessibility report, ready to be printed or sent for review. You can apply the same technique to create a hard copy of any other report generated in Dreamweaver 8.

In this chapter, you worked with various team-building aspects of Dreamweaver 8, including check-in/checkout, Design Notes, and reports. In the next chapter, you'll learn how you can design your pages to work best with the special features and limitations of Contribute.

12

Designing for Contribute

Adobe Contribute is a real door-opener for Dreamweaver 8 designers—but only if they know how to take advantage of its special features. Built on the Dreamweaver 8 platform, Contribute presents an easy-to-use interface that empowers non–Web professionals to modify and publish their own Web pages.

So, where does Dreamweaver 8 come in? Typically, a designer crafts the initial pages in Dreamweaver 8 and, upon completion, turns them over to the client for maintenance in Contribute. This benefits both designers and clients. Designers can concentrate on designing and not get bogged down by a never-ending series of minor content updates. Likewise, clients often prefer to manage their own content, and Contribute allows them to do it in a straightforward environment.

In this chapter, you'll learn how to create Dreamweaver 8 sites from a Contribute perspective. As you'll see, Dreamweaver 8 designers can administer Contribute sites for their clients from within Dreamweaver 8. The techniques in this chapter will help you create pages in Dreamweaver 8 that are easily modified in Contribute. Finally, this chapter shows you how to provide flexible yet controlled styling possibilities using CSS to your Contribute users.

1 | Setting Up Contribute Administration

The Contribute administrative settings, particularly for individual roles, are best decided upon by both the designer and the client. For instance, should writers of content, as well as their supervisors, be able to publish pages to the Web site? It depends on the writer's level of competence and the degree to which the writer is trusted—something only the client knows. Keep in mind, you can also change administrative settings, and the changes take effect the next time a Contribute user works on the site.

Note: To complete this exercise, you'll need to install Contribute, available in Macromedia Studio 8.

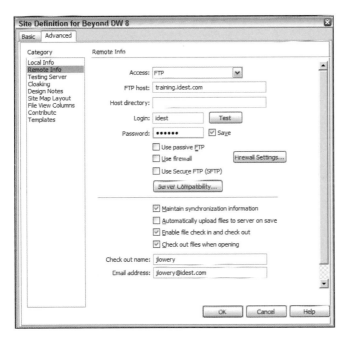

1 In the **Files** panel, double-click the site name, **Beyond DW 8**. In the **Site Definition for Beyond DW 8** dialog box, select the **Advanced** tab. In the **Category** list, click **Remote Info**. Complete one of the following two options, depending on whether you have access to a remote server:

a. If you have a remote Web server available, choose **FTP** from the **Access** pop-up menu, and type the appropriate information in the **FTP host**, **Host directory**, **Login**, and **Password** boxes.

b. If you don't have a remote Web server, choose **Local/Network** from the **Access** pop-up menu, and select the appropriate folder on your local Web server.

If necessary, turn on the **Enable file check in and check out** and **Check out files when opening** check boxes. In the **Check out name** box, type your name, and in the **Email address** box, type your e-mail address.

You'll need to set up a remote server within Dreamweaver 8 to administer Contribute. Contribute works by automatically transferring files from the remote server to the local site, opening them for editing, and then, when the update is complete, copying the files back to the remote server when published.

In the next step, you'll begin to make the current site compatible with Contribute. For this, you'll need to establish a remote server, and you'll need to turn on the check-in/check-out feature.

Note: The check-in/check-out feature is a powerful tool for designing sites with a team. You can find more information about this feature in Chapter 11, *"Working in Groups."*

---

2 In the **Category** list, click **Contribute**. Turn on the **Enable Contribute compatibility** check box. Verify the entry in the **Site root URL** box corresponds to the site information you typed in the **Remote Info** category in the previous step. If it does not, type the Web location of your remote site in the **Site root URL** box. To make sure the entry is correct, click the **Test** button.

After verifying that both Dreamweaver 8 and Contribute are working with the same remote site, you're ready to begin administering the site in Contribute.

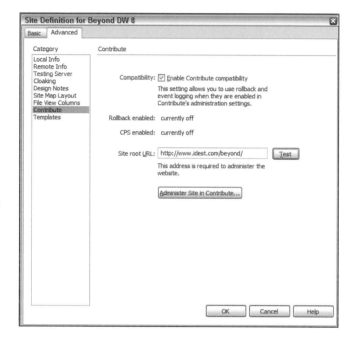

---

3 Click the **Administer Site in Contribute** button. After a brief delay, the **Contribute** dialog box appears. Click the **Dreamweaver-style editing** radio button to turn on this option, and click **Yes**.

The first time you click the Administer Site in Contribute button, Contribute prompts you to verify whether you want to be the site's Contribute administrator.

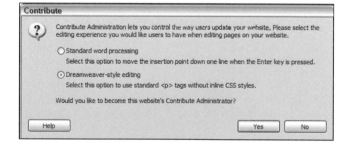

You also can choose between two basic editing methods for your Contribute users. The Standard word processing option uses inline styles, such as `<p style="top-margin:0; bottom-margin:0">`, to simulate paragraph spacing in word processors. Although this is slightly more familiar to the average user, the implementation overrides any similar styling you may have set up in your CSS style sheets. We strongly recommend the second option, Dreamweaver-style editing. If necessary, including a brief note describing how paragraphs are separated on the Web—and how to insert a line break—usually gets all Contribute users up to speed.

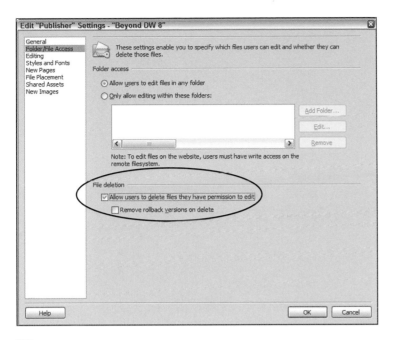

4 In the **Users who have connected** section of the **Administer Site** dialog box, choose **Publisher**, and click **Edit Role Settings**. In the **Edit "Publisher" Settings** dialog box, click the **General** category, and verify the **Allow users to publish files** check box is turned on. Click the **Folder/File Access** category, and turn on the **Allow users to delete files they have permission to edit** check box. Leave the **Remove rollback version on delete** check box turned off.

Contribute offers administrators several options for fine-tuning a site to the client's needs. Contribute allows you to define how different types of users can interact with the site. By default, Contribute defines three roles to start: Administrator, Publisher, and Writer. (You can, of course, create additional roles.) For this exercise, you'll assume the Administrator will use Dreamweaver 8, rather than Contribute, to work on the site, which means concentrating on the Publisher and Writer roles.

Those in the Publisher role should have the most flexibility of all the Contribute users; the ability to publish files is key. In the Folder/File Access category, you could, if you like, limit access to a specific folder and all of its files. In this exercise, however, you've left the site wide open, and you've given the Publisher role the ability to delete files. This is a powerful ability—one you should not provide lightly. When allowing clients to delete files, it's a good idea to always keep a previous version available through Contribute's rollback functionality, described later in this chapter.

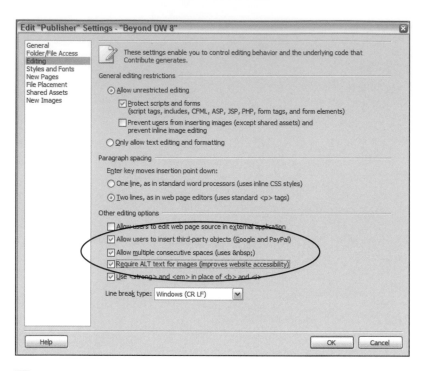

5 Click the **Editing** category. In the **Other editing options** section, turn on the check boxes for these three options: **Allow users to insert third-party objects**, **Allow multiple consecutive spaces**, and **Require ALT text for images**. Leave all other options at their default settings.

First we'll talk about those options you didn't change. Under General editing restrictions, we typically give the Publisher role the most latitude—remember, all Contribute users, including Publisher roles, will be able to change only the content in your template's editable regions. The second section, Paragraph spacing, offers the same options available when you first clicked the Administer Site in Contribute button.

In the Other editing options area, we rarely allow Contribute users to edit the Web page source in an external application—that's tantamount to removing all controls, and it's completely counter to the purpose of using Contribute. The other options in this category give enhanced possibilities, such as inserting a Google search field or PayPal donation button, while keeping the site as standards-compliant as possible.

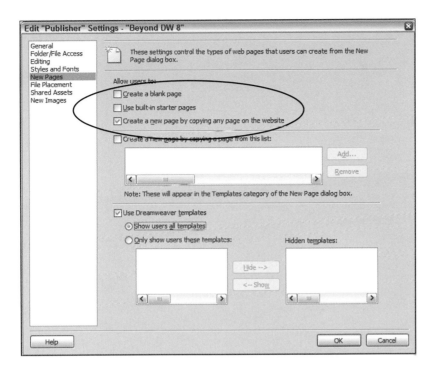

6 Click the **New Pages** category. In the **Allow users to** section, turn off the **Create a blank page** and **Use built-in starter pages** check boxes. Click **OK** to close the **Edit "Publisher" Settings** dialog box.

Contribute allows users to create their own pages in a number of ways. We typically remove all the alternative options except for the one to copy an existing page. This strategy keeps us, as designers, in control of what page layouts clients are using. For more control, you can even restrict new page creation to certain templates.

VIDEO: | **shared_assets.mov**

As a Dreamweaver 8 administrator, you can establish a common library of graphics, Macromedia Flash movies, and **Library** items for your Contribute users called **shared assets**. To learn how to define shared assets, check out **shared_assets.mov** in the **videos** folder on the **Dreamweaver 8 HOT CD-ROM**.

Before you leave this role, you'll need to store a connection key so you can try the Publisher experience yourself later in the chapter.

7 Click **Send Connection Key**. In the **Welcome** step of the **Connection Key Wizard**, turn on the **Include my FTP username and password** check box, and click **Next**. In the **Role Information** step of the wizard, choose **Publisher** from the list of roles, and click **Next**. In the **Connection Key Information** step of the wizard, choose the **Save to local machine** option, and then type **beyond** in each password field. Click **Next**. In the **Summary** step of the wizard, review the information to make sure it's correct, and click **Done**. In the **Export Connection Key** dialog box, leave the default suggested name for the connection key, and navigate to the desktop. Click **Save**.

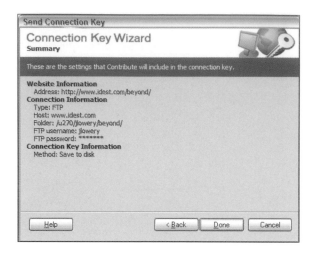

The connection key is one way to give Contribute users in specific roles access to the site in a secure manner. A **connection key** is actually an encrypted file containing the login information—username and password, among other details—for the remote site. When you double-click a connection key to open it, Contribute launches (if necessary), and the appropriate setup dialog box appears. As you've seen, it's password protected, so you'll need to communicate the password to your users. Later in this chapter, you'll use the connection key to experience Contribute—and the Publisher role—for yourself.

Now, it's time to establish some limits for those Contribute users in the Writer role.

---

8 In the **Users who have connected** section of the **Administer Website** dialog box, select **Writer**, and click the **Edit Role Settings** button. In the **Edit "Publisher" Settings** dialog box, click the **General** category, and verify the **Allow users to publish files** check box is turned off.

In the default Contribute settings, the key difference between Publishers and Writers is that Writers cannot publish their files directly to the Web. Instead, they will be offered an option to send the file for review. Typically, they would send the file to their superior, a

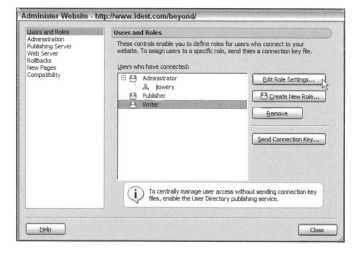

Contribute Publisher, who can either send it back to them for further modification or publish it. Contribute contains an entire approval system for working with drafts in this manner.

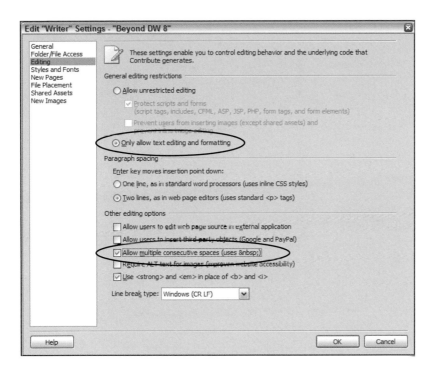

9 In the Edit "Writer" Settings dialog box, click the Editing category. In the General editing restrictions section, select the Only allow text editing and formatting radio button. In the Other editing options section, turn on the Allow multiple consecutive spaces check box.

In this step, you've restricted those in the Writers role to basic text editing and formatting. With this option selected, Contribute users cannot insert or modify tables, images, or links. They can, however, change text content and styles or create unordered and ordered lists.

Whether you opt to allow multiple consecutive spaces is purely a judgment call. On one hand, it does give users some control over the document appearance, similar to the options available in word-processing software, but on the other hand, it opens the door to excessive use of the nonbreaking space code (** **).

10 Click the **Styles and Fonts** category. Turn off the **Allow users to apply fonts and sizes** and **Allow users to apply font color and background color** check boxes.

Text styling is of paramount importance to the designer. It's best to limit the ways content contributors can format the text. As you'll see later in this chapter, the best course is to develop CSS style sheets with the Contribute users in mind. Therefore, you want to allow them to apply pre-designed styles only, thereby preventing them from making unapproved changes to type-faces, font sizes, and colors.

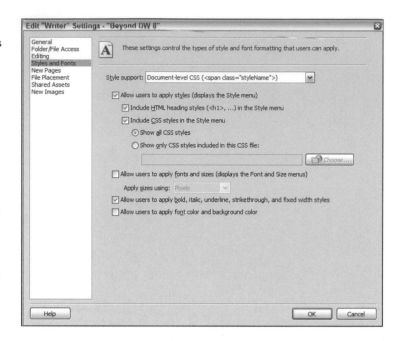

11 Click the **New Pages** category. Turn off the **Create a blank page** and **Use built-in starter pages** check boxes. Still in the **Edit "Writer" Settings** dialog box, click **OK** to confirm your settings for the Writer role and return to the **Administer Website** dialog box.

It's important to realize that changes made in one role, such as the Publisher, do not trickle down to other roles. In almost all cases (the exception is the Shared Assets category discussed in the shared_assets.mov movie in the videos folder on the CD-ROM), you'll need to apply the desired settings in all roles.

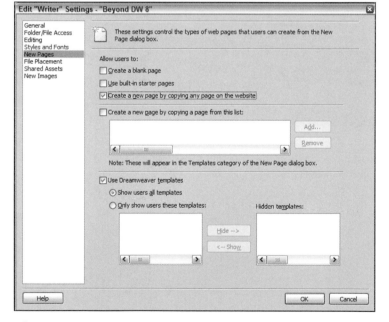

We've just touched on the possibilities for managing your users' options in Contribute. The rule of thumb is the larger the organization, the more Contribute roles you'll need—and the more varied they'll be. As administrator, you're responsible for adjusting other sitewide settings, including two of the most important: passwords and rollbacks.

12 In the **Administer Website** dialog box, click the **Administration** category. Click **Set Administrator Password**. In the **Change Administrator Password** dialog box, type **beyond** in the **New password** box, and then type **beyond** again in the **Confirm new password** box. Click **OK**.

Even if you're the sole designer on a site, it's a good idea to password-protect your Contribute administrative settings. Administrators have a great deal of control over the Contribute experience, and you want to be sure your client's experience is secured and protected.

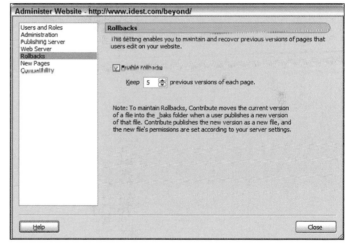

13 Click the **Rollbacks** category. Turn on the **Enable rollbacks** check box, and set **Keep X previous versions of each page** to **5**. Click **Close** to complete the **Administer Website** dialog box, and then click **OK** to close the **Site Definition for Beyond DW 8** dialog box.

In Contribute, a **rollback** is a previous version of a published page. With rollbacks turned on, you're effectively saving a series of snapshots of each page so you can republish if necessary. The number of versions you save is, again, completely up to you and your clients. If you want, you can save up to 99 versions. However, it's important to keep in mind that for each rollback version, you're potentially storing a copy of the entire site, so available server storage may be an issue.

In this exercise, you learned how to set up the administration of a Contribute site in Dreamweaver 8 and how to apply the most common settings, particularly in establishing the different Contribute roles. In the next exercise, you'll develop Dreamweaver 8 templates with the Contribute user in mind.

2 | Building Contribute-Friendly Templates

What's the difference between designing templates for use in Dreamweaver 8 and those for use in Contribute? The end user. If you create a template you know you or another Web-savvy designer will be using to create new pages in Dreamweaver 8, your template can include fewer, more all-encompassing editable regions because you trust the skills and design sense of the user—you.

Contribute users, however, are by and large not Web designers, and they don't want to be. Their goal is to update Web content quickly and without breaking the page or causing any additional work. For Contribute users, templates must expose only those content areas that should be changed while maintaining a high degree of flexibility.

In this exercise, you'll convert a standard HTML page to a Contribute-friendly template with tightly focused editable regions, easily applicable optional regions, and expandable repeat regions. You'll then learn to update Web pages as if you were a Contribute user.

1 In the **Files** panel, open **contribute_example.htm** from the **chap_12** folder you copied to your desktop.

In this example HTML page, you'll find a range of page objects within the content area. A main heading is followed by a subheading and a couple of paragraphs of content. A boxed area proclaiming an occasional special appears above a two-column table of details. On the right are a single photo and a caption—with plenty of room for more. You'll start by converting the page to a template.

2 Choose **File > Save as Template**. In the **Save As Template** dialog box, leave the default suggestion, **contribute_example**, in the **Save as** box, and click **Save**. When Dreamweaver 8 prompts you to update links, click **Yes**.

With the template converted, the first task is to begin assigning editable regions.

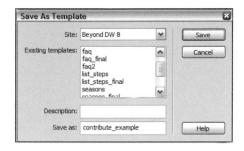

3 In **Design** view, select the **<h1>** text, **London calling…**. In the **Insert** bar, click the **Common** category, and click the button **Templates: Editable Region**. In the **New Editable Region** dialog box, type **Headline** in the **Name** box, and click **OK**. Replace the existing text with **Headline…**. Select the **<h2>** text, **Abbey Road Suites in London, England**, and repeat the same process, naming the editable region **Location** and typing **Enter location here** as the placeholder text.

With both the heading and the subheading, you want to make sure just the text within the tags is editable, not the tags themselves. This method accomplishes several goals. First, you make sure an **<h1>** heading and an **<h2>** subheading are always present. If you enclosed one or more of the tags in an editable region, Contribute users could easily delete them. Second, by keeping the tags outside the editable region, you retain any classes or additional styling. Finally, the editable tag positioning prevents users from inserting their own block-level tags, such as **<h3>** or **<p>**.

Next, you'll use a different strategy—one that allows the user to add as many paragraphs as desired—to set editable regions for the main paragraph areas.

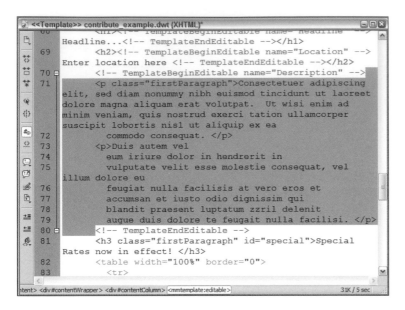

4 Position your cursor in the first paragraph of text, and from the **Tag Selector**, choose **<p .firstParagraph>**. Switch to **Code** view. Hold down the **Shift** key, and then drag to extend the selection to include the second paragraph in the content area. In the **Insert** bar, click the **Common** category, and click the button **Templates: Editable Region**. In the **New Editable Region** dialog box, type **Description** in the **Name** box. Click **OK**.

For this editable region, the outer tags are intentionally enclosed. In Dreamweaver 8 templates, including one or more **<p>** tags allows users to insert additional paragraphs if necessary. To Contribute users, this means increased flexibility.

5 Switch to **Design** view. In the **Description** editable region, select and delete the opening paragraph. Press **Enter** (Windows) or **Return** (Mac) to create a new paragraph. Enter the following text:

Describe the property in a few short paragraphs. Keep your sentences short and lively. To get the right look, put your cursor anywhere in the first paragraph and choose firstParagraph from the toolbar's Style list.

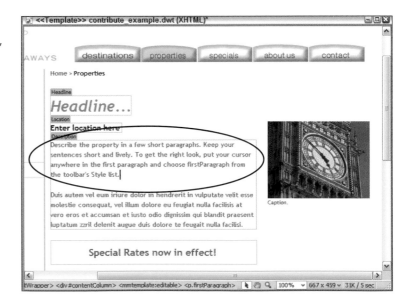

6 In the **Property Inspector**, from the **Style** list, choose **firstParagraph**.

Part of your task as a Dreamweaver 8 designer is to guide the Contribute user however you can. Aside from selectively applying editable regions, you can also name any template region descriptively. So far, you've named each region clearly: Headline, Location, and Description.

Additionally, you can speak to the user directly through the placeholder text and provide any suggestions for content or necessary styles. Although you have a minor risk of the user leaving in the message, the same danger applies to "greeked" text such as Lorem ipsom. Generally, Contribute users quickly catch and fix these errors.

Next, you'll apply a different type of template region to enhance the Contribute page's options.

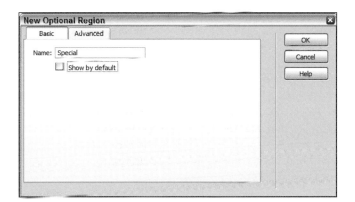

7 Position your cursor in the text **Special Rates now in effect**, and from the **Tag Selector**, choose **<h3 #special>**. In the **Insert** bar, click the **Common** category, and click the button **Templates: Optional Region**. In the **New Optional Region** dialog box, select the **Basic** tab, and type **Special** in the **Name** box. Turn off the **Show by default** check box. Click **OK**.

Optional regions are terrific for both Dreamweaver 8 designers and Contribute users. They provide a method for designers to expand the functionality and content of a page in a controlled fashion—and they're an easy way for Contribute users to add entire blocks of set content, images, or whatever at design time. You can include editable regions within optional regions or, as you you've done here, keep the content locked.

Next, you'll create editable regions for entries in a table.

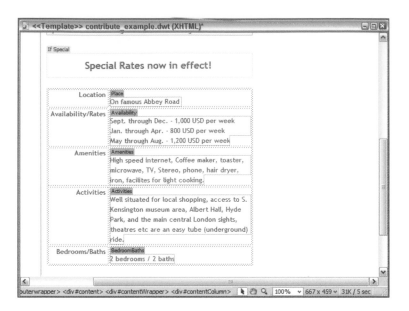

8 Next to the **Location** label, select the content in the table cell. In the **Insert** bar, click the **Common** category, and click the button **Templates: Editable Region**. In the **New Editable Region** dialog box, type **Place**, and click **OK**. Repeat the same procedure for each of the table cells in the same column, and name them **Availability**, **Amenities**, **Activities**, and **BedroomBath**, respectively.

Another way to help the Contribute user is by example. Rather than include greeked text—which would provide no clues as to what type of content is expected—the example content shows the way.

Next, you'll turn your attention to the content area images and captions.

---

9 Select the image in the right column. In the **Insert** bar, click the **Common** category, and click the button **Templates: Editable Region**. In the **New Editable Region** dialog box, type **Image** in the **Name** box, and click **OK**. Select the placeholder text **Caption**, and using the same procedure, create an editable region called **Caption**.

You want to give individual control to Contribute users so they can insert their own images and captions.

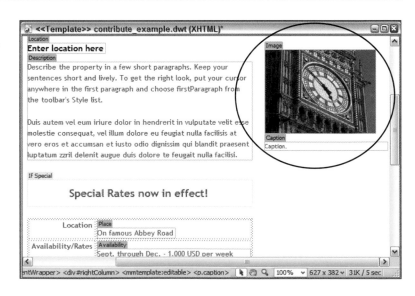

Macromedia Dreamweaver 8 Beyond the Basics : H·O·T

However, you want to make sure both are inserted. An all-too-common mistake made by those creating templates for Contribute users is to group adjacent editable regions. To ensure each section is included, use separate editable regions.

Next, you'll apply a repeat region so Contribute users can insert as many pictures as they'd like.

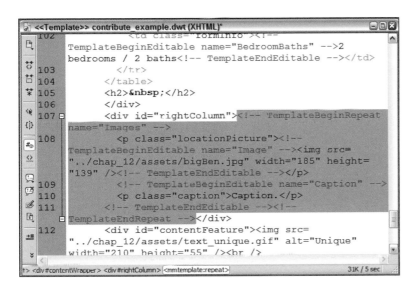

10 Select the image in the right column. From the **Tag Selector**, choose **<p .locationPicture>**. Switch to **Code** view. Hold down the **Shift** key, and drag to extend the selection to include the second **<!-- TemplateEndEditable -->** tag, after the **Caption** placeholder text. In the **Insert** bar, click the **Common** category, and click the button **Templates: Repeating Region**. In the **New Repeating Region** dialog box, type **Images** in the **Name** box, and click **OK**.

Here, both the image and the caption are included in a repeat region. When the Contribute user modifies a page created from this template, a small bar with Add, Remove, Up, and Down controls appears above the repeat region. By clicking the Add button, the user can insert another set of image and caption placeholders.

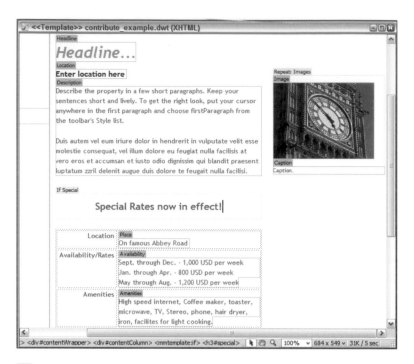

11 Switch to **Design** view. Press **Ctrl+S** (Windows) or **Cmd+S** (Mac) to save your template. If you receive a message from Dreamweaver 8 informing you that you've placed an editable region inside a block element, click **OK**. Choose **Site > Put** to publish **contribute_example.dwt**. If you are prompted to upload dependent files, click **Yes**. When the file transfer process is complete, close **contribute_example.dwt**.

The message displayed when you save your template is a holdover from earlier times when it was thought users would always want to be able to add content to every editable region. This is emphatically not the case, as shown with the Headline and Location editable regions. If you plan on creating templates for Contribute, it's a good idea—and a real time-saver—to turn on the Don't show me this message again check box.

When you're designing for yourself, you don't normally publish the template. However, in a Contribute-based site, you need to put the templates on the remote site so the Contribute users can access them.

In the following steps, you'll test your template in the environment for which it's intended: Contribute.

12 From the desktop, double-click the **BeyondDW8-Publisher.stc** file exported as a connection key in Exercise 1. (If you don't have this file, complete Exercise 1, and then return to this exercise.) After Contribute launches and the **Import Connection Key: Beyond DW 8** dialog box appears, type your name in the first field, your e-mail in the second field, and **beyond** as the password in the third field. Click **OK**.

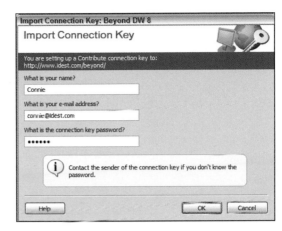

Because the connection key has a Contribute file type, the program automatically launches when you double-click the connection key file. As a designer, it's always a good idea to review your work in the environment in which it will be viewed. Although this often means reviewing your pages in various browsers, in this case, you'll test your page in Contribute. In Contribute, the first step is to create a new page based on the published template.

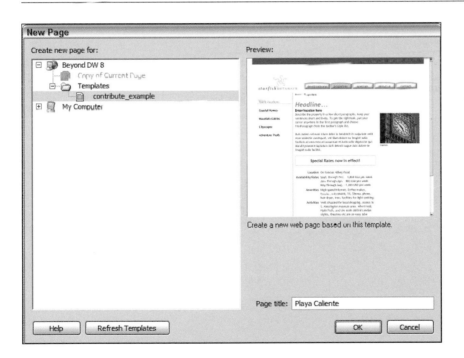

13 In Contribute, choose **File > New Page**. In the **New Page** dialog box, select **contribute_example** from the **Templates** folder. Type **Playa Caliente** in the **Page title** box, and click **OK**.

You'll recall that in Exercise 1, you restricted the method of creating new pages to just copying the current page and the Dreamweaver 8 templates. Because you published the contribute_example.dwt template file in a previous step, it appears listed as a potential template.

14 In the Contribute **Document** window, replace the placeholder text **Headline...** with **Come play on our playa...**, and then replace **Enter location here** with **Playa Caliente, Cabo San Lucas, Mexico**. Replace the first paragraph of placeholder text with the following:

The best beach for the best vacation. Come and relax on our very warm shores.

---

15 Replace the second paragraph of placeholder text with the following:

Playa Caliente offers the modern traveler a unique combination of great climate, upscale activities, unspoiled beauty and incredible cuisine.

Notice how easy it is to add content in Contribute—all users have to do is delete the placeholder text and add their own. Contribute applies the styling automatically. This leads to consistent pages across the entire Web site.

As you'll see next, modifying content in a table is even easier.

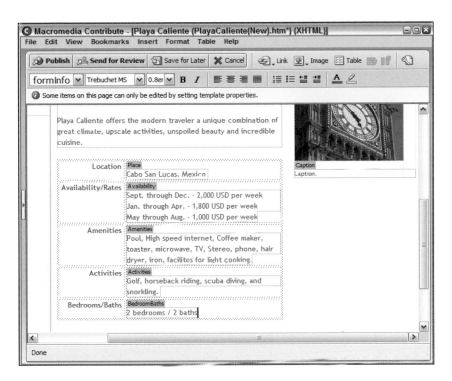

16 Triple-click the placeholder text **On famous Abbey Road** to select it, and replace it with **Cabo San Lucas, Mexico**. Press the **Tab** key to move to the next editable region. Change the following rates: **1,000** to **2,000**; **800** to **1,800**; and **1,200** to **1,000**. Press the **Tab** key, and add **Pool** to the list of amenities. Press the **Tab** key again, and then press **Delete** to remove the entire selected list of activities. Enter the following activities in their place: **Golf, horseback riding, scuba diving, and snorkeling**. Leave the **BedroomBaths** editable region content as is.

A surprising number of word-processing features are built into Contribute, even niceties such as triple-clicking to select a paragraph. Moreover, when editable regions are presented in an orderly fashion like this table, users can use the Tab key to move from one entry to another. The more familiar you become with how Contribute acts, the better you can design for its features.

Next you'll see how you add the optional region to the page.

17 In the message bar at the top of the **Document** window, click the **template properties** link. In the **Template Properties** dialog box, turn on the **Show Special** check box, and click **OK**.

The optional region immediately appears as an integral part of the page. You can easily imagine how you can use optional regions to display images, tables of data, or any other page element.

Next, you'll update an image.

18 Double-click the image in the right column. In the **Image Properties** dialog box, choose **Browse > Images on My Computer**. In the **Open File** dialog box, navigate to the **chap_12/assets** folder, select **pool.jpg**, and click the **Select** button. In the **Description (ALT text)** box, type **Casa Caliente Pool**. Leave all the other fields at their default settings, and click **OK**. In the **Caption** editable region, replace the placeholder text **Caption** with **Our sparkling, refreshing pools await you**.

Even adding images is straightforward in Contribute, when the page is set up prop-

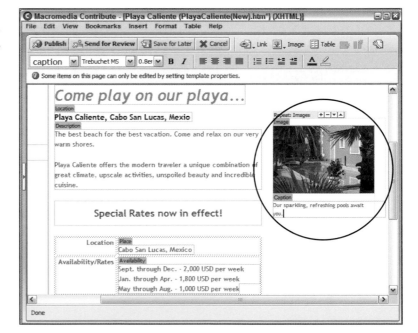

erly. Although it's not obvious to the Contribute user, a style is applied to the paragraph containing the image to assure proper padding and margins. Because the editable region you established contains only the `<img>` tag, Contribute invisibly applies the surrounding style.

Now you're ready to add images, thanks to the repeat region included on the page.

Macromedia Contribute - [Playa Caliente (PlayaCaliente(New).htm*) (XHTML)]

File   Edit   View   Bookmarks   Insert   Format   Table   Help

Publish   Send for Review   Save for Later   Cancel   Link   Image   Table   Table Row

caption   Trebuchet MS   0.8er   B   I

Some items on this page can only be edited by setting template properties.

Repeat: Images   +|−|∨|∧
Image

Playa Caliente, Cabo San Lucas, Mexio

Description
The best beach for the best vacation. Come and relax on our very warm shores.

Playa Caliente offers the modern traveler a unique combination of great climate, upscale activities, unspoiled beauty and incredible cuisine.

Special Rates now in effect!

Caption
Our sparkling, refreshing pools await you.

Image

Location : Place
Cabo San Lucas, Mexico

Availability/Rates : Availability
Sept. through Dec. - 2,000 USD per week
Jan. through Apr. - 1,800 USD per week
May through Aug. - 1,000 USD per week

Amenities : Amenities
Pool, High speed internet, Coffee maker, toaster, microwave, TV, Stereo, phone, hair dryer, iron, facilitor for light cooking

Caption
Spacious modern living rooms included.

Done

19 In the **Repeat: Images** control bar, click **Add (+)**. Repeat the process in Step 18 to replace the placeholder image with **living_room.jpg** in the **chap_12/assets** folder; in the **Description** box, type **Living Room**. Change the associated caption to **Spacious modern living rooms included**. Repeat the entire process to add a third image, using **beach_scene.jpg** for the graphic, **Beach scene** for the description, and **Enjoy pure white, open beaches** for the caption.

Repeat regions offer great flexibility at design time for the Contribute user. On a properly designed page, the user can add as many images as desired, and the layout expands as needed. By grouping the image and the caption in the repeat region, you're assured every image will have a description.

20 In Contribute, click **Publish** on the main toolbar. Contribute will warn you that viewers will not be able to find your page without a link; click **Yes** to continue publishing. In the **Publish New Page** dialog box, accept the suggested page name, and click **Publish**. In the **Congratulations** dialog box, click **OK**. After you've finished reviewing your page, close Contribute.

After the publishing operation is completed, your new page appears in Contribute's built-in browser. The site administrator, or anyone with sufficient editing and publishing privileges, can add links to the page.

This exercise showed you how you can fine-tune your Dreamweaver 8 template skills for a Contribute audience with precisely crafted editable regions, flexible optional regions, and expanding repeat regions. You also practiced updating a Web page from the point of view of a Contribute user. In the next exercise, you'll see how you should craft your CSS styles to further help Contribute users.

3 | Structuring CSS Correctly

You must take special care when creating CSS styles in a Contribute-based site. Although you can restrict any Contribute role to simple text editing with no control over styling whatsoever, this limitation is generally imposed only on the lowliest content contributor in the organization. Most roles are given the freedom to apply available styles—it is up to the Dreamweaver 8 designer to craft the CSS styles in such a way that they are easy to apply correctly.

Contribute users whose roles are CSS-enabled have the ability to use CSS classes only; other selectors such as tags and IDs apply automatically and contextually. For example, if the Contribute user inserts a `<h1>` tag in a particular `<div>` tag with an ID of **mainContent**, and a style rule for `#mainContent h1` exists, that style will be applied without any further action. When creating CSS classes, you want to be sure to name them in a meaningful way so the user can understand how to apply them.

In this exercise, you'll see how you can use Dreamweaver 8 to make your CSS styles Contribute friendly. You'll also learn how to reveal only certain styles in Contribute by using a filter file as defined in your role as Contribute administrator.

---

1 In the **Files** panel, open **contribute_css.dwt** from the **Templates** folder you copied to your desktop.

Although this template is based on the one completed in the previous exercise, it has some key differences. Specifically, we have attached a different CSS style sheet, ct_main.css, so you can undertake this exercise.

However, many of the same lessons you learned in the previous exercise apply. For example, you'll remember you applied both the Headline and Location editable regions to the content within their respective tags. This placement of the editable regions ensures Contribute will apply the proper style regardless of the content.

2 In the **CSS Styles** panel, switch to **All** mode, if necessary. If the style sheet entry **ct_main.css** is collapsed, expand it. In the list of selectors, locate the body entry, **right-click** (Windows) or **Ctrl+click** (Mac), and choose **Go to Code** from the contextual menu. Change the selector from **body** to **body, p, td, ol, ul**.

To make sure your base styles are all the same, it's a good idea to expand the body selector to include the **<p>**, **<td>**, **<ol>**, and **<ul>** tags. These tags represent most of the situations in which text is used. By incorporating them into the same selector as the **<body>** tag, you're preventing Contribute users from, for example, styling an unordered list in a different font.

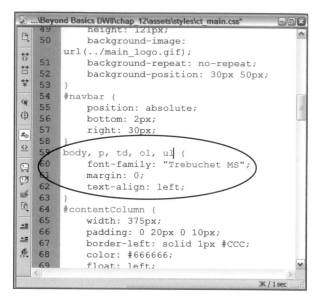

Another good idea for Contribute styles is to give them obvious names. Although you as the designer may remember how you intended a style named **avRed** to be used, the average Contribute user won't have a clue.

---

3 Press **Ctrl+S** (Windows) or **Cmd+S** (Mac) to save the file. Close **ct_main.css**, and return to **contribute_css.dwt**.

In the next step, you'll see how you can use a renaming feature in Dreamweaver 8 to provide more appropriately named styles.

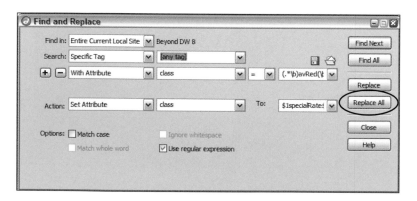

4 In the **CSS Styles** panel, scroll to the bottom of the style sheet. **Right-click** (Windows) or **Ctrl+click** (Mac) the entry **.avRed**, and from the contextual menu, choose **Rename**. In the **Rename Class** dialog box, type **specialRate** in the **New Name** box, and click **OK**. Dreamweaver 8 asks whether you'd like to use the **Find and Replace** feature to rename the class; click **Yes**. In the **Find and Replace** dialog box, click the **Replace All** button. Dreamweaver 8 warns you the operation cannot be undone in closed documents; to continue, click **Yes**.

Dreamweaver 8 recognizes that the class to be renamed is located in an external style sheet and may affect multiple documents in your site. Therefore, Dreamweaver 8 automatically creates a Find and Replace query using the powerful, built-in regular expression engine. With the Use regular expressions check box turned on in the Find and Replace dialog box, you can search (and replace) text patterns, not just text. In this example, Dreamweaver 8 looks for any tag with the class attribute **.avRed** and changes it to **.specialRate**. A separate behind-the-scenes action replaces the class name in the external style sheet.

Note: You must *always* be careful whenever you perform a global search-and-replace operation, and renaming classes is no exception. Be aware that Dreamweaver 8 will replace any instance of the selected class name regardless of the style sheet in which it appears. If, for example, you have used the same class name in two different style sheets for two different templates but want to change only one of them, you should use Find and Replace more selectively, perhaps by opening all the files you want to change and choosing Open Documents in the Find in pop-up menu in the Find and Replace dialog box.

Contribute has the capability to make a subset of all class styles in an attached style sheet available for use. To use this feature, you need to create a separate style sheet that omits any classes you don't want Contribute users to see in their Style pop-up menu. These types of CSS files are called **filter files** because they filter out the classes you don't want.

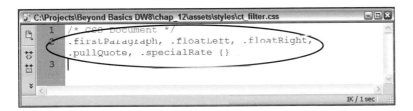

5 Choose **File > New**. In the **New Document** dialog box, select **Basic page** in the **Category** list, and select **CSS** in the **Basic** list. Click the **Create** button. After the new document appears, press **Ctrl+S** (Windows) or **Cmd+S** (Mac). In the **Save As** dialog box, navigate to the **chap_12/assets/styles** folder, type **ct_filter.css** in the **File name** box, and click **Save**. In the **Document** window, type the following code:

.firstParagraph, .floatLeft, .floatRight, .pullQuote, .specialRate {}

A filter file does not need to have all the properties you would normally see in a CSS file, although you could include them if you wanted to do so. You simply need to list the classes you want displayed in a comma-separated list, just as you typically group selectors.

6 Press **Ctrl+S** (Windows) or **Cmd+S** (Mac). Close **ct_filter.css**.

You need to perform a couple more steps before you can use the filter file. You'll need to publish the file to the remote site, and you'll need to establish the proper role settings as the Contribute administrator.

7 In the **Files** panel, expand the **chap_12/assets/styles** folder, and select **ct_filter.css**. In the **Files** panel toolbar, click the **Put** icon.

For the filter file to be assigned, you must put it on the remote site.

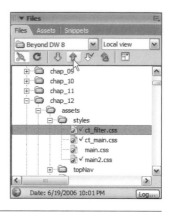

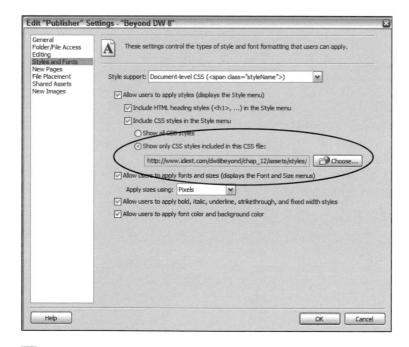

8 In the **Files** panel, double-click the site name, **Beyond DW 8**. When the **Site Definition** for Beyond DW 8 dialog box opens, click the **Contribute** category, and click the **Administer Site in Contribute** button. In the **Administrator Password** dialog box, type **beyond** in the **Password** box, and click **OK**. In the **Administer Website** dialog box, select the **Publisher** role, and click **Edit Role Settings**. In the **Edit "Publisher" Settings** dialog box, click the **Styles and Fonts** category, and turn on the **Show only CSS styles included in this CSS file** check box. Click the **Choose** button. In the **Choose File on Website** dialog box, double-click the **folder** icon to display the uploaded files and folders. Navigate to the **chap_12/assets/styles** folder, choose **ct_filter.css**, and click **OK**. Click **OK** again to close the **Edit "Publisher" Settings** dialog box. In the **Administer Website** dialog box, select the **Writer** role, and repeat this process to assign the filter file. When you're done, click **Close**. In the **Site Definition for Beyond DW 8** dialog box, click **OK**.

To test the effectiveness of the filter file, you'll publish the template and return to Contribute.

9 In the **Document** toolbar, choose **File Management > Put**. After the file transfer has completed, close **contribute_css.dwt**. Open **Contribute**, and click **New Page** on the main toolbar. In the **New Page** dialog box, under **Templates**, select **contribute_css**. Type **cssTest** in the **Page Title** box, and click **OK**. When the page opens, select the **1,200** amount in the **Availability** editable region, and choose **specialRate** from the **Style** list. Notice only those classes in the filter file appear, along with the heading tags. Click **Cancel** in the main toolbar. When Contribute asks whether you'd like to permanently delete your page, click **Yes**. Close **Contribute**.

Filtered CSS styles have the advantage of presenting exactly what the user has to work with and no more. This makes it much easier to apply styles and achieve the result the designer intended.

In this chapter, you learned how to use Dreamweaver 8 to create a better experience for Contribute users. As a Dreamweaver 8 designer, you can administer the Contribute site and tailor the Contribute users' access as needed. As you've seen, you also have the ability to craft your templates to make them easier to use in Contribute. Finally, you learned how to work with CSS—from naming styles to creating a filter file—to achieve the best results in Contribute. In the next chapter, you'll see how to optimize your site to get the most out of search engines.

13

Optimizing for Search Engines

A Web site owner's worst nightmare is a beautiful, costly site with no visitors. Search engines are the Web's primary vehicle for driving traffic to a site—and savvy Web designers construct each page with this in mind. A site properly optimized for search engines will be easier to find both for those familiar with the site and for those seeking its content.

Many experts are willing to tell you—and sell you—the secret to search engine success. Our technique is simple: Help search engines do their job. A search engine's primary objective is to return the most relevant results to a search query. By presenting the information your pages contain in ways a search engine understands best, you're effectively proclaiming, "Here I am!" in a loud, clear voice when everyone else is mumbling.

This chapter explores three levels of site development. First, you'll discover search engine optimization at the page level. You'll see how combining appropriate **<title>** and **<meta>** tags with relevant content, syntactically styled, can make your page stand out in the search results. Next, you'll create a single file—the site map—to help both search robots and Web visitors find what they need. Finally, you'll create an external file to help the biggest search engine of them all, Google, index your site thoroughly. As you now know, a discovered site is on its way to becoming a successful site.

1 | Optimizing Your Pages for Search

When someone types words or phrases in a search engine such as Google, Yahoo, or MSN Search, the goal is to find the Web pages with content matching the search criteria. For us, the key phrase in the prior sentence is **Web pages**. All searches ultimately resolve at the page level. Consequently, it's simply not enough to submit your site to one of these search engines. Search engine optimization starts in the design stage for every page in the site.

In this exercise, you'll learn which tags to target—such as the **<title>** and description **<meta>** tags—and how these tags work with a page's content, particularly when you structure your page correctly with **<h1>** and **<p>** tags.

1 In the **Files** panel, open **seo_example.htm** from the **chap_13** folder you copied to your desktop.

We have purposely stripped this page of all relevant search engine optimization aids for this exercise. You'll start by adding a title.

2 In the **Document** toolbar, type **Affordable Vacations in Paris** in the **Title** field, and press **Enter** (Windows) or **Return** (Mac).

Titles are one of the most important elements a search engine examines when indexing a page. It is extremely important your title contain the most pertinent keywords for the page. The example title, Affordable Vacations in Paris, is brief but, more important, combines a series of keywords; it's easy to see how someone might search for precisely these terms when looking for a Parisian getaway. However, a title alone is not enough; titles are more effective when combined with related keywords.

Note: One of the most common errors by novice Dreamweaver 8 designers is to leave the default title, Untitled Document, when they publish the page. You can avoid this pitfall by choosing Site > Reports and selecting Untitled Documents for the entire current local site. In addition to flagging pages with the default—and meaningless—title Untitled Document, Dreamweaver 8 also reports errors for empty, missing, or multiple title tags.

---

3 In the **Insert** bar, click the **HTML** category, and click the button **Head: Keywords**. In the **Keywords** dialog box, type **Paris vacation, trip, escape, getaway, Eiffel Tower, Champs-Elysee, Louvre, affordable, inexpensive, Starfish Getaways**. Click **OK**.

The keyword `<meta>` tag describes the content on your page in terms that someone might type into a search engine. Simply type a number of words or phrases, separated by commas. Be sure to place your most relevant terms first; search engines are often restricted in the number of keywords they will read.

If your title is adequately descriptive, repeat words used in the title as your keywords. Fill out your keywords with synonyms (for example, trip, escape, and getaway) and specific references to page content (for example, Eiffel Tower, Champs-Elysee, and Louvre). We almost always include a reference to the site name so searchers looking for specific content on a given site will be taken straight to the desired page.

---

4 In the **Insert** bar, click the **HTML** category, and click the button **Head: Description**. In the **Description** dialog box, type **Enjoy the most affordable vacation of your life in beautiful Paris, centrally located near the Eiffel Tower and the Louvre.** Click **OK**.

Search engines use the description `<meta>` tag in two ways. First, they look at its contents in combination with that of the keyword `<meta>` tag and the `<title>` tag to further determine how to index the page. Second, they may use what you type in the description `<meta>` tag in their search results. This gives you an opportunity to speak directly to the Web visitors searching for sites like yours.

Because search engines are limited in the number of words they can display—and the limits vary wildly—it's best to put the most important part of your message in the first part of your sentence and to keep the length of your description fewer than 25 words.

Next, you'll add a lesser-known but search engine–critical `<meta>` tag: robots.

---

5 In the **Insert** bar, click the **HTML** category, and click the button **Head: Meta**. In the **Meta** dialog box, make sure **Attribute** is set to **Name**, and in the **Value** field, type **robots**. In the **Content** field, type **index,follow**. Click **OK**.

The robots `<meta>` tag tells a search engine spider—the indexing tool that crawls through your site gathering information—whether to index the current page and whether to follow the links contained on the page. Because you'll want to have the spider index and follow the links on most of the pages in your site, you'll use the following syntax:

```
<meta name="robots" content="index,follow" />
```

If you were working with a page where you didn't want the spider to index it or follow the links, your robots `<meta>` tag would look like this:

```
<meta name="robots" content="noindex,nofollow" />
```

You can also use this tag to identify pages you want indexed but not followed (`index,nofollow`), or vice versa (`noindex,follow`).

The `<title>`, keyword `<meta>`, and description `<meta>` tags all work together to give the search engine an overview of your page behind the scenes. You can also have an impact on your search engine placement by carefully wording your headings in the visible page content.

6 In the **Document** window, select the placeholder text **Heading**, and replace it with **affordable paris vacations**. Next, replace the placeholder text **Subheading 1** with **Enjoy Paris in the springtime, summertime, anytime**. Finally, replace the placeholder text **Subheading 2** with **See the City of Lights from the ideal location**.

For search engines, if content is king, then semantically correct content is an emperor. When search engine spiders index a page, they examine the entire page, not just the `<head>` area. Content in the page that is placed in `<h1>` tags, such as the example heading, is ranked higher than other content. Similarly, other content in other heading tags—`<h2>` through `<h6>`—is ranked higher than content in `<p>` tags. You'll achieve the maximum search engine optimization by using your primary keywords (previously applied to the `<title>` and various `<meta>` tags) in the content of the page, both in the headings and in the standard paragraphs.

7 Press **Ctrl+S** (Windows) or **Cmd+S** (Mac) to save **seo_example.htm**, and then close the file.

In this exercise, you saw how to approach search engine optimization at the page level, first by properly using the **<title>** tag and then by crafting appropriate content for both the keyword and description **<meta>** tags. Correctly using the robots **<meta>** tag makes sure search engine spiders will index the desired pages on your site. Finally, you saw how to enhance your page's rankings in search engine results by relating your headings to the title and **<meta>** tag content. In the next exercise, you'll learn how to create a site map to help both your site visitors and the search engine spiders find what they're looking for more quickly.

---

2 | Developing a Site Map

A site map is an excellent way to provide your visitors with an overview of your site structure while offering direct navigation. A site map also serves as a great single page to submit to search engines; with one page, you have links to all the pages in your site you want indexed. Typically, a **site map** is a page of links for every key page in your site. In this exercise, you'll expand on an existing site map for Starfish Getaways and then give the site map some much-needed flair with CSS.

1 In the **Files** panel, open **sitemap.htm** from the **chap_13** folder you copied to your desktop.

As you can see, this site map uses unordered lists to structure the links to the various pages in the site. We've completed a good portion of the site map (with pseudolinks) so you can see an example of the basic setup. Next, you'll add a couple of links of your own.

2 Place your cursor after the **Mexico** entry, and press **Enter** (Windows) or **Return** (Mac). Press **Tab** to indent the unordered list, and type **Acapulco**. Press **Enter** (Windows) or **Return** (Mac) again, and type **Cabo San Lucas**. Press **Enter** (Windows) or **Return** (Mac) a final time, and type **Yucatan**.

Unordered lists are perfect for site maps. Not only can you quickly and easily add new entries at any given level, but you can also create a new sublevel by simply pressing the Tab key; Dreamweaver 8 automatically creates a nested unordered list for you.

Naturally, to create an effective site map, you need to convert your entries to links.

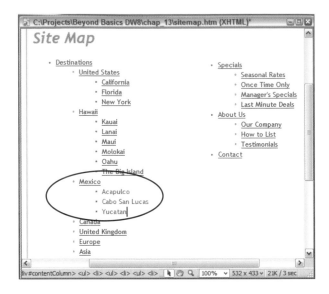

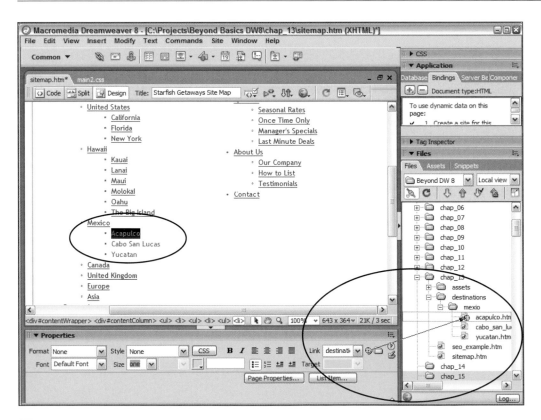

3 Select the **Acapulco** entry just added to the site map. In the **Property Inspector Link** field, drag the **Point to File** icon to the **Files** panel, and point to the **chap_13/destinations/mexico/acapulco.htm** file. (If you need to open a folder, position the dragged target icon over a closed folder, and the folder will expand.) Repeat the process to link **Cabo San Lucas** to **cabo_san_lucas.htm** and **Yucatan** to **yucatan.htm**.

You could, of course, select the Browse for File folder icon instead of using the Point to File method. However, we find the Point to File technique to be much faster, particularly when working with a great number of links, as in a site map.

The site map is perfectly usable as is, both for examination by search-engine spiders and for perusal by human visitors. However, it's a bit mundane for the latter's taste and could use some sprucing up. In the next series of steps, you'll use CSS to add icons for each of the list items. Those links containing other links will have one icon while those pointing to single, contained pages will have another.

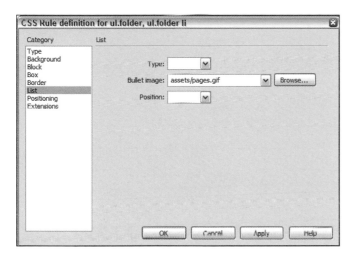

4 In the **CSS Styles** panel, click **New CSS Rule**. In the **New CSS Rule** dialog box, set **Type** to **Advanced**, and in the **Selector** field, type **ul.folder, ul.folder li**. Turn on the **Define in This document only** check box, and click **OK**. In the **CSS Rule definition for ul.folder, ul.folder li** dialog box, click the **Type** category, and set **Line height** to **2 ems**. Click the **List** category, and next to the **Bullet image** pop-up menu, click the **Browse** button. In the **Select Image Source** dialog box, navigate to the **chap_13/assets** folder, and select **pages.gif**. Click **OK**. Repeat the process to create a new CSS rule called **ul li.page**, and select **Bullet image page.gif**, also in the **chap_13/assets** folder.

These style rules define the conditions under which the two icons will appear. The first displays a page icon for any **<ul>** tag with a folder class or any list element under such a tag. Although this may seem a bit broad for a selector, it's necessary to display the multiple page icons for second- and third-level links containing subpages. The key is in application of the classes just defined within the style rules, folder, and page.

5 Place your cursor in the **Destinations** link, and from the **Tag Selector**, choose **<ul>**. From the **Style** list of the **Property Inspector**, choose **folder**. Repeat the process with the **Specials** link in the right column.

As expected, the pages.gif icon appears before every entry because the CSS rule selector includes `ul.folder li`. In the next step, you'll specify which entries are single pages rather than folders.

6 Place your cursor in the **California** link, and from the **Tag Selector**, choose **<li>**. From the **Style** list of the **Property Inspector**, choose **page**. Now, select the remaining list items in this category, **Florida** and **New York**, and apply the **page** style using **Property Inspector**. Repeat this two-step process—setting the **<li>** tag of the first entry in a series to **page** and then selecting the remaining entries before applying the **page** style—for those items under **Hawaii**, **Mexico**, **Specials**, and **About Us**. For example, the first item under **Hawaii** will be **Kauai**, and the first under **Mexico** will be **Acapulco**.

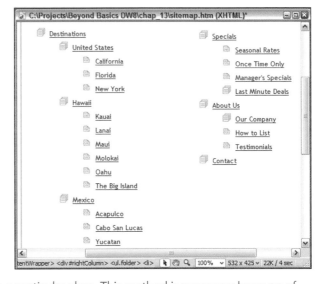

Although this two-step selection and style assignment may seem a bit awkward, it's the fastest way to assign a group of list items to a particular class. This method is necessary because of the way Dreamweaver 8 expands the selection to the parent tag, here **<ul>**, when all the **<li>** tags are selected. Although it takes a little bit longer, all the site map links are now styled appropriately.

7 Press **Ctrl+S** (Windows) or **Cmd+S** (Mac) to save **sitemap.htm**. Close the file.

In this exercise, you learned how to create a site map using unordered lists and the Point to File linking feature in Dreamweaver 8. You also saw how to apply styles to graphically display the difference between links leading to category pages and links leading to end pages. In the next exercise, you'll learn how to construct a Google site map in XML.

3 | Creating a Google Sitemap

With its no-nonsense but whimsical interface—and, most important, lightning-fast search results—Google has quickly become the leading search engine. Since its debut, it has stayed on top by constantly innovating both for visitors typing search criteria and for Web designers submitting sites for indexing. One of its recent innovations is the Google Sitemaps feature. A **Google Sitemap** is an XML (eXtensible Markup Language) file, hosted on your own site, containing information about different pages on your site you want Google to index—including the URL, how frequently the page is updated, and when it was last modified. In other words, a Google Sitemap is a site map intended to help Google do its job better—and help your site at the same time. For more details about the Google Sitemaps initiative, visit **www.google.com/webmasters/sitemaps**.

Like all XML files, the Google Sitemaps format is specific. In this exercise, you'll build a Google Sitemap. The files have only a couple of required XML tags, such as **<url>** and **<loc>**, but they have a number of optional tags, all of which we'll cover throughout the exercise.

Note: This exercise builds on lessons learned in Chapter 8, *"Setting Up an XML Feed."* If you're unfamiliar with XML files and have not completed the exercises in Chapter 8, it is recommended you do so before continuing.

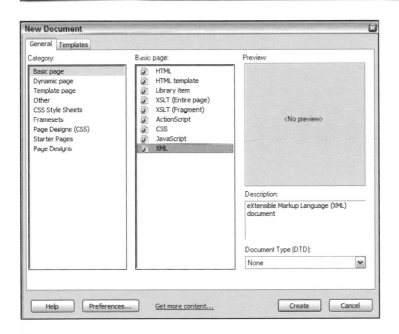

1 Choose **File > New**. In the **New Document** dialog box, click **Basic page** under **Category**, and click **XML** under **Basic page**. Click the **Create** button.

2 Press **Ctrl+S** (Windows) or **Cmd+S** (Mac) to save the file. In the **Save As** dialog box, navigate to the **chap_13** folder, and in the **File name** box, type **sitemap.xml**. Click **OK**. In the XML file, change the **encoding** attribute value from **iso-8859**-1 to **UTF-8**.

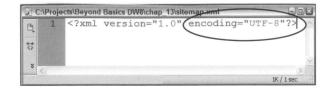

A Google Sitemap requires UTF-8 (**U**niversal **T**ransformation **F**ormat – 8-bit) encoding. The UTF-8 encoding format allows characters from many languages, including Greek, Cyrillic, Armenian, Hebrew, and Arabic, as well as Western Latin.

3 Place your cursor at the end of the initial code line, and press **Enter** (Windows) or **Return** (Mac). Type the following code:

```
<urlset xmlns="http://www.google.com/schemas/sitemap/0.84">
</urlset>
```

The **<urlset>** tag acts as the containing tag for the Google Sitemap file. All additional XML code will appear within the **<urlset>**...**</urlset>** tag pair. Next, you'll add your first site map entry.

4 Place your cursor at the end of the opening **<urlset>** tag, and press **Tab**. Press **Enter** (Windows) or **Return** (Mac) to create a new line, and type the following code:

```
<url>
  <loc>http://www.starfishgetaways.com/destinations/hawaii/oahu.htm</loc>
</url>
```

Each site map entry is enclosed in a **<url>** tag. At a minimum, each entry must further include a **<loc>** tag, short for *location*, with a fully qualified URL, as shown in this step.

NOTE:

Entering Dynamic Links in a Google Sitemap

Although all the links in this exercise are to static pages, it's also possible to link to dynamic pages, even those with parameters. However, you must be sure to encode your URLs properly in the **<loc>** tag. For example, you would type the **http://mydynamicsite.com/products.htm?ID=23&Cat=12** Web address like this: **http://mydynamicsite.com/products.htm?ID=23&Cat=12**. As you can see, you replace the ampersand character (**&**) with the corresponding character entity (**&**). Here's a handy chart of characters requiring character entities when using Google Sitemaps:

Characters for Google Sitemap		
Name	**Character**	**Escape Code**
Ampersand	&	&amp;
Single quotation	'	&apos;
Double quotation	"	&quot;
Greater than	>	&gt;
Less than	<	&lt;

5 With your cursor at the end of the closing **</url>** tag, press **Enter** (Windows) or **Return** (Mac) to create a new line, and type the following code:

```
<url>
  <loc>http://www.starfishgetaways.com/destinations/hawaii/kauai.htm</loc>
  <lastmod>2006-10-18</lastmod>
</url>
```

The **<lastmod>** tag is optional and indicates the date the page was last modified. The date value should be in the YYYY-MM-DD format, as shown in this step.

6 With your cursor at the end of the closing **</url>** tag, press **Enter** (Windows) or **Return** (Mac) to create a new line, and type the following code:

```
<url>
  <loc>http://www.starfishgetaways.com/destinations/hawaii/lanai.htm</loc>
  <changefreq>monthly</changefreq>
</url>
```

The **<changefreq>** tag tells Google how frequently the referenced page is updated. The accepted values are **always**, **hourly**, **daily**, **weekly**, **monthly**, **yearly**, and **never**. Use **always** if your page is continually being updated, perhaps through an external feed, and use **never** if the page has been archived. Google looks at the **<changefreq>** value as a suggestion rather than a command; **<changefreq>** is also an optional tag.

7 With your cursor at the end of the closing **</url>** tag, press **Enter** (Windows) or **Return** (Mac) to create a new line, and type the following code:

```
<url>
  <loc>http://www.starfishgetaways.com/destinations/hawaii/ </loc>
  <priority>0.8</priority>
</url>
```

The **<priority>** tag sets the relative priority of the referenced page to other pages on your site. An optional tag, **<priority>**, is typically used only for those pages you want to rank higher than other similar pages. For example, let's say someone searches Google with the following keywords: hawaii vacation maui. If you'd prefer the search results to go to the main Hawaii page, which has links to all the individual islands, you'd set the Google Sitemap file as shown in this step. Acceptable values are from 0.0 to 1.0, with 0.5 as the default value.

Note: You'll notice you can include a URL pointing to a folder without specifying the default page in a **<loc>** tag. Make sure to include the trailing forward slash after the folder name in the Web address path.

8 Press **Ctrl+S** (Windows) or **Cmd+S** (Mac) to save your file. In the **Document** toolbar, choose **File Management > Put**. After the page has been transferred, close **sitemap.xml**.

If you were working on a standard site, rather than a test site for the exercises in this book, the next step would be to submit your site map to Google. To do so, visit **http://google.com/webmasters/sitemaps/siteoverview/**, and sign in to your Google account. (If you do not have a Google account, follow the instructions for setting one up.) After you've logged in, type the full Web address of the sitemaps.xml file in the Add Site field, and click OK. Although you could type a standard URL as well, we've found that the results begin appearing on Google much faster when submitting a Google Sitemaps file versus the base URL of your site.

In this exercise, you learned how to create a Google Sitemaps file. Google Sitemaps are comprised of required tags, such as **<url>** and **<loc>**, and optional tags, such as **<priority>** and **<changefreq>**.

In this chapter, you learned how to optimize individual pages to get the most out of search engine placement by combining the proper use of the **<title>**, keyword **<meta>**, description **<meta>**, and robots **<meta>** tags with meaningful content, syntactically presented using heading and paragraph tags. You also learned how to develop a site map for presentation on the site and a Google Sitemaps file for submission to the leading search engine. In the next chapter, you'll learn how to maximize the forms on your site for accessibility and stylishness.

14

Building Usable Forms

The more advanced your Web sites become, the more complex your forms are likely to be. Forms are essential for visitor communication; therefore, they should be easy to use, engaging, and functional.

Two problems you'll face when creating complex forms are readability and usability. Getting a visitor's name and e-mail is easy; forms with just a few fields are manageable. However, try getting all the data you need for an online purchase—addresses, shipping options, credit card information, and more—and the form can quickly become difficult to navigate. Fortunately, modern browsers support two tags, **<fieldset>** and **<legend>**, that can help you group related form elements and make visual sense out of a hodgepodge of labels, fields, check boxes, and buttons. In this chapter, you'll learn how to apply these tags to an existing table and how to work with these tags from a clean slate.

CSS can also help you create successful forms. Filling out a big form is often pure drudgery; applying CSS judiciously can make forms more interesting and easier to use. The exercises in this chapter show you how to match your forms to the look and feel of your site while taking advantage of rarely used selectors to guide visitors through the forms. You'll also learn how to apply the **accesskey** and **tabindex** attributes to comply with accessibility standards and enhance usability.

Understanding Fieldsets and Legends

A **fieldset** is a collection of form fields wrapped within a border; a **legend** is the title of a fieldset displayed in the upper-left corner of the surrounding border. You can use the two elements together to distinguish a group of form fields from another in the same form. You might, for example, have one area of an online order form for the billing information and another area for the shipping information. Fieldsets and legends provide a logical grouping for site visitors so they can quickly grasp what's expected.

In Dreamweaver 8, you can insert **<fieldset>** and **<legend>** tags by using the **Fieldset** dialog box. To open the **Fieldset** dialog box, choose **Insert > Form > Fieldset**, or click the **Fieldset** button at the far right of the **Forms** category in the **Insert bar**.

Once the **Fieldset** dialog box appears, all you need to do is specify the legend to use.

Although you can easily add a fieldset and a legend to a Web page in Dreamweaver 8, you must apply a fieldset only under specific circumstances: First, the **<fieldset>** tag must surround a complete table or series of paragraphs; you cannot wrap a **<fieldset>** tag around **<tr>** or **<td>** tags within a table. Second, the fieldset border extends to the width of the containing element. If no **<div>** tag or other such element encompasses the fieldset, its border expands to 100 percent of the browser

Modern browsers widely support the CSS styling of fieldsets and legends. As you'll see later in this chapter, you can control the fieldset's border and background characteristics as well as the legend's text properties, including color, font, and size.

1 | Adding a Fieldset and a Legend

In this exercise, you'll add a fieldset and a legend to an existing table of form elements, and you'll build a complete form with a fieldset and a legend from the start. In both circumstances, you'll see how much easier it is to understand what information is expected in the form once the **<fieldset>** and **<legend>** tags are in place.

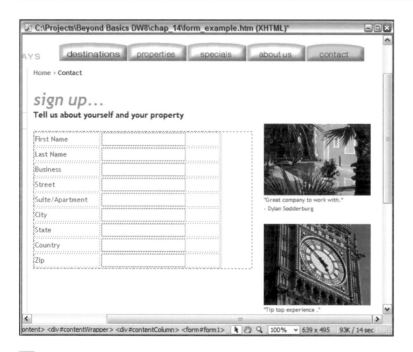

1 In the **Files** panel, open **form_example.htm** from the **chap_14** folder you copied to your desktop. If the red border around the form is not visible, choose **View > Visual Aids > Invisible Elements**.

In the form_example.htm file, a form with a typical series of form elements is already in place. Like many forms, this form uses a basic two-column format, with the labels in the first column. In the next exercise, you'll use CSS to style both the labels and the form elements, but for now, you'll focus on adding the first fieldset.

2 Place your cursor in the form area by selecting any form element, such as the **First Name** field. From the **Tag Selector**, choose the **<table>** tag.

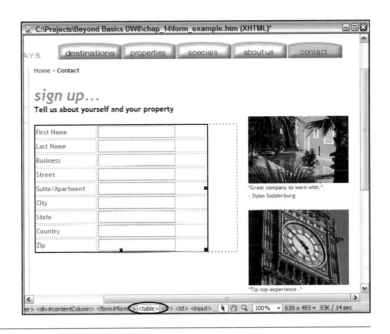

3 In the **Insert** bar, click **Fieldset**. In the **Fieldset** dialog box, type **Your Details** in the **Legend** field, and click **OK**.

4 In the **Document** toolbar, choose **Visual Aids > Hide All** to view the fieldset and legend in Dreamweaver 8.

As you can see, the form fields now appear inside a bordered area with the phrase Your Details. The border is the fieldset, and the phrase is the legend; together they make it much easier to visually understand what the form does. You'll want to keep your legend succinct but informative. The best legends work almost sub-liminally; the site visitor should be able to read and understand them without thinking about them.

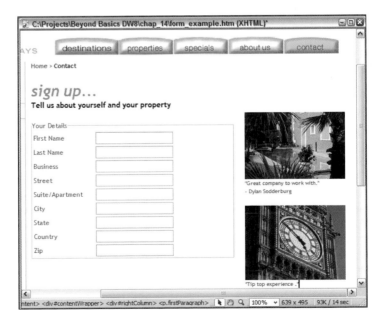

The previous steps work well for existing form elements, but how do you build a fieldset and legend from scratch? In the next series of steps, you'll add the necessary code and the content in the proper places.

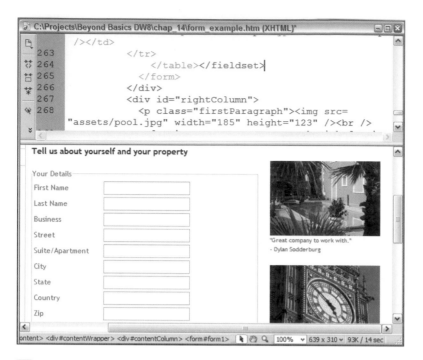

```
/></td>
263        </tr>
264            </table></fieldset>
265        </form>
266    </div>
267    <div id="rightColumn">
268        <p class="firstParagraph"><img src=
"assets/pool.jpg" width="185" height="123" /><br />
```

C:\Projects\Beyond Basics DW8\chap_14\form_example.htm (XHTML)*

Tell us about yourself and your property

Your Details

First Name

Last Name

Business

Street

Suite/Apartment

City

State

Country

Zip

"Great company to work with."
- Dylan Sodderburg

ontent> <div#contentWrapper> <div#contentColumn> <form#form1>   100%   639 x 310   93K / 14 sec

---

5 In the **Document** toolbar, choose **Visual Aids > Hide All** to clear the check mark. From the **Tag Selector**, choose **<fieldset>**; then, switch to **Code** view, and move your cursor to the end of the closing **</fieldset>** tag. Press **Enter** (Windows) or **Return** (Mac) to create a new line. From the **Format** pop-up menu in the **Property Inspector**, choose **None**.

It's best to give separate fieldsets a bit of space so the borders don't run into each other; however, Dreamweaver 8 won't render the fieldset properly if it is inside a **<p>** tag. Choosing None from the Format pop-up menu prevents Dreamweaver 8 from adding an unnecessary **<p>** tag.

---

6 In the **Insert** bar, click **Fieldset**. In the **Fieldset** dialog box, type **Your Property** in the **Legend** field, and click **OK**.

Notice Dreamweaver 8 inserts two sets of tags in a single line:

<fieldset><legend>Your Property</legend></fieldset>

Although it doesn't matter to browsers whether the form content comes before the **<legend>** tags or after, it does to Dreamweaver 8. You'll want to be sure you insert your form elements after the closing **</legend>** tag for best rendering in Dreamweaver 8.

---

7 In the **Code** view, place your cursor after the closing tag **</legend>**. In the **Insert** bar, click the **Common** category, and click **Table**. In the **Table** dialog box, set **Rows** to **5**, **Columns** to **2**, and **Table width** to **325 pixels**. Click **OK**.

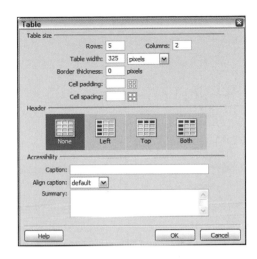

This inserts a table matching the previous one in width and number of columns, but it has fewer rows. The other obvious difference is the width of the columns is different between the two tables. You'll fix that next.

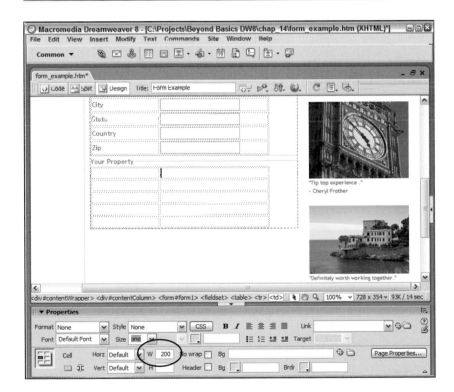

8 Position your cursor in the first cell and first row of the table. In the **Property Inspector**, type **135** in the **Width (W)** field. Move your cursor to the next column in the same row, and type **200** in the **Width (W)** field.

Setting the width of the top cells in the first row establishes the size of each column. Although most browsers will represent the table correctly if you type just one value, we've found it's better in Dreamweaver 8 to set the width for every column in the table.

Now you're ready to begin typing labels and form fields.

9 In the first cell of the left column, type **Location**. Press the **Tab** key. In the **Insert** bar, click the **Forms** category, and choose **Text Field**. With the newly inserted text field chosen, type **location** in the **Name** field of the **Property Inspector**. Repeat the process in the second row of the table to add the label **Facility** and a text field named **facility**.

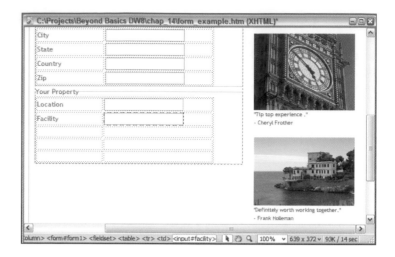

Many form actions depend on the form elements being properly named; for example, an application may examine the value for the text field named zip and react accordingly. We find that unless you get into a habit of naming them as you insert each form element, you will easily forget the names.

In the next step, you'll use select lists rather than text fields—plus you'll take advantage of a Dreamweaver 8 shortcut.

10 In the third row of the left column, type **Bedrooms**. Press the **Tab** key, and press **Shift+F9** to open the **Snippets** panel. Double-click the **Form Elements** folder to expand it, and then expand the **Dropdown Menus** folder. Drag the code snippet numbers **1–12** to the third row of the right column. With the inserted list selected, type **bedrooms** in the **Name** field of the **Property Inspector**. Repeat the process to type labels and the same code snippet for

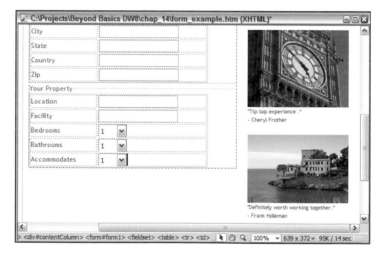

Bathrooms on the fourth row with the list name of **bathrooms** and **Accommodates** on the fifth row with the list name of **accommodations**.

If you had a lot of time on your hands, you could insert a List/Menu object from the Form category in the Insert bar and then painstakingly populate the list with a dozen labels and values—or you could just drop in the snippet provided for you. Dreamweaver 8 offers a wide range of default snippets, and those in the Form Elements folder are among the most useful. You can, of course, customize them after you've added them to the page.

11 Select the **accommodation** list form element. In the **Property Inspector**, choose **2** from the **Initially selected** list. Click **List Values**. In the **List Values** dialog box, scroll to the bottom of the listed values, and select **12**. Click **Add (+)**, and in the newly created entry, type **13** as both the label and the value. Press the **Tab** key to add another entry, and type labels and values for **14** and **15**. When you're finished, click **OK**.

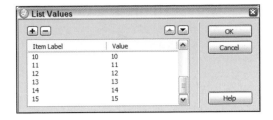

Unlike Library items, you can quickly modify code snippets to fit your needs without affecting the original.

The final element the form needs is a submit button, which you'll add next.

---

12 From the **Tag Selector**, choose **<fieldset>**, press the **right arrow** key to move outside the tag, and press **Enter** (Windows) or **Return** (Mac). In the **Insert** bar, click the **Common** category, and choose **Table**. In the **Table** dialog box, change the number of rows to **1**, leaving the remaining values as they are, and click **OK**. In the **Insert** bar, click the **Forms** category, and drag the **Button** form element to the right column of the new table. In the **Property Inspector**, change the **Value** field to **Send Information**.

Tip: When you have multiple fieldsets on the page, you want to make sure to put the submit button outside both. This placement conveys the impression the submit button applies to the entire form rather than just one portion of it.

---

13 Press **Ctrl+S** (Windows) or **Cmd+S** (Mac) to save the page. Leave **form_example.htm** open for the next exercise.

In this exercise, you applied a fieldset and a legend to existing form elements by selecting the containing element—the table—first. Then you added a new fieldset and legend to the page and built the form elements within it, using precoded snippets for easy lists of numbers. Although the fieldsets and legends have really begun to take shape, a great deal more styling is possible, as you'll discover in the next exercise.

2 | Styling Form Elements

Forms go well with CSS because you can style so many distinct components. In addition to the form elements and the labels—typically stored in table cells—you can also style the enclosing form and, as demonstrated in the previous exercise, fieldsets and legends. Moreover, when you have a series of text fields, you can often present them at the same width. This consistency makes it easy to create a single class to style many of the form elements. In this exercise, you'll get a chance to really make your form stand out as you create and apply styles for everything from fieldsets to text fields.

1 If you followed the previous exercise, **form_example.htm** should still be open in Dreamweaver 8. If it's not, complete Exercise 1, and then return to this exercise.

You'll start the CSS makeover of the form by styling the labels and form fields first.

2 In the **CSS Styles** panel, click **New CSS Rule**. In the **New CSS Rule** dialog box, set **Type** to **Class**. In the **Class** field, type **.formLabels**, make sure **Define in** is set to **This document only**, and click **OK**. In the **CSS Rule definition for .formLabels** dialog box, click the **Block** category, and set **Text align** to **right**. Click **OK**.

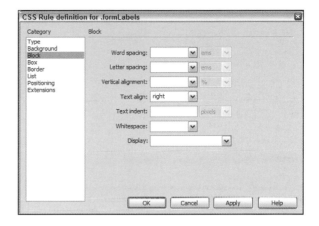

We almost always right-align labels in forms. Forms are much easier to read with this stylistic choice, particularly on a line-by-line basis. Applying this style—even to a number of labels—is quick in Dreamweaver 8.

3 Click the table cell of the first label, **First Name**, and drag your cursor all the way down to the last label, **Zip**, to select all the labels. From the **Style** pop-up menu in the **Property Inspector**, choose **formLabels**. Repeat the process in the second table, starting with **Location** and ending with **Accommodates**.

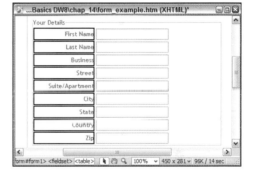

Because you're applying the class to the table cell containing the label, you can easily style many **<td>** tags in a single step. You'll define the classes for the form elements next.

Note: If your table cells are not all in a row, as shown in this example, you can press Ctrl (Windows) or Cmd (Mac), click the first cell, and then click additional cells to select noncontiguous cells.

4 In the **CSS Styles** panel, click **New CSS Rule**. In the **New CSS Rule** dialog box, set **Type** to **Class**. In the **Class** field, type **.formInput**. Make sure **Define in** is set to **This document only**, and click **OK**. In the **CSS Rule definition for .formInput** dialog box, set **Color** to **#333333** in the **Type** category. Click the **Box** category, and set **Width** to **195 pixels**. Turn off the **Padding Same for all** check box, and then set **Top** to **2 pixels** and **Left** to **3 pixels**. Click **OK**.

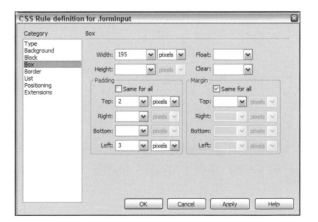

You are defining the .formInput class to give the text fields a unified, distinct appearance. You are using a dark, but not black, color to match the existing font styles and a uniform width. A bit of padding helps complete the look.

Next, you'll create a similar style to be used for the three list elements.

5 In the **CSS Styles** panel, make sure you're in **All** mode. **Right-click** (Windows) or **Ctrl+click** (Mac) the just-added **.formInput** class, and choose **Duplicate** from the contextual menu. In the **Duplicate CSS Rule** dialog box, change **Name** to **.formInputsLists**, and click **OK**. In the **CSS Styles** panel, in the list of styles, select **.formInputsLists**. In the **Properties** pane, change **Width** to **50 pixels**, and remove the values for both **padding-left** and **padding-top**.

Because the list elements contain numbers up to only two digits, a full-width box would be overkill, so you've set the width to 50 pixels. Likewise, you don't need the padding properties; removing a value in the Properties pane removes that property, as you can see the next time you display the style.

With your styles defined, you're ready to apply them.

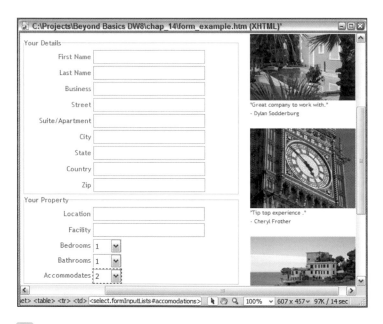

6 Choose the **firstname** text field. In the **Property Inspector**, select **formInput** from the **Class** pop-up menu. Repeat for each remaining text field. Now, select the **bedrooms** list element, and choose **formInputsLists** from the **Class** pop-up menu. Repeat for the two other list elements. Finally, place your cursor in the table cell next to the **bedrooms** list element, and drag to select the two cells below it. In the **Property Inspector**, click **Align Left**.

Although the operation is a bit tedious, it's necessary to apply each class individually to each form element. You cannot, as with the labels, select multiple items and apply the style in one step. You added the left text alignment to the **<td>** tags containing the list elements to handle some aberrant behavior by Microsoft Internet Explorer 6; without it, the list items move to the center of the table cell.

The form is really beginning to take shape. Next you'll establish some styles for the fieldset and legend to really give them some flair.

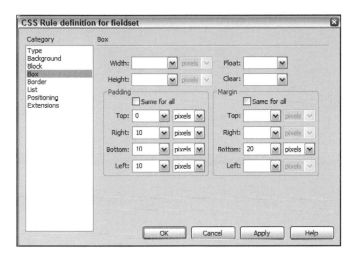

7 In the **CSS Styles** panel, click **New CSS Rule**. In the **New CSS Rule** dialog box, set **Type** to **Tag**. In the **Tag** field, type **fieldset**. Make sure **Define in** is set to **This document only**, and click **OK**. In the **CSS Rule definition for fieldset** dialog box, click the **Background** category, and set **Background color** to **#609DC9**. Click the **Box** category, and turn off the **Padding Same for all** and **Margin Same for all** check boxes. In the **Padding** area, set **Top** to **0 pixels**, **Right** to **10 pixels**, **Bottom** to **10 pixels**, and **Left** to **10 pixels**. In the **Margin** area, set **Bottom** to **20 pixels**. Click **OK**.

The big change here is adding a background color, the color chosen is the same as used in the `<h1>` tag and the `.currentLink` class. The padding properties are designed to move the table—and the contained form labels and elements—in from the edge of the fieldset. You add the `bottom-margin` value to separate the two fieldsets from each other and from the submit button. Next, you'll add a bit of style to the legend tag and adjust the labels so they work better with the fieldset background color.

Note: You may be curious why you set the `padding-top` value to 0; the table would certainly benefit from a little space from the top border of the fieldset. Dreamweaver 8, unfortunately, has a problem rendering a fieldset with any `padding-top` value other than 0: Dreamweaver 8 mistakenly moves the legend down with the enclosed elements, such as the table. To work around this visual problem, you'll add a new rule later in this exercise to add a `margin-top` value of 10 pixels to the tables within the fieldsets.

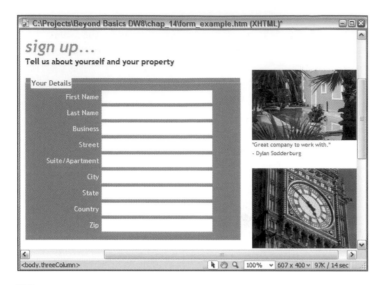

8 In the **CSS Styles** panel, click **New CSS Rule**. In the **New CSS Rule** dialog box, set **Type** to **Tag**. In the **Tag** field, type **legend**. Make sure **Define in** is set to **This document only**, and click **OK**. In the **CSS Rule definition for legend** dialog box, in the **Type** category, set **Weight** to **bold**. Click the **Background** category, and set **Background color** to **#609DC9**. Click **OK**. In the **CSS Styles** panel, select the **.formLabels** entry, and in the **Properties** pane, click **Add Property**. Type **color** in the open field, and press **Enter** (Windows) or **Return** (Mac); type **#FFF**.

With a white background and bold font, the legend stands out much better. Similarly, the white color for the `.formLabels` class adds a nice contrast to the background color of the fieldset.

All that's left to define are a couple of styles to fine-tune the look and feel of the form.

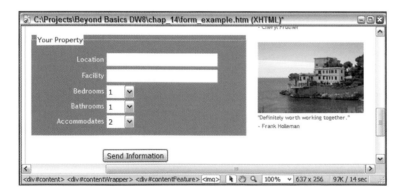

9 In the **CSS Styles** panel, click **New CSS Rule**. In the **New CSS Rule** dialog box, set **Type** to **Tag**. In the **Tag** field, type **form**. Make sure **Define in** is set to **This document only**, and click **OK**. In the **CSS Rule definition for form** dialog box, click the **Box** category, and turn off the **Padding Set for all** check box. In the **Padding** area, set **Top** to **20 pixels**. Click **OK**. Repeat the process to create another new rule with the **Advanced** selector, **fieldset table**; in the **Margin** area, set **Top** to **10 pixels**. Click **OK**.

By adding a `padding-top: 20px` declaration to the form tag style, you're providing a bit of separation between the `<h2>` tag and the top of the form. Similarly, the rule defined second—`margin-top: 10px`, which affects tables within a `<fieldset>` tag—adds some padding between the top of the fieldset and the top of the enclosed table. This is the aforementioned workaround for the rendering problem in Dreamweaver 8.

Time to check out your work in a browser!

10 Press **Ctrl+S** (Windows) or **Cmd+S** (Mac) to save your file, and then press **F12** to preview it in your browser. Type sample data in the any of the text fields to see how the styles appear. Select any of the pop-up lists to verify the applied color and styles change. When you're finished, close your browser, and return to Dreamweaver 8.

Browsers render fieldsets somewhat differently, so your form may appear different from the Firefox browser on Windows, as shown in the illustration here.

11 Leave **form_example.htm** open for the next exercise.

In this exercise, you learned how to apply styles to the various form elements, as well as the fieldset and legend, to create a personalized, inviting form. In the next exercise, you'll learn how to add accessibility options to your forms to make them easier for site visitors to navigate.

Making Forms Accessible

Forms are one of the most difficult aspects of the Web for the physically challenged to navigate. Ironically, forms also have the most tags and attributes available for overcoming those difficulties. You can integrate three basic tags/attributes with form elements to enhance accessibility: the `<label>` tag and the `accesskey` and `tabindex` attributes. Unfortunately, Web professionals rarely apply these elements. In this exercise, you'll learn how to upgrade an existing form to be more accessible by adding these attributes and values through the **Quick Tag Editor**.

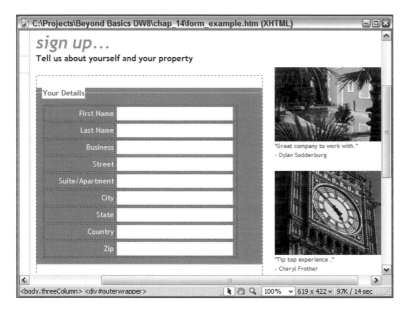

1 If you followed the previous exercise, **form_example.htm** should still be open in Dreamweaver 8. If it's not, complete Exercise 2, and then return to this exercise.

2 In the **Document** toolbar, choose **Visual Aids > Hide all Visual Aids** to turn on Dreamweaver 8's visual aids.

The first goal is to bring all the form labels into accessibility compliance.

3 In **Design** view, select the label **First Name**. Press **Ctrl+T** (Windows) or **Cmd+T** (Mac) to open the **Quick Tag Editor** in **Wrap** mode. In the **Quick Tag Editor**, type **label for="firstname"**, and press **Enter** (Windows) or **Return** (Mac). Repeat the process for each of the remaining labels in both fieldsets, using the adjacent form element name as the **for** attribute value. (For example, when adding a **<label>** tag to the **Last Name** text, set the **for** attribute to **lastname**; for the **Location** text, set the **for** attribute to **location**.)

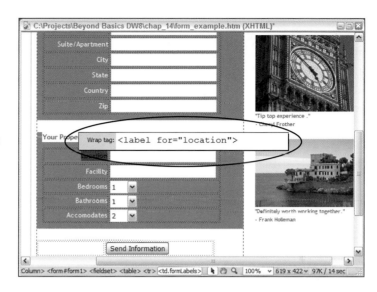

The **<label>** tag makes it possible for screen readers to properly identify the referenced form elements. Without a **<label>** tag, screen readers would pronounce the name of the form element, which may or may not describe the field meaningfully. The **for** attribute makes it possible to place your labels in one table cell and the form field in another. The other approach to using the **<label>** tag is to wrap it around the target form field; we find the **for** attribute method much more flexible and vastly prefer it.

Note: If you're not sure what form element name to use as the **for** attribute, select the form element, and look at the Name field of the Property Inspector.

Next, you'll begin to make it easier to navigate to a specific field with the **accesskey** attribute.

---

4 Select the **firstname** text field, and press **Ctrl+T** (Windows) or **Cmd+T** (Mac) to open the **Quick Tag Editor** in **Edit tag** mode. Press the **Tab** key to reach the end of the tag, and type **accesskey="f"** before the closing tag characters (**/>**). Press **Enter** (Windows) or **Return** (Mac) to confirm the change. Repeat the process for each form element in the two fieldsets, and select a relevant key for the **accesskey** value.

Note: Make sure not to duplicate **accesskey** values for any two form elements on the page.

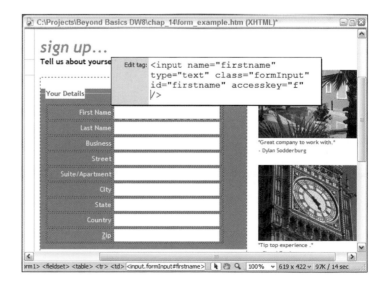

The **accesskey** attribute allows the user to jump directly to a specific form element by pressing Alt (Windows) or Ctrl (Mac) plus the **accesskey** value. For example, if you wanted to go directly to the firstname text field on a Windows XP system, you'd press Alt+F. One of the challenges in defining **accesskey** values for a form is making sure you don't have any duplicate values. Whenever possible, we use the first letter of a corresponding label (F for First Name and L for Last Name). When the first letter has been previously used, we use the second letter, and so forth.

Because this is not always intuitive when working with complex forms, you need to perform another step to help identify the **accesskey** values for any form element.

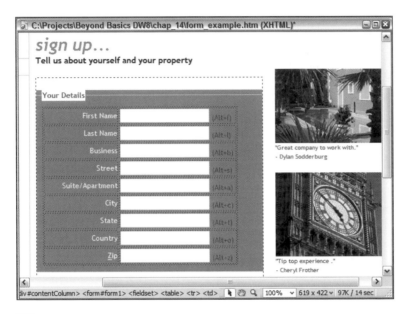

5 In the **CSS Styles** panel, select the **.formInput** entry. In the **Properties** pane, change the **Width** value to **140 pixels**. Place your cursor directly after the **firstname** text field, and type **(Alt+f)**. Repeat this process for each form element, typing **Alt** plus the **accesskey** value for the form element, enclosed in parentheses.

With the form fields slightly shortened, you added the parenthetical phrase to identify the **accesskey** value for each form element. You're intentionally leaving these small bits of help text in the default style so they won't distract from the overall form appearance but will remain visible. Screen readers will read the text after announcing the form element's name so the page visitor can jump to any desired field.

The final accessibility attribute to add, `tabindex`, ensures the visitor can move quickly from one field to the next.

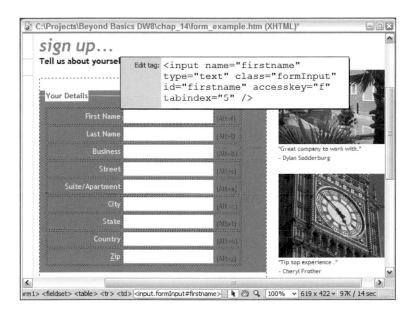

6 Select the **firstname** text field, and press **Ctrl+T** (Windows) or **Cmd+T** (Mac) to open the **Quick Tag Editor** in **Edit tag** mode. Press the Tab key to reach the end of the tag, and insert **tabindex="5"** before the closing tag characters (**/>**). Press **Enter** (Windows) or **Return** (Mac) to confirm the change. Repeat the process for each form element in the two fieldsets, and type a greater value for each successive **tabindex** value. Make sure not to duplicate **tabindex** values for any two form elements on the page.

Tip: When typing greater values for successive **tabindex** values, we suggest using multiples of 5. This gives you a bit of leeway to insert other **tabindex** values if you want to include new form elements later without renumbering the existing values.

The **tabindex** attribute makes it possible to direct your page visitors' form experience. After filling out one form text field, your visitors can use the Tab key to move to the next field. On a form like the one in this example, you won't notice any changes, but should the form increase in complexity—with side-by-side form elements, for example—the **tabindex** property will help guide visitors through the form process.

You'll try it next.

7 Press **Ctrl+S** (Windows) or **Cmd+S** (Mac) to save your file, and then press **F12** to preview it in your browser. Press any indicated **accesskey** (**Alt+accesskey** [Windows] or **Ctrl+accesskey** [Mac]) to jump from one field to another. Once you're in any given field, press the **Tab** key to proceed to the next form element. Press **Shift+Tab** to go to the previous form element.

---

8 When you're finished practicing navigating the form, close your browser. Return to Dreamweaver 8, and close **form_example.htm**.

This exercise showed you how to add tags and attributes to form elements to make them accessible. You can properly identify labels with a **<label>** tag and **for** attribute; adding an **accesskey** attribute allows for instant access to any form element, and inserting a **tabindex** attribute defines the tab order of the form elements.

VIDEO: | **validating_forms.mov**

To make sure you're getting the proper data in the desired format, it's a good idea to add validation to your form. To learn more about adding JavaScript validation to your form elements, check out **validating_foms.mov** in the **videos** folder on the **Dreamweaver 8 HOT CD-ROM**.

In this chapter, you learned how to structure and style forms to make them easier to comprehend and quicker to complete. You separated primary sections of the form with the **<fieldset>** and **<legend>** tags and then styled the entire form all the way down to the form labels. You also learned how to make forms more accessible by using **<label>** tags and other specialized attributes. In the next chapter, you'll explore the advanced media possibilities of Dreamweaver 8.

Integrating Multimedia Content

Multimedia, particularly in the form of podcasts and video, has exploded on the Web. If relevant, multimedia can serve as a significant attraction for your intended audience. A **podcast** is audio content, typically prerecorded, that you can syndicate over the Web. Video on the Web comes in a multitude of formats. Adobe Flash video, with the ubiquity of the Adobe Flash Player, has greatly popularized the medium as a Web-based phenomenon.

In this chapter, you'll get a chance to integrate both podcasts and video into a Web site. Along the way, you'll learn how to prepare your own audio recordings for podcasting and how to create a podcast-ready RSS (**R**eally **S**imple **S**yndication) feed for syndicating your content. On the video front, you'll learn how to encode your video to get the best quality at the lowest file size and how to insert Flash video—standard or streaming—into your Web page.

Understanding Podcasts

Podcasting is a movement that grew from the popularization of a technological innovation. As Apple iPods and other similar portable digital music players became more common, Web professionals wanted to provide more content types in addition to music. Former MTV VJ (**V**ideo **J**ockey) Adam Curry created the first podcast; today you can find podcasts on topics ranging from astrology (**http://cosmicweather.blogspot.com**) to zoology (**www.mnzoo.org/podcasts**).

Each podcast is essentially an audio file, typically in MP3 format. What elevates podcasting above the long-standing ability to play audio clips over the Web is the combination of RSS feeds and podcasts. As described in Chapter 8, *"Setting Up an XML Feed,"* an **RSS feed** is an XML (e**X**tensible **M**arkup **L**anguage) file containing metainformation about the available recordings—such as who created them and where they are stored—as well as details about individual podcasts, such as a title, brief description, and, most important, a link to an audio file. When a Web visitor subscribes to the RSS feed using software such as Apple iTunes, they can automatically download and listen to new content, as described in the RSS feed.

iTunes, available for free on both Mac and Windows, makes it easy to subscribe and listen to podcasts.

Preparing Content for Podcasting

One of the reasons podcasting is spreading so quickly is that it is inexpensive to get started. All you need is a little bit of hardware—a microphone and a pair of headphones compatible with your computer—and some software to record your audio. Although you can use pretty much any microphone and headphones to do your recording, the adage "you get what you pay for" applies to recording equipment. If the sound quality of your recordings is not what you're expecting, look into getting a better-quality microphone. Headphones are necessary so your microphone won't pick up the sound of your computer speakers.

Many audio-recording software packages are available, including free alternatives for both Windows and Mac platforms. On Windows, we recommend Audacity (**http://audacity.sourceforge.net**), an open-source sound editor. You'll also need to get the LAME MP3 encoder for exporting MP3 files (you can find links for downloading and instructions for use on the Audacity site). For Macs, OS X includes Apple GarageBand, which offers a number of podcast-specific features, such as a speech enhancer, as well as basic sound-recording capabilities.

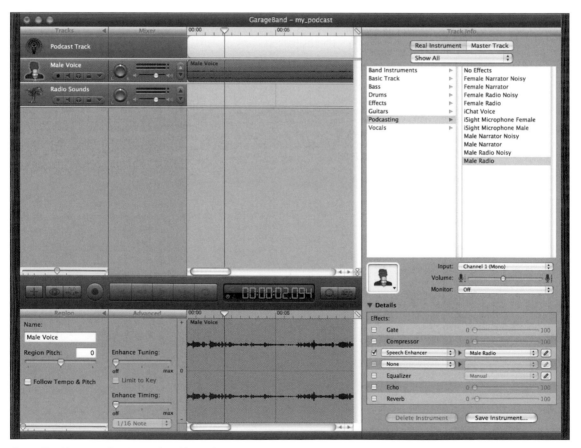

GarageBand has several settings tailored for podcasting.

Regardless of the application you use, establishing the proper settings is important. We recommend you record your audio as mono; recording voice in stereo is good only for doubling the file size. If you're using Audacity, you'll be able to choose the sample rate and format. A sample rate of 44,100 Hz (**Hertz**) with a 16-bit format works well for voice recording. Save your recording as a WAV file (which is an uncompressed audio format that retains the highest sound quality when editing). If you're using GarageBand, create a Real Instrument track with your preferred preset vocal setting, such as Male Speech. It's a good idea to enable the Gate option at the default setting; this enhancement helps to cut extraneous noise.

After you've recorded and edited your podcast, the next step is to export it as an MP3 file. The MP3 format is the de facto standard for podcasts and provides excellent fidelity at a relatively small file size. Again, most software offers a range of sample bit rates to choose from: The higher the bit rate, the better the sound quality and the larger the file size. Think of choosing a bit rate as similar to optimizing a JPEG image. In Audacity, start within the recommended range of 32 to 64 for your MP3 bit rate, and find an acceptable sound quality (and file size). GarageBand has special settings for podcasts.

The final step in preparing your audio file for podcasting is to add identifying tags called **ID3 tags**, which are similar to **<meta>** tags in HTML and can include information such as the name of the podcast and the creator. You insert all the ID3 details into the MP3 file. iTunes provides a direct way to type and modify the ID3 tags: Simply import the file into your iTunes **Library**, and choose **File > Get Info**; then add or modify your details, and click **OK**. Audacity presents a dialog box for typing ID3 tags when you export the file as an MP3. When you publish your podcast to the Web, any recent MP3 player will be able to display the ID3 information in the file.

In the following exercise, you'll learn how to create the XML file that defines an RSS feed. You'll also set up your Web page to play the file individually as well as offer an RSS feed option.

VIDEO: | **encoding_MP3.mov**

For a complete A–Z recording and encoding session, check out **encoding_MP3.mov** in the **videos** folder on the **Dreamweaver 8 HOT CD-ROM**.

1 | Structuring an RSS Feed

If you followed the exercises in Chapter 8, *"Setting Up an XML Feed,"* you're familiar with XML files and RSS feeds. The latest RSS specification is RSS 2.0, and one of the main benefits of this specification is that it allows **enclosures**, such as an MP3 file, which are just the ticket for podcasts. In this exercise, you'll create an RSS feed file from the ground up so you can better understand how to structure and use each tag and section. You'll start by creating a basic XML file in Dreamweaver 8.

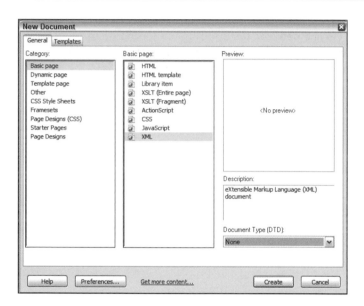

1 Choose **File > New**. In the **New Document** dialog box, select the **General** tab if necessary. In the **Category** list, select **Basic page**, and in the **Basic page** list, select **XML**. (Leave the **Document Type (DTD)** setting at the default, **None**.) Click the **Create** button. After Dreamweaver 8 creates the XML page, press **Ctrl+S** (Windows) or **Cmd+S** (Mac) to save the page. In the **Save As** dialog box, navigate to the **chap_15** folder you copied to your desktop, type **podcasts.xml** in the **File name** field, and then click **Save**.

Unlike the XML file created in Chapter 13, *"Optimizing for Search Engines,"* for the Google Sitemap, an RSS feed does not need to use a specific encoding.

```
C:\Projects\Beyond Basics DW8\chap_15\podcasts.xml*
1    <?xml version="1.0" encoding="iso-8859-1"?>
2        <rss version="2.0">
3            <channel>
4
5            </channel>
6        </rss>
                                                    1K / 1 sec
```

2 Position your cursor after the opening code line, and press **Enter** (Windows) or **Return** (Mac). On the new line, press the **Tab** key, and type **<rss version="2.0">**. Press **Enter** (Windows) or **Return** (Mac) two times, and type **</rss>**. Move your cursor to the line between the opening and closing **<rss>** tags, and press the **Tab** key. Repeat the process to type the **<channel>…</channel>** tag pair. Position your cursor on the line between the opening and closing **<channel>** tags, and press the **Tab** key again.

The **<rss>** and **<channel>** tags form the overall structure of your RSS feed. As you might expect, the **<rss>** tag identifies the file as an RSS feed using the specified version, 2.0. The **<channel>** tag refers to all the podcasts on your site collectively and is subdivided into two major sections: one holding all the metadata about your channel and a series of other tags describing each podcast.

Next, you'll add the required metadata tags.

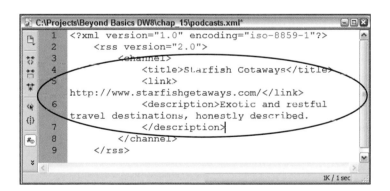

```
C:\Projects\Beyond Basics DW8\chap_15\podcasts.xml*
1    <?xml version="1.0" encoding="iso-8859-1"?>
2        <rss version="2.0">
3            <channel>
4                <title>Starfish Getaways</title>
5                <link>
     http://www.starfishgetaways.com/</link>
6                <description>Exotic and restful
     travel destinations, honestly described.
7                </description>
8            </channel>
9        </rss>
                                                    1K / 1 sec
```

3 Type **<title>Starfish Getaways</title>**. Press **Enter** (Windows) or **Return** (Mac), and type **<link>http://www.starfishgetaways.com/</link>**. Press **Enter** (Windows) or **Return** (Mac) again, and type **<description>Exotic and restful travel destinations, honestly described.</description>**.

The three tags and their content begin to describe your site for the RSS feed readers. The **<title>** tag contains the title of your overall site, **<link>** contains an absolute URL to your site's home page, and **<description>** provides an overall view of your site's podcast content.

You'll add a couple of optional metadata tags next.

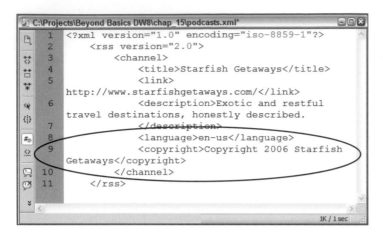

```
C:\Projects\Beyond Basics DW8\chap_15\podcasts.xml*
1   <?xml version="1.0" encoding="iso-8859-1"?>
2       <rss version="2.0">
3           <channel>
4               <title>Starfish Getaways</title>
5               <link>
http://www.starfishgetaways.com/</link>
6               <description>Exotic and restful
travel destinations, honestly described.
7               </description>
8               <language>en-us</language>
9               <copyright>Copyright 2006 Starfish
Getaways</copyright>
10              </channel>
11      </rss>
                                          1K / 1 sec
```

4 Press **Enter** (Windows) or **Return** (Mac), and type **<language>en-us</language>**. Press **Enter** (Windows) or **Return** (Mac) again, and type **<copyright>Copyright 2006 Starfish Getaways</copyright>**.

Podcasts are truly an international phenomenon, and it's helpful to identify which language your podcast uses. In this case, **en-us** identifies the podcast as having been recorded in the United States flavor of English. For a complete list of acceptable language values, see **www.rssboard.org/rss-language-codes**. Also, whenever you're broadcasting original content in any public forum such as the Web, it's a good idea to label it with the appropriate copyright information.

Note: RSS 2.0 has many optional **<channel>** tags. With them, you can convey the relevant categories, the Webmaster's e-mail address, or even an image to be displayed representing the site. You can find a complete list at **www.rssboard.org/rss-specification**.

Now you're ready to create the structure for referring to a specific podcast.

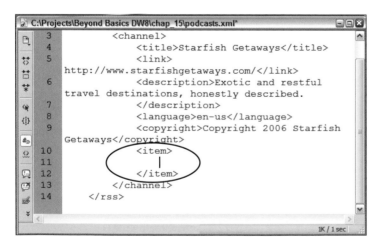

```
C:\Projects\Beyond Basics DW8\chap_15\podcasts.xml*
3           <channel>
4               <title>Starfish Getaways</title>
5               <link>
http://www.starfishgetaways.com/</link>
6               <description>Exotic and restful
travel destinations, honestly described.
7               </description>
8               <language>en-us</language>
9               <copyright>Copyright 2006 Starfish
Getaways</copyright>
10              <item>
11
12              </item>
13          </channel>
14      </rss>
                                          1K / 1 sec
```

5 On the new line, press the **Tab** key, and type **<item>**. Press **Enter** (Windows) or **Return** (Mac) two times, and type **</item>**. Move your cursor to the line between the opening and closing **<item>** tags, and press the **Tab** key.

Details about individual podcasts are stored in an **<item>**...**</item>** tag pair. You'll need to add a new **<item>** group whenever you publish a new podcast; you can include as many **<item>** tags as you'd like.

Next, you'll add the key details about the podcast. You'll find them similar to those detailed for the overall channel.

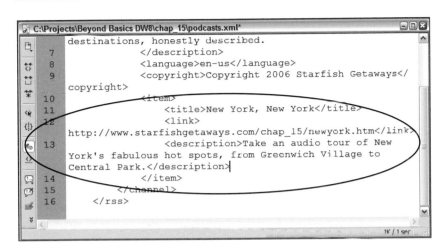

6 Type **<title>New York, New York</title>**. Press **Enter** (Windows) or **Return** (Mac), and type **<link> http://www.starfishgetaways.com/chap_15/newyork.htm</link>**. Press **Enter** (Windows) or **Return** (Mac) again, and type **<description> Take an audio tour of New York's fabulous hot spots, from Greenwich Village to Central Park.</description>**.

The three tags you typed are identical to those you typed for the **<channel>** tag, but the values are specific to a particular podcast. The **<link>** tag points to the page hosting the individual podcast where a site visitor can go for more detailed information about the podcast and related subjects. Later in this exercise, you'll add to the page referenced in the **<link>** tag to create a direct connection to the MP3 file.

Next, you have just one more, extremely important tag to go.

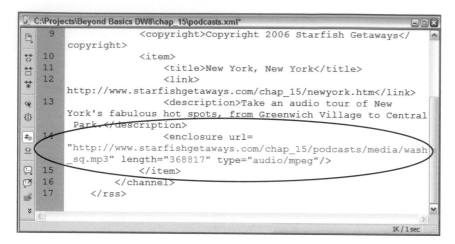

7 Type the following code:

```
<enclosure url="http://www.starfishgetaways.com/chap_15/podcasts/media/wash_sq.mp3" length="368817" type="audio/mpeg"/>
```

The `<enclosure>` tag is what separates an RSS podcast feed from a standard RSS text feed. The `<enclosure>` tag has three attributes: `url`, `length`, and `type`. The `url` attribute requires a fully qualified URL to the MP3 file on the Web, the `length` attribute lists the size of the file in bytes, and the `type` attribute refers to the standard MIME (**M**ultipurpose **I**nternet **M**ail **E**xtensions) type, which for MP3 files is `audio/mpeg`.

---

8 Press **Ctrl+S** (Windows) or **Cmd+S** (Mac) to save your file. Close **podcasts.xml**.

With the RSS file prepared, you'll include a couple of links on a Web page so visitors can subscribe to your podcasts or listen to the individual MP3 file.

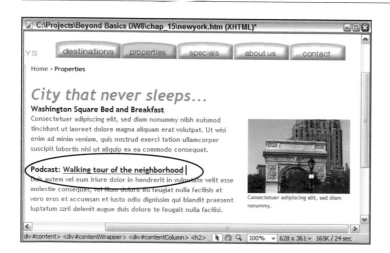

9 In the **Files** panel, open **chap_15/newyork.htm**. Select the text **Walking tour of the neighborhood**, and in the **Property Inspector**, drag the **Link Point to File** icon to **chap_15/podcasts/wash_sq.mp3**.

Because of the ubiquity of media players able to handle MP3 files now (including Apple QuickTime, RealNetworks RealPlayer, and Windows Media Player), it's pretty safe to link directly to the individual podcast file. When a visitor clicks the link, the player will load the document and begin playing the file.

Next, you'll add a link to a full slate of podcasts offered by the site.

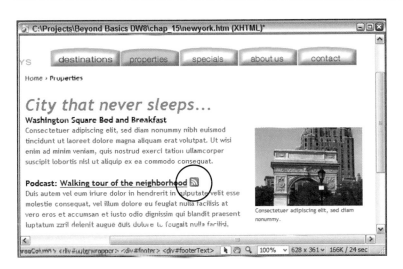

10 Place your cursor after the text you just linked. In the **Insert** bar, click the **Common** category, and click the button **Images: Image**. In the **Select Image Source** dialog box, open the **chap_15/assets** folder, and select **feed.png**. In the **Property Inspector**, drag **Link Point to File** to **chap_15/podcasts.xml**. In the **Alt** field, type **RSS Podcast Feed**.

The RSS feed icon serves a couple of purposes. First, its visual design draws attention to the adjacent podcast link to make it stand out more than just a regular link. Second, the icon acts as a link to the RSS XML page, an emerging standard practice for indicating the location of syndicated content on the Web.

Note: Although there is no set standard for the icon, more and more sites are using the feed icon shown in the illustration here. The Firefox team developed this icon, and Microsoft also recently designated it as the default icon to be used. You can find a good collection of feed icons at **http://feedicons.com**.

11 Press **Ctrl+S** (Windows) or **Cmd+S** (Mac). Leave **newyork.htm** open for the next exercise.

In this exercise, you learned how to create an RSS file in XML format to syndicate your podcasts. The RSS file has two major sections: one describing your overall channel and another detailing each podcast or item. Once you have created the RSS file, you can use standard links to provide a connection to the MP3 podcast file and the RSS XML file. In the next exercise, you'll learn how to add Flash video to your media-rich site.

Publicizing Your Podcasts

What's the big difference between creating podcasts and creating audio files? Syndication. The concept behind podcasts is your content is available to be publicized and distributed over a syndicated network. The number of podcasts on the Web is increasing extraordinarily quickly. For people to hear your podcasts, they'll first need to hear *about* them, so publicizing your podcasts is important.

You should consider submitting your podcast to a number of primary resources. In most circumstances, this is as easy as submitting the URL to your published RSS XML file. Here are a few of the most notable podcast directories:

iTunes Directory: When a recent version of iTunes began supporting podcasts, the format really exploded. In iTunes, switch to the **Podcast** category, and click the **Podcast Directory** link. When the **Podcast Directory** page loads, click **Submit a Podcast**.

Podcast.net: This directory (**www.podcast.net**) offers a wide range of podcast categories.

Yahoo! Podcasts: Yahoo! has recently jumped on the podcast bandwagon and offers a free listing service at **http://podcasts.yahoo.com/publish**.

Feed-Directory.com: This site (**http://www.feed-directory.com**) is a vast and ever-growing collection of text and podcast feeds.

Podcast Alley: This site (**http://podcastalley.com**) is a general podcast portal with easy searching and ongoing rankings.

Understanding Flash Video

From the perspective of long time Macromedia (and now Adobe) supporters, the Flash video revolution has been a joy to behold. When Flash Player 6 introduced the potential to display video, the player adoption rate increased dramatically—largely so people could see the cool new ways sites were integrating video. With each successive release, the Flash engineers have improved the quality and performance of Flash video playback. Today, Flash video has gained wide acceptance across the Web, and Flash Player is the default player for such major sites as Google Video and YouTube.

One of the biggest barriers to video on the Web is file size. With many formats still prevalent, a significant amount of time is required to download a sufficient amount (if not all) of the video clip to begin displaying the movie. Flash addresses this problem by offering several delivery modes through its video format, FLV (**FL**ash **V**ideo). The two best Flash alternatives are progressive download and streaming. The **progressive download** method sends the initial video segment to the requesting Web page, which begins playing as soon as possible while the video is continuing to download. The delay before the video appears is relatively short, but this downside is largely offset by the key advantage the progressive download offers: No specialized media server is required.

Streaming Flash video, on the other hand, requires separate server software such as Flash Media Server (previously Flash Communications Server). However, if your site budget can bear the burden, the payoff is tremendous. Streaming video begins immediately and is highly interactive. You can, for example, move the video playhead to any location—forward or backward—in the video stream for instant viewing; with progressive download, viewers can move the playhead only to previously downloaded video. In addition, streaming video gives you other advanced features such as live broadcasting and video messaging.

Note: For the sake of completion, we should acknowledge that you can deliver Flash video in a third method, as embedded video. **Embedded** Flash video combines the SWF video player with the FLV video file in a single SWF. This method requires the entire video be downloaded before it can be played and therefore is seldom used and not recommended.

Once you have acquired your video footage, you need to compress, or **encode**, it in a Flash Player–compatible format. Flash video uses a format different from standard Flash movies. Whereas Flash movies and animations—and the player skin and controls showing Flash video—are SWF files, Flash video is stored in an FLV format. Major digital video editors such as Adobe Premiere Pro, Adobe After Effects, and Apple Final Cut Pro support the FLV format. This support gives video editors the best possible quality by exporting their uncompressed source video directly to FLV.

You can also encode FLV files using the Adobe Flash 8 Video Encoder, which is bundled with Flash 8 Professional. The process is straightforward. You simply drag your source video files—supported formats include AVI, MPEG, MP4, DV, MOV, and WMV—to the Flash 8 Video Encoder, choose your settings with output file names, and click the **Start Queue** button. (Encoding is a computing-intensive process, and if you have a number of files to encode or if the files are large, you should do your encoding when you are not otherwise using your system.)

The Flash 8 Video Encoder gives you complete control over your output video through the **Flash Video Encoder Settings** dialog box. To make a complex subject easier to master, the Flash 8 Video Encoder offers a series of preconfigured encoding profiles broken down into versions supporting Flash 7 and newer and those supporting Flash 8 and newer, each in a range of quality choices. Unless you know your audience requires Flash 7 support, it's best to select one of the Flash 8 options. Flash 8 supports a more advanced compression scheme known as the On2 VP6 video codec. If you need more finely tuned control, click the **Show Advanced Settings** button.

Once the Flash 8 Video Encoder has completed its operation, you'll be able to add the FLV file to your site for use in your Web page—as described in the next exercise.

The Flash 8 Video Encoder offers several predefined settings, complete with previews.

2 | Adding Flash Video

In Dreamweaver 8, Flash video is extremely straightforward to insert and a dream to modify. By using a single object, aptly named **Flash Video**, you can include any kind of FLV file, whether progressive download or streaming, complete with video playback controls. Once added to the page, the custom **Flash Video Property Inspector** allows you to modify almost all the parameters. Get ready to add some video!

---

1 If you followed the previous exercise, **newyork.htm** should still be open in Dreamweaver 8. If it's not, complete Exercise 1, and then return to this exercise.

Dreamweaver 8 has greatly simplified the process of integrating video into a Web page. As you'll see in the subsequent steps, the Flash Video object combines inserting the FLV video file and inserting the SWF video player in a single operation.

2 Place your cursor at the end of the second placeholder paragraph in the main content area, and press **Enter** (Windows) or **Return** (Mac). In the **Insert** bar, click the **Common** category, and click the button **Media: Flash Video**. In the **Insert Flash Video** dialog box, make sure **Video type** is set to **Progressive Download Video**. Click the **Browse** button. In the **Select File** dialog box, navigate to the **chap_15/assets** folder, and select **park_video.flv**. From the **Skin** pop-up menu, choose **Halo Skin 3**. Click **Detect Size**, and make sure the **Constrain** option is turned on. Leave the rest of the options at their default settings, and click **OK**.

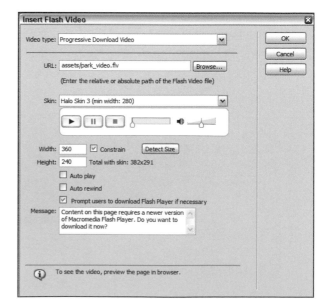

Because not everyone will have access to a Flash Media Server, you're using the Progressive Download video type in this step. The Insert Flash Video object offers a good selection of controls through the Skin pop-up list. As you'll see, you can change the skin at any point. In addition, the video size is embedded in the FLV file. We find it's always better to detect the original size and use it if possible; you can also change the dimensions.

This object also gives you the option to automatically start and rewind the video for the user, if you'd like. We rarely see anyone take advantage of these options; somehow, it feels a little pushy to do so. On the other hand, we heartily recommend you take advantage of the Flash Player detection option. The Insert Flash Video object also adds Flash detection routines to make sure your site visitor has the proper Flash version required by the FLV encoding. You can customize the message that appears if a new version is needed.

VIDEO: **streaming_video.mov**

To learn more about how to set up a streaming video, check out **streaming_video.mov** in the **videos** folder on the **Dreamweaver 8 HOT CD-ROM**.

3 Notice the Flash movie is too wide for the current layout, and the right column is pushed out of place. With the Flash placeholder selected, in the **Property Inspector**, make sure the **Constrain** option is turned on, and change the **Width (W)** value to **340**.

It's often difficult to tell whether your video will fit properly in your layout without trying it. As long as the Constrain option is turned on, you can modify the values to fit without fear of the video becoming distorted. Next, you'll look at the video in action.

4 Press **Ctrl+S** (Windows) or **Cmd+S** (Mac) to save your file, and then press **F12**. When the page opens in your browser, click the **Play** button on the video controller. Test the other video controls as it plays, including the volume control. When you're finished, close your browser, and return to Dreamweaver 8.

The video fits nicely on the page now and is fully functional. It's time to try another skin for a different look and feel.

5 With the Flash placeholder selected, in the **Property Inspector**, choose **Clear Skin 3** from the **Skin** pop-up list.

6 Press **Ctrl+S** (Windows) or **Cmd+S** (Mac) to save your file, and then press **F12**. When the page opens in your browser, click the **Play** button on the video controller, and then move your cursor away from the video. Move your cursor over the video again to make the controller bar reappear. When you're finished, close the browser, and return to Dreamweaver 8. Close **newyork.htm**.

The Clear Skin option is a nice one when space is limited and you want the full frame of the video—without the controller bar—to appear.

Note: When it's time to publish your page, you'll need to publish several files in addition to the HTML page and its standard dependent files such as the included graphics. Specifically, you'll need to publish the FLV file and the two SWF files generated by the Insert Flash Video object: FLVPlayer_progressive.swf and Clear_Skin_3.swf. The first is the core SWF file that loads all the other moving parts (pun intended) and handles the delivery of the Flash video. The second is, obviously, the controller skin. Because you initially tried Halo Skin 3, you'll notice a SWF file for that skin in your folder. You don't need to upload it; you can delete it without consequences.

This exercise detailed how to add Flash video to your page. Through the Insert Flash Video object, you selected the desired FLV file and set the initial skin and size. As you've seen, the Flash Video Property Inspector allows you to change most parameters including the dimensions and skin.

In this chapter, you learned how to integrate different media components into your Web pages. You can include podcasts, which are syndicated audio files, by creating an RSS file with the proper tags pointing to the individual MP3 files. Video is even easier to add, thanks to the power and sophistication of Flash video. You saw how simple it is to add and modify Flash video in any Web page, and you learned about the encoding process.

I hope you've enjoyed taking Dreamweaver 8 to the next level by following the exercises in this book. I'm sure you'll find as I have that the more you uncover in Dreamweaver 8, the more you'll realize what there is to discover. Enjoy the adventure!

Troubleshooting FAQ and Technical Support

If you run into problems while following the exercises in this book, you might find the answer in the "Troubleshooting Frequently Asked Questions" section. If you don't find the information you're looking for, use the contact information provided in the "Technical Support Information" section.

Troubleshooting Frequently Asked Questions

Q When I preview my files locally, why do I get an error that a file or image cannot be found?

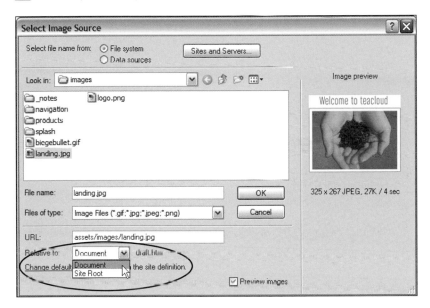

A This is one of the most common problems beginners encounter when creating links in Dreamweaver 8. This almost always occurs when you create a link that is site-root relative instead of document relative. Creating a site root–relative link means a slash (/) appears at the beginning of the path to the file, which will cause images to disappear, frames to function incorrectly, and file links to break when previewed locally. You can correct this problem by relinking the file/image and making sure you choose the **Document** option from the **Relative to** pop-up list in the **Select Image Source** dialog box.

Q I can't find a feature that existed in previous versions of Dreamweaver. What happened?

A Some features from previous versions of Dreamweaver aren't available in Dreamweaver 8. This is because these features were obsolete or they recommended a workflow that is no longer current with modern Web practices.

Q How do I open the **Property Inspector**?

A If you can't see the **Property Inspector** or, for that matter, any of the Dreamweaver 8 panels, choose the **Window** menu, and select the panel you want to open. The **Window** menu also lists the shortcut keys you can use to quickly access all the Dreamweaver 8 panels.

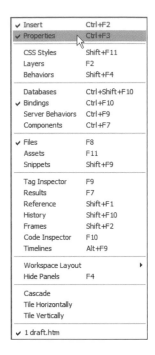

Q I defined my site for the exercises, but files that are listed in the exercises aren't there. What happened?

A When you were defining the site, you may have specified a chapter folder instead of the folder containing the chapters. Go ahead and redefine the site.

Note: The process of selecting the correct folder is different on Mac and Windows: In Windows, when you're browsing in order to define the chapter folder and the **Choose Local Folder** dialog box opens, select the chapter folder, and then click **Open**. After Dreamweaver 8 opens the folder, click **Select**. On a Mac, when you're browsing in order to define the chapter folder and the **Choose Local Folder** dialog box opens, select the chapter folder, and click **Choose**.

Q Where's the **color picker**?

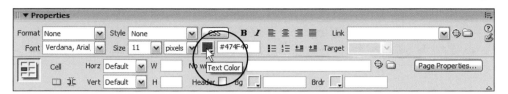

A Because it's context sensitive, the **color picker** appears when you click one of the Dreamweaver 8 color swatches. Color swatches appear in the **Property Inspector** and in the **Page Properties** dialog box. You can also find the **color picker** in Dreamweaver 8's **Code** view by **right-clicking** (Windows) or **Ctrl+clicking** (Mac) and choosing **Code Hint Tools > Color Picker** from the contextual menu.

Q Why do I get the message, "To make a document-relative path, your document should be saved first"?

A It would be nice if the dialog box simply stated, "Save your file now, or Dreamweaver 8 can't keep track of your files," because that's all it's asking you to do. All you need to do is click **OK** and save your file (in the defined site), and Dreamweaver 8 will write the path correctly.

Q Why do I get the message that my file is located outside the root folder?

A Dreamweaver 8 is asking you to move the file into the root folder you've defined as your site. If you work with files outside your defined root folder, Dreamweaver 8 cannot keep track of your links or manage your site, which is counterproductive to the way the program is structured and to your workflow. Though this message is annoying, it is actually helping you maintain a healthy site without experiencing broken links and problems uploading your files when you publish it.

Note: You can handle this message in different ways, depending on the system you are running: In Windows, click **Yes**, and Dreamweaver 8 will automatically put you in the correct folder. Click **Save**, and Dreamweaver 8 will move the file. On a Mac, click **Yes**, and then browse to the correct folder. At that point you will be prompted to save, which you should do.

Q When I try to locate files, why can't I see the file extensions at the end of file names, such as **.gif**, **.jpg**, and **.html**?

A On Windows, you will need to change your Preferences to view file name extensions. See the introduction at the beginning of this book for instructions about how to do this.

Technical Support Information

The following sections contain technical support resources you can use if you need help.

lynda.com

If you run into any problems as you work through this book, check the companion Web site for updates:

www.lynda.com/books/HOT/dw8btb

If you don't find what you're looking for on the companion Web site, send Joseph Lowery an e-mail at the following address:

dw8btbhot@lynda.com

We encourage and welcome your feedback, comments, and error reports.

Peachpit Press

If your book has a defective CD, please contact the customer service department at Peachpit Press:

customer_service@peachpit.com

Macromedia Technical Support

If you're having problems with Dreamweaver 8, please visit the Macromedia technical support center at the following location:

www.macromedia.com/support/

B

Dreamweaver 8 Resources

Many great resources are available for Dreamweaver 8 users. You can access a variety of newsgroups, conferences, and third-party Web sites to help you get the most out of the new skills you've developed by reading this book. In this appendix, you'll find the best resources for further developing your skills with Dreamweaver 8.

lynda.com Training Resources

lynda.com

lynda.com is a leader in software books and video training for Web and graphics professionals. To help further develop your skills in Dreamweaver 8, check out the following training resources from lynda.com.

lynda.com books

The HOT (**H**ands-**O**n **T**raining) series was originally developed by Lynda Weinman, author of the revolutionary book *Designing Web Graphics*, first released in 1996. Lynda believes people learn best from doing and has developed this series to teach users software programs and technologies through a progressive learning process.

Check out the following books from lynda.com:

Designing Web Graphics 4
by Lynda Weinman
New Riders
ISBN: 0735710791

Macromedia Dreamweaver 8 Hands-On Training
by Daniel Short and Garo Green
lynda.com/books and Peachpit Press
ISBN: 0321293894

Macromedia Flash Professional 8 Hands-On Training
by James Gonzalez
lynda.com/books and Peachpit Press
ISBN: 0321293886

Macromedia Flash Professional 8 Beyond the Basics Hands-On Training
by Shane Rebenschied
lynda.com/books and Peachpit Press
ISBN: 0321293878

lynda.com video-based training

lynda.com offers video training as stand-alone CD-ROM and DVD-ROM products and through a monthly or annual subscription to the lynda.com Online Training Library.

For a free, 24-hour trial pass to the lynda.com Online Training Library, register your copy of Dreamweaver 8 Beyond the Basics HOT at the following location:

www.lynda.com/register/HOT/dreamweaver8btb

Note: This offer is available for new subscribers only and does not apply to current or past subscribers of the lynda.com Online Training Library.

To help you build your skills with Dreamweaver 8, check out the following video-based training titles from lynda.com.

Specifically, the following are Dreamweaver video-based training titles:

Dreamweaver 8 Essential Training
with Garrick Chow

Dreamweaver 8 New Features
with Garrick Chow

Dreamweaver 8 Beyond the Basics
with Daniel Short

Dreamweaver 8 Dynamic Development
with Daniel Short

Learning Macromedia Dreamweaver MX 2004
with Garo Green

Intermediate Dreamweaver MX 2004
with Garo Green and Daniel Short

Dynamic Development with ASP and Dreamweaver MX 2004
with Daniel Short

The following are Web design video-based training titles:

Studio 8 Web Workflow
with Abigail Rudner

Photoshop CS2 for the Web Essential Training
with Tanya Staples

Fireworks 8 Essential Training
With Abigail Rudner

The following are Web development video-based training titles:

Learning CSS 2
With Christopher Deutsch

Learning XHTML
With William E. Weinman

Learning HTML
With William E. Weinman

Learning JavaScript
With Charles G. Hollins

Flashforward Conference and Film Festival

The **Flashforward Conference and Film Festival** is an international educational conference dedicated to Macromedia Flash. Flashforward was first hosted by Lynda Weinman, founder of lynda.com, and Stewart McBride, founder of United Digital Artists. Flashforward is now owned exclusively by lynda.com and strives to provide the best conferences for designers and developers to present their technical and artistic work in an educational setting.

For more information about the Flashforward Conference and Film Festival, visit **www.flashforwardconference.com**.

Online Resources

Dreamweaver Support Forums
www.adobe.com/cfusion/webforums/forum/index.cfm?forumid=12

Web Sites

WebAssist
www.webassist.com

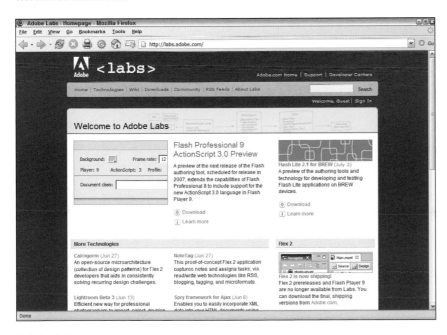

Adobe Labs
http://labs.adobe.com

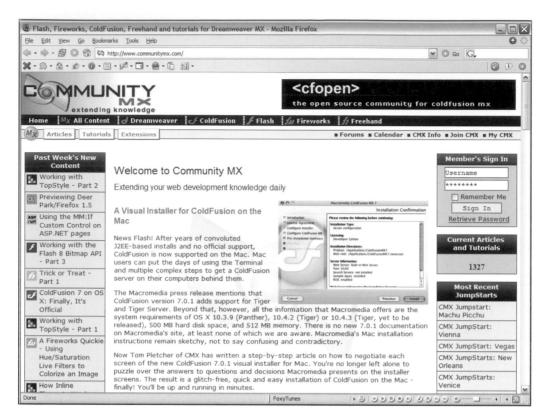

Community MX

www.communitymx.com

Books

Dreamweaver 8 Bible
by Joseph Lowery
Wiley Publishing
ISBN: 0471763128

CSS Hacks and Filters
by Joseph Lowery
Wiley Publishing
ISBN: 0764579851

Design and Deploy Web Sites with Macromedia Dreamweaver MX 2004 and Contribute 3
by Joseph Lowery
Macromedia Press
ISBN: 032128884

Macromedia Dreamweaver MX 2004 Killer Tips
by Joseph Lowery and Angela C. Burgalia
New Riders
ISBN: 0735713790

Joseph Lowery's Beyond Dreamweaver
by Joseph Lowery
New Riders
ISBN: 0735712778

Index

C

Cascading Style Sheets (CSS), 10

applying comp images to layouts, 29–33

designing layouts, 3

float property, 28

magazine style layouts, 87–89

navigation, 4, 56

applying hacks, 90–93

basics, 57

horizontal navigation bars, 57–62

sliding panels with JavaScriipt, 69–75

tabbed, 64–68

vertical CSS navigation, 63

position property

absolute declaration, 25–26

fixed declaration, 26

relative declaration, 24–25

static declaration, 24

slicing graphics, 11

exporting slices, 23–24

foreground elements, 18–20

preparing background images and gradients, 21–22

visualizing layout, 12–17

structuring for Contribute, 219–223

templates

expressions, 106–112

integration, 77–81

nested, 82–86

three-column layouts, 51–55

two-column layouts, 35

building header, 41–43

content area, 44–48

footers, 49–50

page structure setup, 36–39

CD-ROM

attach_rss.mov, 147

encoding_MP3.mov, 261

photoshop.mov, 24

shared_assets.mov, 201

spry_widget.mov, 161

streaming_video.mov, 271

validating_forms.mov, 257

vertical_nav.mov, 63

<CDATA> tags, 167

Change Administrator Password dialog box, 205

<channel> tags, 263

check in/check out systems, groups, 177–181

check_in_out_example.htm, group check in/check out system, 177–181

Choose Remote Root Folder dialog box, 178

Chosen Font pane, 40

Clone command (Edit menu), 21

Close All command (File menu), 105

code collapse, 114, 121–123

Code view, 5, 114

Coding toolbar, 115–116

collapsing code, 121–123

commenting code, 124–126

comparing code, 127–128

quick tag selection, 117–120

codes

customizing toolbars, 129–131

rapid use techniques, 114

Coding toolbar, 115–116

collapsing code, 121–123

commenting code, 124–126

comparing code, 127–128

quick tag selection, 117–120

Coding command (View menu), 115

Coding toolbar, 5

basics, 115–116

tools, 116

coding_example.htm, codes

collapsing code, 121–123

commenting code, 124–126

customizing toolbars, 129–131

Collapse Full Tag tool, 116

Collapse Selection tool, 116

collapsing codes, 121–123

color picker, troubleshooting, 277

M

N

U–V

W

X–Y–Z